Outdated

Outdated

A Novel

Nathan Wolff

ISBN-10 1937887480
ISBN-13 978-1-937887-48-3
Printed in Israel
First Edition 2015

Typeset and Cover Design: Rachel Jacobs
racheljacobss@gmail.com
rachel-jacobs.com

nathannwolff@gmail.com

For Drew T. Fishman

Chapter One

Joe

WHEN JOE CHARNOFF turned the corner onto his block, he breathed a deep sigh of relief. Through the orange streetlights he could see his apartment—or at least the Gruberman's two-story box of a house whose basement he rented—and was eagerly anticipating the moment he wouldn't have to drag along his clunky, secondhand rolling suitcase and could collapse into his bed. Just as he was passing by the walkway to his landlords' side entrance, he heard the familiar squeak of their door and saw Mrs. Gruberman's broad figure emerge onto her small square porch. With a plastic watering can held at her side, she bent over to check the soil in the planters hanging over the railing.

"Good evening, Mrs. Gruberman," Joe cordially called, loudly enough for her to hear. She immediately turned her head in his direction and squinted from behind her Armani glasses.

"Oh, good evening, Joe," she replied casually. Without hesitation she rested the watering can on the ground and ambled towards him. As she approached, she rubbed her arms with her hands, as if she felt chilly on this pleasant evening in early June. "I wasn't sure if it was you. How was your trip?"

"Fine," he answered, too tired to elaborate. She looked into his eyes, but he turned away.

She pointed towards his suitcase. "Just getting home now?"

"Yeah," he exhaled. "Six hours door-to-door."

"My gosh," she shuddered, covering her mouth with her hand. "Why so late?"

"It's normally a four-hour trip, but the train was delayed leaving DC, and then we stopped for no reason whatsoever outside just Philadelphia." He mustered a heavy smile. "So it felt very long."

"I'm so sorry to hear that," she said in a motherly tone. "You must be starving."

"No, my family had its ritual Sunday brunch just before I left, so I'm fine."

"That's good. You know, I wanted to make a brunch with my sisters this morning too, but by the time I got around to contacting them, one had to take her son to get his wedding suit, and the other had to fix her Smartphone, so...*b'kitzur* it didn't happen."

"Yeah." As he listened, Joe glanced quickly at the watering can and felt something amiss. Weren't their flowers watered by an automatic hose system? And why would Mrs. Gruberman tend to her garden at 10 PM in a skirt-suit? Her charade didn't fool him. She probably heard the plastic wheels of his suitcase scraping along the sidewalk and probably even peeked from behind the blinds in her front room to be sure it was him. Maybe, he hoped, she was coming to report on what he'd asked her to find out.

He couldn't just broach the subject abruptly, though. "Did you have a lot of guests over Shavuos?"

"We did," she said matter-of-factly. "You missed some great meals."

He glanced down the street at the traffic light changing to yellow. "Did Daniela come, by any chance?"

"Yes, actually," she answered with wide eyes. "I think she came for two meals, if I'm not mistaken. I'm pretty sure she was at our *milchig* meal. She's always ordering into the office from one of the cafés in the neighborhood and it always smells so good."

Joe stood there, a smile frozen on his face while Mrs. Gruberman rambled on like she usually did. Had she not been his landlord and his frequent Shabbos meal hostess he would've interrupted her long ago. A car passed behind him and he started blinking rapidly to revive himself.

"Anyway," she said finally. "You're probably wondering whether I was able to ask her."

Joe nodded nonchalantly. "I mean, I can understand with so many guests that you might not have had the chance…"

"No, I did," she said, accenting the "did" in a way that said everything. Her sudden look of compassion didn't help Joe feel any better, but he allowed her to continue. "While she said that she thought you were very nice, she wasn't interested in going out."

He scratched the stubble around his chin, but then cupped his hands behind his back and looked down at his scoffed shoes. "Well, thank you anyway."

"I wanted to let you know so that you didn't get all…expectant."

"Yeah, I guess it's good that you asked her and I didn't." He exhaled. "OK then."

Mrs. Gruberman, though, seemed to have taken it harder than Joe. With a frown, she said, "I don't think that she's really ready for marriage, to tell you the truth. I don't mean like that…I just don't even know if she's dating at all. I mean, maybe she should be, but there's only so much I can say to her as her boss."

Now can I go home? he thought but didn't say. He took the handle of his suitcase, as if to subtly drop a hint to Mrs. Gruberman.

"What are you doing next Shabbos?" she asked. "Maybe you'll come to us?"

"We'll see. It's only Sunday."

She went back inside, without watering any of the flowers, while Joe lugged himself and his suitcase to the other side of the house. The entrance to his apartment was at the back of the driveway and to get there he had to maneuver between the Gruberman's Grand Cherokee and the exterior siding of the house. Though his suitcase was packed pretty lightly, it clomped loudly as he dragged it behind him down the stairs. He unlocked the door and was immediately hit with the stench of stale air. He went to the small window next to the door and heaved it open.

After rolling his suitcase inside the apartment, he slid his suit jacket off his shoulders and hung it on the back of one of two chairs around the table. He reached into his pockets and dropped all the contents on the table, the coins hitting the table with a loud crash and scattering in all directions and onto the floor. With a shrug, he went to the kitchen, which was really just the back corner of the one main room. He pulled out the Brita from the refrigerator and poured himself some water. Standing above the sink, he emitted a long sigh and made a *bracha* before drinking. He drank half before spiking the tumbler into the sink. After another sigh, he hobbled over to his bedroom to get undressed.

As he was unbuttoning his white Oxford shirt, he couldn't understand why he was in such a funk. So Daniela, whom he had met at least ten times at the Gruberman's Shabbos table, didn't want to date him. He had thought there was a rapport developing during their conversations but apparently she didn't. It shouldn't have been such a big deal. He looked around and for the first time felt dissatisfaction with the mess. There was the pile of clothing in the corner that never seemed to get put away, the line of shoes along the wall, his desk cluttered with a disarray of graduate text books, work papers, science magazines, *seforim* and various gadgets for his phone and camera. After brushing his teeth, he tumbled onto his mattress and fell asleep.

At 6:40 AM the next morning his alarm clock jolted him awake, but he turned over and stared at the ceiling for nine minutes until rolling out of bed when the snooze alarm went off. Joe washed his hands and face in the kitchen sink and looked up at his reflection in the small mirror his former roommate had hung on the wall. He had never been that confident with the way he looked, though he knew of girls who described him as "cute." His short hair had no particular style to it—it was just short—and his eyes were a dull green that looked bluish when he wore blue shirts. He was exactly the average height for American males his age but slightly thinner, and he felt out of shape. Depressing thoughts were uncharacteristic for Joe and so he rubbed his face with the closest towel and announced to his reflection, "But I'm alive!" It didn't motivate him for very long, so he dressed slowly, filled his messenger bag with his work papers and headed towards the *shul* on the corner.

After *davening*, he stopped in the kosher bakery to calm his grumbling stomach. With a heave he opened the door and walked straight up to the counter, relishing the rarity of it being so empty at this normally busy hour. When the woman behind the counter indicated she was ready to serve him, he ordered a small hazelnut coffee with milk and on impulse a corn muffin. She turned with a nod to make his coffee, and at that moment his cell phone rang. It was Sharon, his friend from college. He didn't answer immediately.

"Hey Joey," she said in a pleasant sing-song. "Good morning."

"Yeah yeah," he replied morosely. "I'm at the bakery."

"Already? Early riser…"

"Not really," he said with a grumble. The door to the back opened and the baker carried in a large tray of marble cake to the counter, bringing with him a scent of fresh cake and sweat. "Why are you up so early?"

"I don't know," Sharon answered behind a yawn. "I couldn't go back to sleep."

Joe hummed, his attention captured by the colorful pastries spotlighted in the display case in front of him. "So, what's up?"

"I didn't see you online for a few days. Everything all right?"

"I went down to Potomac last Wednesday," he explained. "My parents' computer is painfully outdated."

"Oh. Well, you probably had a better time than my cheesecake binge at home." She laughed, but Joe didn't.

"Probably," he said blankly. He glanced to his left where an older woman with huge sunglasses and a shopping cart at her side was standing next to him and flailing her arm to draw the attention of the woman behind the counter.

"How long do I have to wait to be serviced?" she demanded of the clerk, who was busy putting Joe's muffin in a small brown paper bag.

"What did you say?" Sharon asked.

"It wasn't me," Joe told her. "Look, I'm heading to the subway. Can we talk later?"

"Sure," she said. "I was actually calling to say that I'll be down-town later."

"Really? What for?"

"Oh, nothing really. Just, you know, meeting someone…"

"Someone?" He took the phone away from his ear as the woman placed the paper bag with his muffin and presumably his coffee on the counter. He pulled out a five-dollar bill from his pocket and returned the phone to his ear. "Is it a guy? Is it a…date?"

"Nooooo," she denied. "Just a guy I met at this surprise party — you know Evelyn from my building?"

"No," Joe said decisively.

"Well, whatever, he was there and Evelyn introduced us and then wandered off, and we talked and he…asked for my number, and—"

"That's nice," Joe interrupted her. He held his phone with his shoulder and collected his change from the counter. "Have fun."

"So, you wanna meet for dinner at the spot?" Sharon asked.

Joe's nose twitched as he picked up his coffee and muffin. "I learn nights now, remember?"

"Oh, right," she said, with a short laugh. "I forgot."

"Another time," he offered as he placed his breakfast on a small table in the corner of the bakery. "Look, I gotta go."

"OK. What's up for Shabbat?"

He rolled his eyes. "How do I know? It's only Monday."

"I'm just asking. You don't have to be so terse."

He held the phone away from his ear and sighed. "I meant that I never know this early."

"So come for Shabbat," she offered. "There's a get-together this week at Frankel's."

"No thanks," Joe said pointedly. "Have a good time with Frankel."

Sharon clicked her tongue. "Don't be so cynical. You used to enjoy going."

"Maybe when we were undergrads," he said as he took the plastic cover off his coffee and blew on it. "I'll be there in a few weeks for Rob's *aufruf* anyway."

"That's in a few weeks," she pointed out. "I figured that you'd be lonely now that your roommate's left. Are they bringing in someone else?"

He made a bracha over his coffee and tasted it before answering. "I don't think so. My landlords haven't said anything."

"Aren't they losing money?"

"I don't know if they even need my money," he said, taking a sip.

"Oh, why don't you live uptown?" she blurted. "I don't know why you still live there."

He threw back his head in exasperation. "We've been through this before. Number one," he was counting with his fingers, "It's still cheaper to live in Brooklyn. Two, it's closer to my job and school—"

"But you have to ride the subway through all those bad neighborhoods," she whined.

"New York isn't what it was in the eighties."

"Fine. But at least don't spend your Shabbat alone."

He took out his muffin from the bag and peeled off the paper. "I'll see. Let me go."

It was another minute before he could finally hang up. Even though Joe had basically cut contact with girls, he hadn't gotten around to telling Sharon yet. When he first arrived at NYU as a scared freshman from Maryland, she befriended him and showed him the ropes of college, New York City, and helped him acclimate to the Orthodox lifestyle he'd chosen in Israel that summer after high school. They became close friends, but nothing more, because while Sharon seemed content with her level of observance, Joe was always growing, and wanted a girlfriend who was also interested in seeking a stronger connection to her *yiddishkeit*. When she graduated after his second year, he felt he'd the time had come for him to distance himself from the girls he was friendly with and from hanging out in mixed crowds, but since Sharon wasn't on campus and didn't see Joe in his new isolation, she continued to call and Joe never got up the nerve to tell her he wasn't keeping female friends anymore. Instead he placated her, finding excuses not to meet up, sporadically answering her calls but never initiating, hoping that eventually she'd get the hint. As he drank his coffee and stared out the big windows at the synchronized changing of the traffic lights, he concluded that he couldn't continue doing nothing indefinitely, but couldn't imagine hurting her like that either. He finished his breakfast with his stomach still unsettled and disposed of his trash on his way out to join the morning march towards the subway.

As Joe strolled down Nostrand Avenue, glancing into the store windows as he passed them and enjoying the cool air, his train of thought switched tracks and he agonized over where he went wrong with Daniela. Was it the right thing to use Mrs. Gruberman? Maybe Daniela didn't feel comfortable with her boss intruding into her personal life. Was he misreading her interest in their conversations? She seemed to be engaged when speaking with him, despite the frenetic background action typical to a Gruberman Shabbos meal. Perhaps he was someone who she didn't even think of as a potential date and immediately relegated him to at best a friend? When he reached the station and settled into a seat on a waiting-to-depart 2 train, he concluded that he simply didn't know, and the uncertainty soured him for the duration of his ride into Manhattan.

Eventually the train passed through most of Brooklyn and entered the last leg of his journey in the tunnel under the East River. Joe perked up a bit as the automatic voice announced, "The Next Stop is…Wall Street." He stood up heavily, coming to terms with having to spend the day at work instead of moping in his apartment. The subway doors opened upon their two-tone chime and for five minutes Joe joined a dense mass of commuters shuffling towards their respective jobs, breaking from the herd when it passed his building on Water Street.

Joe waved to the doorman, who nodded in response. Nobody from his office was in the elevator so the twenty-four-second ride was shared in silence with a young guy giving off a strong whiff of the same cologne Sharon once tried to persuade him to spend way too much money for. When he reached his floor, he pulled out his electronic keycard from his wallet and opened the glass doors to the offices of Stadler & Klein. He managed to get to his little cubicle without being drawn into any conversations, and as he sat down at his swivel chair, he dropped his bag at his feet and emitted an audible sigh that he hoped nobody else heard.

Once Joe started working, though, he forgot about the image of Daniela laughing at his corny sarcasm and focused on his task. Currently he was spending three days a week interning at a stock market research firm while he finished his Master's. Joe was extremely grateful to have found work in his undergraduate major—statistics—doubly so that Stadler & Klein was predominantly a religious Jewish company. He took his lunch at one and then went to the conference room where there was a daily *minyan* at 1:30.

Afterwards, he was about to return to his number crunching when he was approached by Mr. Siegel, head of acquisitions.

"How is everything Joseph?" he asked jovially, extending a

large hand and offering a warm smile. He was a tall man, some-where in his forties, clean-shaven, appeared to be in good shape, and always wore a *kippah* over his balding hairline. While he wasn't one of Joe's bosses, he did pass on Joe's resume to the statistical analysis department when the internship liaison at NYU contacted him and for that Joe owed him a debt of gratitude. Since then he always maintained an interest in Joe's progress—when he was around.

They shook hands. "Very good, Mr. Siegel." It was common for Mr. Siegel to approach Joe after mincha, the only time they would run into each other. "How was your weekend?" he asked.

"Nice, and yours?"

"Pretty good, Baruch Hashem. I visited my parents," he admit-ted, though he didn't know why.

Mr. Siegel leaned on the back of a chair. "Where do they live again?"

"In Maryland…in a suburb north of DC."

"That's not such a bad trip. Did you take the train?"

Joe nodded. "I left last Wednesday after work."

Mr. Siegel gave a puzzled look. "You were here last Wednes-day? Wait, where was I?"

"I always come in Mondays, Wednesdays, and Fridays."

"You're still only part-time?" he exclaimed. "I've got to speak to Barry about that."

Joe didn't want to get anyone in trouble. "No, I'm still working on my Master's, Mr. Siegel. It's better this way."

"Oh, all right then." Mr. Siegel looked around, as though to en-sure no one was within earshot. The conference room was mostly empty, except for two men who always sat at the head of the table for fifteen minutes after mincha huddled around a pocket sefer.

"Listen, are you running anywhere after you leave the office?"

Joe quickly calculated how much time he could spare to still get home, eat dinner, and be on time to meet his evening learning partner. "No, not really."

"So come to my office before you leave then."

"No problem, Mr. Siegel," he said with a smile.

"All right. I'll see you then."

Mr. Siegel quickly left the conference room, leaving Joe standing in place bewildered. He could think of no reason why Mr. Siegel would want to speak with him, especially in the privacy of his office. For the two years since his initial hiring, they had only shared pleasantries or general work inquiries ("How's Mr. Robinson treating you?"), so what was so important that it couldn't be said in the conference room? Was he going to get reprimanded? For nearly half-an-hour after he got back to his cubicle, Joe stared at his computer, unable to understand why the same calculations he breezed through all morning suddenly didn't make any sense. He went to get a drink from the coffee room and as he gulped some cold water, he felt his hand shaking and his left eyelid twitching. With a few deep breaths, the shaking ceased and he went back to his cubicle to find the numbers back to their old selves.

At the calculated time of 5:09 he made his way to the corner offices and announced his presence to Mr. Siegel's secretary. She was probably Joe's age, if not younger, a slender and pretty brunette who Joe thought dressed too stylish for their boring office. She was busy examining dresses from a bridal magazine when he approached and barely looked up when she indicated with her hand that he was free to proceed to Mr. Siegel's office. The door was open a small crack and made a creaking sound when Joe knocked.

"Come in," Mr. Siegel called from inside.

Joe opened the door and stepped in.

Mr. Siegel looked up from his computer. "Ah, Joseph. Take a seat."

He was typing rapidly as Joe entered the office and closed the door behind him. He walked over to the chair opposite Mr. Siegel and settled into the leather while glancing around. There was a polished wood desk with a flat-screen computer and a line of framed photos, but besides a small tree Joe couldn't identify, the only other furniture was a bookcase filled with colorful binders and a few seforim. Joe surmised the panoramic view of the East River compensated for any need of furnishings. The entire downtown Brooklyn skyline was Mr. Siegel's backdrop, with the two bridges named after the two connecting boroughs to the north and the shipyards and townhouses of Brooklyn Heights to the south. With a view like that Joe tried to guess how much the company must've been making just to handle the rent.

"So, Joseph," Mr. Siegel finally said. He increased the speed of his typing, made one dramatic Enter, and slid his chair away from the computer. "How are things going in statistical analysis?"

"Fine," Joe replied. "Great."

"I saw your name on a first-quarter report last month. It looked pretty thorough."

"Thank you," Joe said sheepishly. Joe's eyes looked around the room as he anxiously awaited Mr. Siegel's mystery business. He concluded that the tree in the corner was probably a fern.

Mr. Siegel leaned forward and stared at Joe. "You're probably scared to death to know what I called you in for."

"I am," Joe felt safe to admit.

Mr. Siegel smiled and picked up his phone. "Joanie, could you bring in a bottle of seltzer and two glasses, please?" After he hung up, he told Joe, "It's nothing work-related, I can assure you."

Still Joe felt weird. All this suspense must have been for something important. The secretary entered with the requested drink and two glasses. Mr. Siegel thanked her and waited for her to leave before continuing. "Look, I'll get to the bottom line. I'm not exactly your boss, so I feel I can…I can ask you this…"

"OK," Joe answered, scratching his stubble.

"You see," he paused, exhaling quickly. He grabbed the bottle of seltzer with the speed of a ninja. "Do you want a drink?"

"Sure," Joe answered.

Mr. Siegel looked completely at ease as he busied himself with pouring Joe his drink. "Look, I hope I'm not prying into your business, but I ran into a relative of mine before *yom tov* who's a *shadchan* who asked me if I knew of any guys. I wasn't in the proper mindset to offer her any names then, but when I saw you at mincha I thought that you might be interested. Have you thought about getting married?"

For a moment, Joe sat dumbfounded. He couldn't believe that this was the climax to his hours of suspense. He wanted to laugh very hard, but held back. He reached for his glass and made a bracha before drinking. After his first sip, he replied, "Who at my age isn't thinking about it? But a matchmaker?"

"You've never been set up?" Mr. Siegel asked, settling back into his chair with his glass.

"No," Joe admitted.

"How old are you"

"Twenty-two."

He laughed a hearty laugh and Joe couldn't help laughing with him. "Twenty-two? How is a young guy like you already finishing a Master's?"

"I took a lot of APs in high school," Joe answered simply.

"Oh, I see. I didn't get to take any of those in *yeshiva*. So what do you say?"

Joe was slow to answer, which Mr. Siegel must have understood as a hesitation, because he added: "Listen, at worst it's an hour meeting a very nice woman in Borough Park. You live in Brooklyn, right?"

"For now, at least."

"And at best, you could find your wife. She's made dozens of matches — she's a professional, you know, not just some newly-married *kallah* trying to set up her single friends. Here," he opened a drawer, pulled out a business card and started writing on the back. Then he handed the card to Joe. "Give her a call."

Joe took the card, glanced down at the writing, and quickly put it into his pocket. "I really…had no idea this was what you wanted to speak about."

Mr. Siegel leaned back in his seat and sipped his seltzer. "I didn't think that it would be appropriate to bring this up in the conference room."

"You're right," Joe said, nodding. He then felt his phone vibrating again but he maintained a straight smile.

"All right. Otherwise, everything is all right?"

"Yes, Mr. Siegel."

"Good. I've kept you long enough."

Joe made an after-bracha and stood. "Thank you for thinking about me, Mr. Siegel."

"It could turn out very good. I have the same feeling about this as I had when I first got your resume, and look at what you've done." Mr. Siegel got up from his chair and accompanied Joe out of the office. When they reached the door, he slapped Joe on the shoulder. "Go finish your Master's already," he commanded. "I'll see what I can do about getting you a real position." Mr. Siegel smiled widely at Joe before closing the door.

As Joe walked to his cubicle to get his bag, he felt his heart beating heavily. Mr. Siegel's guarantee of a job didn't even register because he was more perplexed over the rest of their conversation. It wasn't the first time someone tried to help him get married. Last year at a friend's wedding, the bride, in so many words, enthusiastically told him she would set him up with a girlfriend. The girl, who was in earshot, overheard the bride's plan and blushed and Joe felt that somehow the boundaries of modesty had been breached with such a public announcement. Nothing transpired from the suggestion, and it seemed strange to him to make his private life such public business. Although Joe appreciated Mr. Siegel looking out for him, he wouldn't do anything with the number.

When he reached his desk and bent down to pick up his messenger bag, he discovered that he was still holding Mr. Siegel's glass. He backtracked and ran it to his secretary, who actually looked up as he approached.

"Oh, thanks," she said with a smile as he put it on her desk.

He was so surprised that she even spoke to him that he smiled back and nervously murmured, "You too." Realizing his slip, his face turned red and he turned and hurried out of the office.

Chapter Two

Sharon

OF ALL PLACES, Sharon thought as she sat unnaturally straight in her seat, trying to pay attention to her date. They were sitting in the lobby of a trendy hotel on Park Avenue that she and Joe used to frequent when she wanted to dress up and feel posh. All the furniture was white but the floors and window frames and inner walls were jet-black, with tall glass windows showing off their happenings to the pedestrians on the sidewalk. There was upbeat music playing at a volume just short of loud, and with the conversations of the other patrons, she used the noise as an excuse for not being all there.

"Do you want another drink?" her date asked her as he hailed a passing waiter. "You're still nursing your first rum and Coke."

"I'm fine," she told him, taking a slow sip from the thin straw. He ordered a second Vodka tonic for himself, which she hoped would be the last. He was cute enough, with no obvious turn-offs like acute baldness or facial asymmetry, but she wasn't gathering enough in terms of compatibility.

"I normally don't drink this much," he explained when the waiter left. "I just figured that in a place like this—"

She put up her hand. "No need to explain. You told me you

were an accountant," she then asked. "What else do you do, like, outside of work?"

"If I even get a chance!" he exclaimed. He was trying to be funny, but Sharon only granted him a thin smile. "I'm just kidding. Seriously, though, because I'm still starting out I stay at the office pretty late. I try to get to a gym but, you know, it just doesn't happen. I'm an early riser, so I get to sleep early." He crossed his eyes. "I guess I'm kind of boring."

She coughed. "It's good to get enough sleep."

"Certainly. It's a necessary foundation to a healthy lifestyle."

That sounded like a magazine advertisement, she thought. Moreover, such a rigid schedule didn't mesh with her nocturnal lifestyle. She tested this theory of hers: "Would you call yourself 'health-conscious,' or you just try to keep in-shape?"

"Well, I definitely try to be healthy," he replied. "I don't eat fried food or drink coffee."

Doesn't drink coffee! While she didn't live off it, she couldn't understand how anyone could pull a nine-hour day without a bit of a boost. Sharon glanced around, unable to find a clock. "If you get to sleep so early," she asked him, "when do you get a chance to socialize? To enjoy life?"

He was taken aback. "Who says I'm not enjoying life?"

"I just figured that such dedication to your job leaves you without much free time."

His drink arrived and they silently watched the waiter remove the old glass and place the new one in front of them on a fresh black napkin. Her date thanked the waiter and took a big gulp. "Like I said, I'm just starting and have to put in additional hours to find my niche. But I do other things. I'm very particular with davening, I learn *daf yomi*..."

"Really?" she asked, raising her eyes to fight off a yawn. "Like, you go to a *shiur*?"

"Every morning before *Shacharit*."

"That must be at like 5:30!" she said, astonished. He nodded silently, as if he had been waiting for her to understand. "I see why you get to bed so early. Coming out to meet me must be taking you out of your schedule."

He looked away and smiled shyly. "Well, I figured that meeting up with you was worth a coffee in the morning..."

It was a line and it was too much. She knew she was being harsh, but then she walked into the date on bad terms. As soon as she realized where her date was taking her, Joe popped into her mind and she couldn't get him out. Why was he so grumpy on the phone? And why didn't she know that he was going to his parents for Shavuot? Two years ago, when they had both been at NYU, she had known everything about him. Once he moved to Brooklyn last year, he started acting differently, almost not like himself. Unfortunately for this guy, she didn't have the energy to focus on what he had to offer, and so she let the date continue on autopilot until he would make the gesture to leave or 10 PM, whichever came first.

As hoped, at around 9:30 they shared a taxi to her building on West End Avenue, where he told the driver to wait as he walked her to the door. She thanked him for the evening and complimented him by calling him "a gentleman from beginning to end." He smiled and waved and disappeared into the cab and from her life.

Upstairs she went straight to her room and fell into her bed. It was her grandmother's bed—in fact, the whole apartment had been her grandmother's before she had a stroke and went to a home in Lakewood, New Jersey. For the last eighteen months or so, Sharon was "occupying" the space, living it up on the Upper West Side rent-free. Besides for a few additions to the décor, Sharon's presence was only detectable by her piles of clothing on the bedroom floor and her computer on her grandmother's vanity. She stared at the ceiling for a moment before reaching into her purse to call her mother from her cell phone. She had made the mistake of mentioning her date and no matter how late she would return home she knew her mother was waiting for her call.

"Hi honey," her mother said quickly after two rings. "You're home?"

"Yes," replied Sharon.

"Short date?" She sounded disappointed.

"All first dates are meant to be short, Ima."

"Hmm," was all she heard. It was enough. "How was he?"

"A gentleman from beginning to end," Sharon said sardonically as she rolled over onto her stomach to kick off her shoes.

"That sounds good."

Sharon sighed. "He had three drinks."

A pause. "Well, with tax season and everything—"

Sharon sat up and started unbuttoning her blouse. "Tax season ended in April, and that's no excuse."

"I don't know why you are so picky, Sharon."

The bottom button was refusing to squeeze through its hole, frustrating her. "Would you want me dating someone who drinks that much?"

"Was he incoherent?"

"No, just…I didn't like it. I kind of let it dive-bomb after the second."

"How did you get set up?"

"Set up?" she repeated incredulously. "Please, Ima."

"What? What's wrong with getting set up?"

She clicked her tongue. "I can take care of myself, and would you like me spending $2,000 for someone to make a few phone calls?"

"OK, honey," her mother said quickly. "Sorry for mentioning it. I'm actually waiting up for your brother. He didn't tell us where he went and he doesn't answer his cell phone."

Sharon rolled off the bed to find her pajamas. "It's senioritis. He's basically graduated."

"But still, he didn't tell me where he was going."

She lifted all the clothing off the back of her computer chair and was surprised that her pajamas weren't there.

"So I'm planning your brother's Shabbat next week," her mother then added. "You're coming, right?"

Sharon knew that it was less a question than an affirmation. "Right."

"Maybe you'll come to the graduation Thursday night? Your father wasn't sure if he could make it..."

Whatever. She opened up the dresser and found no pajamas there either. "OK, but the week after I've got to be here."

"Why?"

"Friend from college's getting married. He's having a whole thing." She finally found them under a pile of other clothing. With a huff, she said, "Look, I'm pretty tired. I'll talk to you tomorrow."

"OK, honey. Don't worry. There are other men out there."

"Thanks, Ima."

Chapter Three

Joe

JOE NORMALLY STAYED LATE at his office on Fridays, finding the relative quiet more conducive to getting his work done. Besides, he wasn't in any rush to get back to prepare for Shabbos. He had no definite plans, only a hope of an invite from someone he befriended from the shuls in the neighborhood he frequented, supplemented by a meager purchase from Gourmet on J in case of a shutout. Still, he much preferred it to crashing on the couch of one of a string of friends from college who lived in more popular neighborhoods for young professionals around the city. Once in a while he availed himself of a bit of revelry, but to spend his entire Shabbos engrossed in party games and hanging out didn't excite him. He much preferred using his time for learning Gemara or getting his graduate reading done than being tied to someone's social schedule.

He had been hoping to avoid Mr. Siegel ever since their meeting last Monday because he wasn't planning to call the shadchan. However much Daniela might've set back his confidence, he wasn't desperate enough to need a matchmaker. He'd heard all about shidduchim from Sharon, and didn't need to be escorted through a relationship or cajoled into a marriage with someone he barely knew when he could take care of himself. Just because he hadn't yet been successful finding someone to love didn't ruin his chances forever. He was still optimistic; his future wife might bump into him around the next corner. He had resolved to destroy the business card, but procrastination prevented him from acting so hasty.

After work, he got on a downtown 2 train and squeezed into the standing space of the crowded car with his messenger bag. At Atlantic Avenue he switched to the Q to procure some Shabbos foods in case Mrs. Gruberman's offer had been conditional to a follow-up phone call. As he approached the platform he heard the exhaust of the train brakes and so he ran down the stairs and hopped into the closest door. Satisfied with his accomplishment, he looked around the subway car to show his face of triumph and saw someone he knew and went over. Millions of people pass through the subways in New York every day, so even running into the faintest acquaintance is a treasured occurrence.

"Hi Nati," Joe said after squirming through the crowded car.

"Hey there Joe," Nati replied, offering the hand that wasn't holding a briefcase. Whenever Joe found himself around the Upper West Side, somehow Nati was always there, and upon the third such instance Nati introduced himself and they discovered that they both were raised in the suburbs of DC. "How's it going?"

"Fine. Just finishing work?"

"Yep. Live around here?"

"In Flatbush. I take it that you're visiting someone."

"You got me," he said.

"I went down to Potomac for Shavuos," Joe told him.

"Yeah?" Nati nodded in an understanding way. "Nothing

changes down there."

"Nope. But our parents like it."

"Oh sure, sure." They both began to look around the car, as if something needed to fill the silence. Never had they met out of a large group context where escaping to another conversation was always an option, and the intimacy that comes with being thrown in the same crowded Q train was an unfamiliar burden.

"So then I take it that you're not going down for the wedding," Nati said.

"What wedding?" Joe asked.

"Isn't Rebecca Hoffman getting married in two weeks?"

"What?" Joe exclaimed. Half the people in the subway car turned upon hearing his outburst, and so he quickly composed himself, mustering a weak smile. "Did you say Rebecca Hoffman?" he asked Nati more quietly.

"Yeah," Nati told him, expressionless. "Wasn't she in your year at JDS?"

"Yes, yes she was. I just…hmm." He scratched his chin.

"I didn't get an invitation," Nati said absently. "I didn't know her so well. My cousin told me about it. The *hattan* is from Westchester; they met in college."

"At Harvard," Joe added hollowly.

"Is that where she went? Wow, smart girl."

"Yeah," Joe agreed. "I didn't know." Wanting to change the subject, he quickly asked the only thing that came to mind. "So who are you visiting?"

"You know my friend Jessica?" Nati asked.

Joe blinked his eyes rapidly. He couldn't think of a time he saw Nati without her. "Yes, Jessica. Where does she live?"

"Well, she lives on 92nd, just off Broadway, but her parents live in Sheepshead Bay. She went there for Shavuot and caught something nasty; she's been in bed all week."

Joe winced. "I'm sorry to hear that."

Nati looked away. "Yeah, well, thank G-d she's feeling better, but she's been so bored out there she asked me to come cheer her up."

"That's nice of you," Joe told him as he patted Nati's shoulder. Then he realized something. "But how are you going to get back in time?"

Nati eyed Joe with a puzzled face. "Get back?"

"How are you going to get uptown before Shabbos?"

Nati laughed. "Nah, I'm not going anywhere. Besides, her mother is an excellent cook. Tonight she's making duck." He closed his eyes and hummed as if he could taste it there on the subway.

"I take it this isn't your first time going out there," Joe surmised.

Nati laughed gruffly, almost coarsely. "No. Not at all."

The subway stopped and Joe had to back up to let passengers exit. When the doors closed, Joe returned to where he was standing, bringing back the conversation by saying, "Wow…a whole Shabbos."

Nati shrugged one shoulder and closed his eyes. "When you know someone for so long," he said blankly, "it doesn't register any more. I've known Jessica since college—six, seven years. You reach a stage when it's just natural."

Joe nodded. He recalled the time in his senior year when he dropped everything and jettisoned uptown to bring Sharon some soup when she was sick in bed at her grandmother's apartment. He laughed to himself, thinking that it wasn't so long ago he would do something like that, and yet now he couldn't imagine himself doing the same. The nostalgia quieted them both until the train announced its imminent approach to Prospect Park.

Nati straightened his back. "I'm going to get off and take the express."

"You really know the deal," Joe joked.

He looked into Joe's eyes and sighed. "I guess so."

"You're doing a real *hessed*," Joe told him.

Nati nodded tiredly as the train came to a stop. "You don't know the half of it," he said.

Joe hid his curiosity as the train door opened and Nati waved goodbye as he walked onto the platform.

Chapter Four

Sharon

FIVE MINUTES AFTER the time for candle-lighting, Sharon was still unsure what she could squeeze in before accepting Shabbat. Her face was already smoothed with a thin layer of cream and her eyelashes were already mascara-ed, but her eyes still needed shadowing and her lips were completely untouched—no lipstick or pencil. Could she do all three? But then she didn't even choose an outfit. Were the candles even set up? No. OK, that is essential. Then again, so is eye shadow...all right, not really, but she couldn't leave her eyes completely bare. Fine, eye shadow and just lip gloss—no lipstick or pencil. Wait, is the light off in the fridge?

"Tamar!" she yelled to her roommate. "Is the light out in the fridge?"

"Yes," she heard from the other room. "Do you want me to set up your candles?"

"Please!" Sharon screamed back. Great, another minute...but she already glossed her lips. So she'll get dressed before lighting; she remembered one of her high school teachers saying that it's more *kavod* to Shabbat to finish everything before lighting, but then again, so is lighting on time. But what to wear? Her eye shadow was turquoise, but the turquoise blouse was in the laundry pile. She could Febreeze it…no time. Why did she choose that eye shadow? Didn't she get it that time she ran into that guy Jake at Macy's? Maybe he'd be at O-Z tonight…can't think about him, no, not now…Fine, then what else will match the turquoise? Maybe just go with black, but which black top went with her boutique skirt?

Sharon eventually stepped out of her bedroom into the living room/dining room where the candles were set up above her grandmother's dresser. Tamar had already lit her candles and was setting the table, also wearing a black cardigan and a gypsy skirt. Sharon froze, looking to see that there were still three minutes to change.

"Just light," said her roommate, also noticing her 'mirror.' "It's not like we're eating together tonight anyway."

"But we will be walking together," said Sharon as she dashed to the candles. She lit her two tea lights and said the bracha, concluding with an elongated sigh and a collapse onto the loveseat. Through the window in front of her, she could see between the buildings a nice strip of the western sky above the Hudson River. The sunset was already colored with deep oranges and pinks at the horizon and for the first time she noticed how nicely the setting sun and its sky fit with the new curtains she put up. It was part of her attempt to take the interior design of her grandmother's apartment out of the 1970s. She had already covered the brown couch and matching loveseat, stored the shag carpet in the hall closet, and added a necessary halogen light to the reading corner, but the bulky coffee table and the wooden bookshelves and their collection of cheap novels with fading covers just couldn't be ignored. Looking around the house, she delighted in seeing the kitchen sink empty of its perennial pile of dishes. She realized that she could really do a lot around the house when she didn't have any real work.

She was jolted out of her half-asleep musings by Tamar's voice. "Do you want to walk together?" she was asking. "Where are you going?"

"O-Z," Sharon replied with a grimace. "Esther told me to meet her outside."

"Well, I'm headed towards the Center, so you don't have to worry about matching."

Sharon felt very blessed to have ended up with such a personable roommate. She'd heard all the horror stories, but she didn't want to live alone and leave a bedroom entirely unoccupied. So Tamar's rent money paid for Sharon's utilities and a few other expenses, giving Sharon a chance to live on the Upper West without the burden of having to work to pay an exorbitant rent. She kept from complete boredom by taking freelance magazine writing or editing jobs and an occasional translation of an official Hebrew document for her uncle's law firm, but she was essentially enjoying her time hanging out with whoever was available, uninterested in pursuing a career or any particular hobby.

"Hey, what happened to Joey?" Tamar then asked. "He keeps popping up on your screensaver and I can't remember the last time he was here."

"Don't ask," Sharon sighed. "I don't know what's wrong with him. He seems to prefer isolating himself in his basement apartment in the middle of nowhere."

"He hasn't come around in a few weeks now, right?"

"Try a few months," she said sadly. "He got upset the last time I arranged for us to eat by this friend from college who ended up having a whole soiree for, like, two dozen people. Joey's been living in Brooklyn for so long that he forgot how social he was at NYU."

"Well, I wouldn't worry too much. Friday night parties aren't for everybody."

"I guess not," agreed Sharon. She lifted herself from the couch. "Let's go out together," she suggested to Tamar. "I'll wear my denim jacket."

She took the bottle of Chenin Blanc that she had found at the wine store from the refrigerator. It was advertised in the store as having won some Chairman's Award, whatever that was. She put her trust in the chairman's tastes and hoped that her host would enjoy it. Then she left with Tamar down the eleven flights of stairs to the lobby and out to stickiness of the humid evening.

Sharon was off to Ohav Tzedek, a popular synagogue in the Upper West, though not because anything extraordinary went on inside the walls. With the departure of the congregants after the service, the sidewalk of 95th Street became the flocking ground for scores of Upper West Side Jews and their guests and well-wishers exchanging salutations and sound-bite conversations before leaving for their respective Shabbat evening meals. It was such a neighborhood attraction that the police even stationed a lone officer to ensure its safety. For some reason, this was where her host told her to meet her.

Already as she turned off Amsterdam Avenue, she glanced down the block and found that the davening had ended and the sidewalk was already filled with people. She passed a few older men in dark sport coats as she made her way towards the shul, eventually arriving at the edge of the crowd. The sidewalk was thick with people all trying to hear themselves above the din of so many simultaneous conversations. She stepped on her tip-toes to search for her host but could only see hair, hats, and kippot. Still in the air, from her right she was addressed by the unmistakable voice of Devorah Marcus.

"Hello darling," Devorah said in British-sounding way. Sharon lowered her heels and turned to find Devorah extending her arms. Sharon accepted the embrace, reciprocating lightly. "Shabbat Shalom, how are you?"

"Very good Devorah," Sharon had started to say, but Devorah interrupted by turning to a short balding man with thick frameless eyeglasses and sweat beading on his forehead.

"Sharon, meet Ralph." He waved enthusiastically with a full smile, which Sharon almost had to mirror. She lifted her hand that was holding the wine in a similar salute.

"That's a pretty special wine you have there," Ralph then said, pointing to the bottle in Sharon's hand. "It won the Chairman's Award in 2002."

"Wow," she faked surprise. "Does it taste like the Bartenura Moscato?"

"Not at all," Ralph answered, pulling out a handkerchief and wiping his forehead. "Completely different. Make sure you present this to your host *before* the dessert. It's really more of an aperitif."

"Thanks for telling me," Sharon tried to say with enthusiasm. "Hey, Devorah, do you know Esther Jacob?"

Devorah shook her head. "No, I don't think so. Does she daven here?"

"I don't know," Sharon said, looking around. *There's that guy Jake...* "She told me to meet her here."

"Sorry," Devorah said. "Good luck. How is everything?"

Sharon responded absently, thinking that she saw Esther on the other side of the crowd. Without noticing that she left Devorah and

Ralph, she walked around the police barriers and into the street. In the middle of the street she realized that the well-dressed woman she was looking at was in fact Esther and so she doubled her pace. The solitary police officer was standing by the barrier, watching Sharon's odd behavior, and upon realizing his suspicious glance she assured him with a gesture that she knew she was in the middle of the street and that she was returning to the sidewalk.

Esther was older than Sharon, somewhere in her thirties, but she carried her age with a maturity that Sharon hoped to emulate one day. She even looked the part: her dark curly hair was held up by a big spider clip and she wore what looked like an evening gown with matching pumps. It was as if she had on no make-up, or very little, but nonetheless looked put-together and fully in touch with her position as hostess of the evening. As Sharon got closer, almost exactly at the right moment Esther turned to Sharon and her face brightened.

"Shabbat Shalom Sharon!" Esther beamed, her enthusiasm unmistakably genuine.

"I'm sorry I'm late," Sharon said as they hugged. "Were you waiting long?"

"No, I also just got here," Esther answered. "I go to the Sephardic shul."

Before Sharon could ask why they had to meet here, two guys intercepted Esther from the side and Sharon waited patiently for Esther to greet them. They were a strange pair, completely mismatched, but they seemed to know each other well, as Esther wasn't addressing them individually. The shorter looked older than his companion, his light-brown hair parted to one side rather conservatively. He wore a white shirt and simple dark gray pants with a pattered red tie clashing with his white-and-blue knit kippah. The other guy had short hair, stylishly flipped up from his forehead, and wore a suit with no tie. After a moment he noticed that Sharon had previously been speaking with Esther and his glance lingered on her eyes.

"Esther, who's your friend?" he asked, still looking at Sharon. His dark-blue eyes penetrated into Sharon's, and for a moment she lost her gall and inwardly hoped that Esther would hurry up and introduce them.

"Andy, this is Sharon. She's my guest for the evening."

"My loss," he conceded. Then he smacked the other guy on the arm. "Last time I let you make my Shabbat plans."

Sharon knew that he was trying to humor her but she still felt flattered. "Next time. Your name is Andy?"

"That's right. I'm sorry about your meal tomorrow."

"What do you mean?"

"After eating Esther's cuisine you won't be able to enjoy anything else for a while…maybe by next Shabbat."

"Oh stop," Esther pleaded. "Take your compliments and find yourself a girlfriend already."

He was looking at Sharon when he said, "Whatever you say." Turning to his companion, he again smacked him on the arm. "Let's go, David."

"Shabbat Shalom, Andy," Esther said. "Shabbat Shalom, David."

Esther and Sharon watched the guys as they walked down towards Amsterdam Avenue, pushing each other as they walked. After a few moments the girls turned to each other and rolled their eyes.

"They're all the same," Sharon told Esther.

"Yeah, but what can you do?"

"They're friends of yours?"

Esther thought for a moment. "You could say that."

Sharon then suspected that Esther turned them down because of her. "Look, they don't have to eat alone. I don't want to be the reason…"

"Don't worry," Esther assured her. "I don't have guys over for meals." Then she added, more quietly, "not anymore."

Sharon turned to Esther and was surprised to find her wearing a stern face. "Oh," she added nervously.

"Come," Esther then commanded, squinting at the crowd and pivoting away from it. "Let's get out of this heat."

Chapter Five

Joe

AS JOE WATCHED NATI pass by through the windows, his head suddenly felt very heavy. He didn't know what Nati meant by his parting statement, but he was too bothered by a different piece of their conversation to dwell on it. Little did Nati know that mentioning Rebecca's name would affect Joe so much, as to consume his thoughts for the rest of his way home.

He and Rebecca Hoffman had been in the same grade, in the same honors classes, in the same Jewish day school from first grade and all throughout high school, living two streets apart but knowing very little about each other. They were both "over-achievers," smart kids who focused their time and attention on studying and academic achievement and didn't devote their time to thinking about the opposite sex in the way teenagers their age did. At least Joe never thought anything more about her; he was too busy filling his college applications with positive accomplishments.

Everything changed when their whole class went to Poland for its post-graduation senior trip. Their school was unique in that the seniors took all their required coursework by January and spent the remainder of the spring term in Israel, along the way subduing their hearts with the perfunctory March of the Living. With all the college applications in and their diplomas merely awaiting print, Joe and Rebecca were able to finally meet, now released from the constant preparation for the next test or project. On the plane they found that they had a lot in common, finally able to talk when before they had never exchanged more than a quick chat or school-work assistance. This gave them each someone to share the emotional onslaught that comes with touring post-war Poland, and by the time their class reached Israel, they were deeply attached. They walked together on hikes, ate together, requested to be assigned the same tasks together when they volunteered, all the while believing that they were different than their peers in having saved their first relationship for the mature age of seventeen.

Their bliss was tested when the acceptance letters reached home in early April and everyone's parents relayed the results. Rebecca had been accepted to her first choice at Harvard, but Joe's shooting for the moon with MIT hadn't worked out, his only remaining options being his mother's alma mater at NYU or College Park. At first Rebecca decided to go to Columbia so they could both be in Manhattan, but Joe refused to let her settle and turn down her first choice. Only after a week of debating Rebecca agreed to allow them to matriculate five hours apart. However close they now were, they'd only really been together a few months and Joe didn't feel that it was enough to risk her entire future on their short relationship. Though she appeared to understand that he was only thinking of her best interests, he worried whether she inwardly translated his adamancy to suggest that he really didn't want to be with her, and from then he realized that their relationship would need to answer the looming serious question.

However, she never granted them the chance to ask it. When

she surprised him a few days later by telling him that she would be returning home for Passover, he knew that she was already giving up on whatever they had built. Why should they continue to string each other along when the inevitable distance would do its damage in a few months? He didn't fight her. He accompanied her to the airport, the two of them silently staring out the bus window at the Negev Desert in the night, mentally preparing for what would come. For three months they had never been more than a few meters apart, and now each sand dune the streetlights illuminated denoted another step towards separation. He struggled with his decision even as they waited for her boarding pass. Was he doing the right thing? Would they give it a shot if he would try to convince her? Was anyone else in the throng of people at the terminal also passing such an ordeal? They promised to call, a last attempt at denying the truth of the moment, and Rebecca looked him in the eye to give him one last chance.

"I love you Joe," she said for the first time. "I had the best time of my life and I'll never forget it."

"Neither will I," he said back.

There were a number of minutes while she probably waited for him to say three different last words but he didn't. She finally turned and went, tears soaking both of her cheeks. He loved her too much to not let her live her own life, and when she finally disappeared from his sight he resolved to never forget his sacrifice.

He tried to return to his classmates but everything reminded him of her. When his father's cousin invited him to Jerusalem for the sedarim, he packed all of his things and bid everyone farewell. It was more than opportune that he would meet an MIT graduate at the second-day minyan who persuaded Joe into spending his summer learning in yeshiva; Joe was doubly relieved to have a pretext to explain why he wasn't going back to volunteering.

His short experience in yeshiva gave him a new and invigorating perspective on Judaism, and he left for home with a kippah permanently atop his head and a desire to learn more. Still, he didn't forget the fondness that he had towards Rebecca and longed to meet up with her once he returned to Potomac. They kept in touch through e-mail and even got together the day after he got back, but without the original tenderness to blind him, Joe was turned off by Rebecca's lack of enthusiasm towards his new religious lifestyle. He never forgot the first moment when they saw each other after four months and she just stared at his black velvet kippah, without even saying hello, for five embarrassing seconds. From then, Joe started college knowing that he'd made the right decision.

Now she was getting married. In his three years dorming at NYU, he had been trying to fill the void left by Rebecca with a religious girl, and all his attempts had proven to be failures. He had thought religious girls would be similarly seeking a committed guy and yet they only seemed to want someone to hang out with and have a good time. He knew from Rebecca that he couldn't be satisfied with silly flings or with girls who weren't serious about eventually committing, but as he grew older he was becoming frustrated at not getting anywhere in his pursuit. He'd followed all of Sharon's advice and yet never seemed to find the right girl. Joe now felt worse being in last place, knowing that Rebecca had already reached the finish line.

Only when Joe heard the conductor's announcement did he realize that the train had reached Avenue J. With a jolt, he jumped up and leaped out the door as the closing bell was ringing. The time was just about five and he dashed down the stairs and up the street to Gourmet on J. He was able to obtain a small portion of roast chicken and a kugel as they were putting the food away and afterwards headed towards Duane Reade for drinks and other supplies. In the paper goods aisle, his mother called him.

"How are you doing, Joe?" she asked him, in a way that reminded him of the stereotypical therapy session. "How was your week?"

"Fine. I've been catching up at work."

"That's good. Where are you for Shabbos?"

"Home." He examined the selection of plates with a pensive glance. "Right now I'm trying to choose paper plates."

"Get the coated ones."

"They're twice the price!"

"They don't fall apart."

He grunted. "I don't have the money for such luxuries."

"You didn't want to go to Sharon?"

Ever since Sharon invited him to her parents' house for Shabbos when he had a final one Friday before Winter Break, his mother thought they must've spent every Shabbos together. "Nope," he said decisively.

"Why not?"

"I do have a life here in Brooklyn, you know," he said indignantly. "Besides, it's not like I have a standing invitation to crash by her neighbors."

"I just thought that it was somewhat lonely with your roommate gone."

Realizing that he probably spoke too harshly with his mother, he admitted, "Sometimes it feels that way."

"What are you going to do?"

"My landlords aren't insisting I find anyone," then adding, "yet."

"That's nice of them."

"Yeah, it is." He picked his brand—the cheapest—and started towards the checkout. "What are you doing for Shabbos? Is dad home yet?"

"No, not yet. We might go up to Ellen and Michael tonight, depending on how he feels. It's been a long week for him, too."

"Yeah," Joe said distractedly. He was standing in front of the Snapple stand, figuring out how he would be able to grab a bottle while talking on his phone and holding his Gourmet on J shopping bag and paper plates in the other hand.

Then his mother said, "I found out today that Rebecca Hoffman is getting married in two weeks. Did you know about this?"

As he clenched his phone between his ear and his shoulder to reach for a bottle of raspberry Snapple, he answered in a strained voice, "I just heard about it."

"Well, I take it that you aren't going. Did you get an invitation?"

He could sense from his mother's tone that she felt snubbed. "No, but don't think Mrs. Hoffman has anything against you. She probably…there's a good reason I didn't get invited."

"Why? I thought you two were good friends. You got together with her when you came down."

"Not in a long time," he stated. He knew he would have to explain at least some of the story to his mother to prevent her from bearing a grudge against Rebecca's mother. However, he was standing in Duane Reade with his hands full and Shabbos fast approaching. "I never told you what happened between me and Rebecca, mom. We became…pretty close in Israel."

"Oh," she said, followed by a long silence. Joe chose his drink and got on a checkout line behind a religious man who reminded him of Mr. Siegel. "But that was years ago. It still isn't awkward between you, right?"

"No, but…I guess…I can't really speak for her but it wasn't, like, an easy break. Not like that."

"I see. I'm sorry. Is it hard for you to hear she's getting married?"

"No," he sighed. "I wish her much success and happiness."

"What about you? Are you dating anyone?"

How ironic that we have never spoken about this area of my life until today. "Look, I'm standing in Duane Reade with my hands full. Can I perhaps call you back?"

"Certainly, dear. I know that it's probably hard to talk about it."

"It is, especially in public." The Mr. Siegel look-alike turned around and glared at Joe.

"OK then."

"I'll try to call when I get home."

"Whenever you're settled."

A bus drove past as he left the pharmacy, so he painstakingly walked the dozen or so blocks to his street in the thick humidity. At home, he dropped his bags on the table and fell into his bed.

Some time later he woke up with a jerk—his first instinct was to make sure he didn't sleep into Shabbos and miss davening. With only twenty minutes until candle-lighting, he quickly set the timer on his toaster oven and slid the chicken and kugel inside. If an invite didn't pan out he would at least have warm food. He jumped in the shower and emerged to shave with his electric shaver with ten minutes before candle-lighting. He got dressed in his Shabbos suit and turned off the fridge light while fumbling with his tie. With no woman to light for him, he lit two tiny tea lights and went to mincha, leaving his key hidden in its Shabbos hiding-place to the side of the door behind a broken lantern.

Davening was an exercise in anxiety because as each congregant entered the *shul* Joe turned towards the door to see if his hope for an invite would be fulfilled. He was a regular at two neighborhood benefactors who davened at this shul, but neither of them had arrived yet and things weren't looking too good. Joe was beginning to resolve to enjoy his warm dinner when he saw Mr. Gruberman, his upstairs neighbor and landlord, clamor into the shul and begin his silent *Amidah*. While he could always count on Mr. Gruberman to cajole Joe into joining their meal, he didn't want to get into any awkward situation were Daniela to also be there and so he'd wait for Mr. Gruberman to make the offer. Joe enjoyed the davening with at least the thought that he didn't choose the wrong shul.

Afterwards Joe confidently went over to wish Mr. Gruberman a Good Shabbos. He was very happy with his landlord, a stocky but jovial man in his late forties with a full head of short silvering hair who wore starched cufflink shirts everyday, but never with a tie. The Grubermans, both husband and wife, were lawyers, and spent their wealth on lavish Shabbos meals with many dishes and many guests. Because of his physical condition, Mr. Gruberman could no longer indulge in his wife's delicacies as much as he had at the beginning of their marriage, but he didn't allow his limitations to affect his guests' *oneg Shabbos* and passed around dishes he couldn't eat without a touch of sorrow. There were Hassidim somewhere in his ancestry and Joe had to politely refuse after his first *l'haim*, which he only downed to please his host's desire to give.

As Joe approached, Mr. Gruberman was shaking hands and smiling widely at the *chazzan*. "I haven't heard that *niggin* in two years," he told him. "If you come back here in a month I'll get you up to sing it for me again."

"Why only a month?" the chazzan asked him, noticing Joe and

giving him a wink.

"Because you aren't a member." Without turning, Mr. Gruberman let go of the chazzan's hand and reached for Joe's, grasping it so that Joe couldn't move. "Once you start paying dues, maybe you'll get a more regular gig."

"I'll think about it," the chazzan replied as he turned towards the exit.

"Please do." Then he released Joe's arm but engaged his attention. "What about you, Joe? When are you going to start paying dues?"

"I didn't know that single guys were allowed to become members."

"That's exactly my question." Mr. Gruberman gave Joe a look that basically asked *nu?* "How was Shavuos?"

"Fine."

"You learned all night?"

Joe made a face. "I was awake. I learned most of the time."

"That sounds about right. Are you joining us?"

"You mean on the walk home?"

"Yes, to my home." He indicated the direction to the door.

"Your wife invited me earlier in the week but I didn't speak to her since."

Mr. Gruberman countered Joe's doubt with his raised hand. "Doesn't matter. You know you don't need an invitation."

Joe wasn't sure whether Mr. Gruberman was in on the whole Daniela thing. He therefore confirmed, "Your wife asked to see if I'm coming?"

Mr. Gruberman walked towards the door. "I don't need her approval to invite one of our children," he said. As he walked out, he shook hands with the other congregants. Over his shoulder, he beckoned Joe. "Come, it's late enough."

Joe still didn't know whether Mr. Gruberman was warmly assuring Joe that he had nothing to worry about or whether he was overriding anything his wife might've told him. With no way to find out he acceded to at least accompany him to his house and perhaps gage the issue on the way.

As they stepped out the door they were approached by another regular of the Grubermans who Joe had met on several previous occasions. This guy was older than Joe, somewhere in his mid-thirties, an ambitious lawyer who quickly engaged Mr. Gruberman in some political discussion that Joe listened to with vague interest. When they reached the house, the man bid them farewell with an explanation that he'd made other plans. Mr. Gruberman scolded the man for getting his hopes up. "I thought you'd keep me company while Yosef here occupies the women."

"And what about me?" he asked as he walked down the block. "I still need to find myself a shidduch."

"Take some time off and do some serious dating," Mr. Gruberman called to him. Then, more quietly, he added, "he's too busy for a wife." He turned off the sidewalk and onto the thin stone path alongside the front room towards the side-door entrance. As he walked, he said, "that goes for you too, Yosef. I want to make a l'haim already and get back a second tenant into my basement— and I don't mean another guy, if you catch my drift."

"I'm too busy for a wife," Joe quipped. "I still have to finish my graduate degree."

"Feh," Mr. Gruberman dismissed Joe's claim with a wave of his hand. "It's the summer. Find yourself a wife."

"I'm trying," Joe answered, then admitting, "I've been trying for years."

"Have you been to a shadchan?"

Joe looked away, not wanting to get into a debate. Mr. Gruberman didn't pursue the matter any further. "Well, you never know," he said encouragingly. "Maybe something will happen soon."

Joe sighed. "It's always maybe."

Mr. Gruberman opened the door and the two of them were hit with cool air from the AC and an aroma of chicken soup blending with potpourri. To the left was the stairway to the second floor and after it a hallway to the kitchen and the back of the house. Immediately in front of them was the small outlet of the front room that met the dining room and the foyer in which they presently stood. Joe lingered in the foyer while Mr. Gruberman closed the door, the loud crash resonating to the kitchen. "Good Shabbos Tatty!" they heard Mrs. Gruberman's voice call from the kitchen, shortly followed by the thumps of teenage feet clunking down the wooden stairs.

"Good Shabbos Shira-leh!" Mr. Gruberman said to his youngest daughter as she landed into him. "What are you doing with your bas mitzvah album?"

"I'm showing it to Daniela," she replied proudly. She was a just-turned-teenager who had energy to spare, addressing Joe with a number of waves and a wide show of her braces. Joe mustered a strained smile as he suddenly felt an entire butterfly exhibit move into his gut. Daniela was here!

"She's never seen it?" Mr. Gruberman asked wondrously to his daughter.

"Nope. I mean, I couldn't find it for, like, a year, but she asked and I looked."

"Great!"

"Shira, could you come here?" Mrs. Gruberman called from

the kitchen.

She made a teenage face of annoyance, but Mr. Gruberman gently took her shoulders and marched her towards the kitchen. "Daniela isn't going anywhere," he assured her as they headed down the hallway. "Joe, make yourself comfortable."

He turned towards the living room, waiting for some prompt that would tell him how to act. He was hoping his hosts would realize the awkward situation in the making and somehow Mr. Gruberman would excuse Joe with a rain-check and let him silently slip out without Daniela knowing he'd even entered the house. However, when he heard Mr. Gruberman's loud voice echo from the kitchen, saying, "I know what you told me but Joe's as much a regular here..." he figured that Daniela had also heard and he might as well face her. He lifted his foot but stopped in mid-step when he heard female voices in the living room.

"I'm TELLing you," Daniela said emphatically, "I'm not even THINKing of dating now."

That confirms Mrs. Gruberman's story. Joe felt as if eavesdropping on their conversation was violating some type of halacha, but since they were brazen enough to speak so candidly in earshot of others, and he wanted to hear more, he resumed his position in the front hallway and listened without moving.

"Yeah, sure," came the voice of Aliza Gruberman, age eighteen. "You're probably inundated with suggestions."

"From where do you know a word like 'inundated'?"

"SATs."

"Touche."

"Nu, come on. I thought we were friends," Aliza whined.

"We are. I'm telling you the truth."

"No you're not."

"Why? What do you know?"

"What do you mean?"

There was a pause. Eventually, Daniela said, "Nothing."

"You're lying. What am I supposed to know?"

"No, I can't say."

"Come on! You can tell me!"

"Nooooooo."

"Yeah! Tell me...you were suggested someone? I know the person?"

"Kind of..."

"Who?"

Daniela lowered her voice and Joe crept up to the corner of the foyer to hear. "You know that guy that comes here? I think he lives downstairs."

"Who? Joe?" Another pause. "Really? Who suggested?"

"Your mother."

"I could see that."

"Really?"

"Yeah. He's a good guy—he works, has a degree, and he learns. Plus he's from out-of-town."

"Whatever that's supposed to mean."

"Fine, right. So, what did you say?" Another pause. "Why?"

Yeah, why? Joe also wanted to know.

"I don't know," Daniela said slowly. "I thought...when I first met him here, but then...I don't know..."

Joe's heart was beating like an African drum circle, so much that he feared the girls in the other room could hear it. He was confused; was she interested at all in finding a guy or not? Why was she even scrutinizing him at all if she was so busy? It sounded as if their conversations had been potentially more than friendly, but then what had she said before about not even thinking about guys? He needed to sort out these incongruent statements, and he certainly couldn't do that during the meal.

Then Mr. Gruberman made his presence in the dining room known by dragging his chair from under the table. "Aliza," his voice beckoned, "just because you've nearly graduated and are going to Israel in two months, you aren't excused from helping mommy."

"I was entertaining our guest," Aliza explained.

"Oh, well then," he replied. "Good Shabbos Daniela. Where's Joe?"

"Joe?" Daniela asked nervously. "What Joe?"

"What Joe? Is there any other Joe we know? Ha, a rhyme! Didn't he come in?"

"No," the girls answered together.

Joe knew that if he didn't think of something fast, the girls would assume that he'd heard everything. He was beginning to shake as Mr. Gruberman called, "Joe? Are you still in the hall-way?" On an impulse, he opened the front door from the inside and closed it a second later, loud enough to make an echoing slam. He hesitated a second, until he heard Mr. Gruberman ask, "Is that you coming in, Joe?"

"Yeah," he called to the dining room. "I'm sorry. I...uh, had to go downstairs for a minute." As he walked towards the dining room, he deliberately avoided making any glances towards Daniela and Aliza on the couch. "I had a kugel in the toaster that I didn't want to get super-dry. Were you waiting for me?"

"No. We're a bit behind—thanks to our growing young wom-en."

Joe then turned towards the couch to find the two girls sitting there motionless with blank expressions on their faces as if they had been spared tremendous embarrassment. He gave the most unassuming "good Shabbos" he could muster, which they meekly responded to.

"Why did you have a kugel in the toaster?" Mr. Gruberman then asked him. "Don't you know you're always invited here?"

"I do. But…I didn't know if I'd find you on the corner or at the *shteibel*."

"Nah," he dismissed Joe's claim with the wave of his hand. "Come sing *Shalom Aleichem* with me. But don't pull any harmonies."

"It'll be enough for me to stay on key," Joe said as he took his normal seat.

Chapter Six

Sharon

SHARON AWOKE SOME TIME on Saturday night to a dark house. When she squinted in the direction of her night-glow alarm clock and discovered it was 9:30 PM, she sighed and declared *Hamavdil bein kodesh l'hol*. She opened the drawer of the night stand next to the bed and turned on her phone. Almost immediately its ring pierced through the silence and startled her. She was further surprised to see Joe's name on the Caller ID.

"So nice of you to call," she said, sweetly.

"Hi Sharon," he replied quickly. "How was Shabbos?"

"Fine," she said with a stretch. "I just woke up."

"From the morning?" he asked astounded.

"No. I just went to sleep around five. But tell me, Joey, to what honor do I owe this call?"

"Ha ha. Stop laying it on."

Sharon yawned and got out of bed. "No, I honestly can't recall the last time I heard your ringtone playing from my phone."

"Enough, Sharon," he said, annoyed.

She opened her eyes widely. "What's that supposed to mean? And why are you so serious?"

He stammered for a moment. "I'm just…confused." She heard him sigh. "I need your advice."

His tone alarmed her. "Really? What's wrong?"

For about five minutes, she listened to the history of his latest crush while locating what she needed for *havdalah*, her heart sinking as he told over his oft-repeated story. *He's never going to learn*, she told herself.

"Look, I don't know enough about her," she said when he concluded. "But it sounds as if she doesn't know the game. You caught her by surprise and she got scared."

"I didn't even bring it up," he said. "She was saying this to one of my landlords' daughters."

"Maybe she was just trying to placate her."

"No, she knew there was something going on. But when it actually came down to the reality of an actual date, she covered herself by showing no interest in dating…if Mrs. Gruberman was telling me the truth."

"You're making too much of this. She said no. Who cares why? Leave it. Move on."

There was a pause, which Sharon used to pull out the bottle of Kedem grape juice from the back of the refrigerator. "Maybe I was reading more than there actually was," Joe eventually admitted, defeated. "You know, I thought about it all day today. Since college began I haven't had any success with girls."

"You're *shomer negiah*; you haven't touched a girl in, what, four years? That's cause for celebration."

"OK," he conceded, "but I haven't even had a girlfriend, not even a girl who liked me."

"That's not true," she said automatically, though she knew he was telling the truth. She had placed her grandfather's silver *kiddush* goblet on the table, the Kedem, the cinnamon sticks from the spice cabinet and the end of a Safed Candle Factory havdalah candle on the table and was waiting, unsure whether Tamar would also need to hear. She went to the living room and sank into the couch. "What about my friend Erica from Cooper Union…you remember her?"

"Erica?" he scoffed. "She didn't really like me. She was probably hallucinating from all the lab fumes."

"She was a Fine Arts major," Sharon corrected him. "She definitely liked you and she's cute…in a sense."

"Ah, there you go. She's a perfect example, because the whole time she tried hanging around with us I was chasing Elisheva Ashkenazi."

"I've told you before that whole Elisheva thing was a mistake."

"In hindsight," said Joe. "But I was so distracted I didn't care that Erica was at all interested, and who knows what could've been?"

"You wouldn't have liked her," Sharon decided for him. "And so what if you didn't find your wife from the gaggle of immature girls at NYU? You're still young, with a graduate degree and a shoe-in at a firm on Wall Street. I'm telling you, Joey, if you moved up here you'd be grabbed in a second. Any girl with a brain would be clamoring for you."

"But that's not enough," he whined. "If I don't know how to play the game, which my experience shows I can't, I'd only hit fouls despite being pitched slow balls down the center."

Sharon understood his baseball reference, but said nothing. It was true that he had never been able to turn any of his crushes into a relationship the entire time he was in college, and Sharon felt that she was somehow responsible for a lot of his failures, inflating his confidence only to be disappointed each time. Often he would romanticize what he believed were signs of real interest when Sharon knew that he never had a chance. She didn't understand why already in college he needed a serious girlfriend and wouldn't be satisfied with just hanging out like everyone else, but she couldn't shake him of his dream and so she tried to help him in the best way she could, hoping that one day he would succeed with enough experience. Yet instead of growing wiser with his setbacks, he reverted to a feeling of inadequacy. This latest episode was simply a continuation of the same story with Joe, and Sharon feared that he would one day realize the pattern and blame her...or do something more drastic like speed dating or mail-ordering a bride from Singapore.

"Well, Sharon, I called you this Saturday night to declare that I am giving up. I'll just wait until I can buy myself a trophy wife."

"Don't talk like that. Don't let one misjudgment throw you out of the game." Sharon heard the front door open and saw Tamar turn on the hallway light. "Here, my roommate just walked in. Let's get her opinion."

Tamar must've heard Sharon's voice because she approached the living room with a puzzled face. "Why are you sitting in the dark?" she asked Sharon.

"I just got up," she explained. Extending the phone out to Tamar, she said, "Here, Joey wants to ask you something. Joey, you're on speakerphone."

He got right to the point. "Is there ever a way that a guy can tell whether a girl is interested? I mean, if it isn't obvious. Does he just have to go out on a limb every time?"

"Am I supposed to be some expert on the matter?" Tamar retorted.

"No, just…come on, I'm not asking for the secrets of womanhood. I just want to know if there are any signs a guy can use to size up a girl's interest…not what they are, but whether they exist at all."

Both girls looked at each other and shared a smile. "No," they both said.

Then Joe whined, "Then how is a guy to know whether a girl's checking him out or not?"

"Sometimes it's obvious," Sharon said. "And sometimes not. Right, Tamar?" Tamar agreed with a gesture before turning and going out of the room. "She nodded. Listen, Joey, I'm starving and we haven't done havdalah." He mumbled something that she hoped was his understanding of her hunger. "Can we talk later? You'll be all right? You're not going to go call a shadchan over this?"

"Again with the shadchan?" he exclaimed. "Leave it alone already!"

"Sorry," she laughed awkwardly. "Can't take a joke?"

"You never seem to think there's anything funny about it."

Sharon was growing impatient. "You don't agree?"

"I really don't know," he said matter-of-factly. "I only know what you've told me."

"Well, don't even go investigating. It'll ruin your reputation." Sharon laughed at her own sarcasm as Tamar reappeared and jerked her head in the direction of the table. "OK, Joey. Gotta go. Get some sleep and calm down." He huffed. "We'll talk."

"Bye," he grumbled.

Chapter Seven

Joe

JOE IMMEDIATELY REGRETTED calling Sharon, even as the phone was ringing, but he was desperate. All Shabbos afternoon Daniela's words to Aliza bounced around his head, leading him to review his entire relationship history and conclude that he didn't know a thing about girls. Three years in college trying to find a girlfriend and all of Sharon's advice didn't get him anywhere. And when he reached out for help, she dismissed his concerns and gave him no hope. When he finally fell asleep around midnight, his last thought was that he was done asking Sharon for advice.

On Sunday morning he couldn't fully concentrate on his davening. Instead of speaking to Hashem, he found himself getting angrier at Sharon, blaming her for his current conundrum. She had taught him everything about his religious lifestyle, and with her latest defection, he questioned what else she had told him that he had to reevaluate. When Mr. Siegel's business card fell out of his wallet as he took out a dollar to give *tzedakah*, he saw the scribbled number on the back and took it as a sign. He set an appointment with the matchmaker as soon as he got back to his apartment.

"If you're free, come today," she insisted in a thick Brooklyn accent. "We're going to the Mountains any day now, and who knows what'll be this week with my kids needing this for the end of the year and that for camp."

He hung up and roared out loud, as if going against Sharon was a symbolic assertion of some sort. As he waited for the bus an hour later, his internal dialogue started to speak out his second thoughts:

> I don't have the money for this – Don't believe everything Sharon says. Mr. Siegel boss wouldn't suggest it without mentioning the money – Still, I don't need someone to find me a girl: I meet plenty of them – But then what success have I had in getting a date? – What, I'll never meet anyone? That G-d would make me suffer when He really wants me to get married? – Maybe He wants me to find her this way, though. Plenty of religious Jews use this method and they're successful – But will she have any girls like me or will I have to change and be more frum than I really am? I really have no idea what this entails, but I've already gone this far... – But how can I marry without really knowing her? – OK, slow down. It's probably simply an interview of sorts, which I have experience with. All she's going to do is suggest someone to meet, and that's all. No big deal...

Joe listened as he stood rigidly on the packed bus, his eyes roving about as he observed the other riders. One particularly boisterous pair of brothers, at most seven years old, attracted his attention as they spoke with each other in rapid Yiddish about something of great importance. He was envious of their enthusiasm, carefree to argue about complete nonsense without a care in the world. Joe, on the other hand, was stunned at how quickly he had made the decision. Without Sharon's vitriol against *shidduchim* to prevent him, he not only called but was on the way to meet her. He took a deep breath and was glad Sharon hadn't blown his confidence by texting or calling him.

Finally he got off the bus and started walking up 13th Avenue, amazed at what he saw. While it was an avenue lined with businesses like any other in Brooklyn, the particular make-up of the heavily religious neighborhood made everything seem to stand out. The uniformity of the Hassidic men in their black felt hats and *bekeshes* and the conservative, modest dress of the women with wigs under their pillbox hats characterized the shoppers, eager to get their supplies for the upcoming sojourn to the Catskills. One newly-married couple attracted Joe's eyes in particular: the husband stood out as the only one on the street with his fox-fur *shtreimel* and a shining black long-coat contrasting his radiant white knee socks while his bride had on her best Shabbos suit and a stylish kerchief adorning her short wig. Even the stores all had a Jewish feel, either from the kosher menus or the *tznius* clothing or the business owners curling their *peyos*. The sidewalks were filled with young girls with shoulder bags hanging from their elbow joints, mothers holding whining children as they talked on their cell phones, fathers pushing strollers and the occasional out-of-place person of color. It all reminded Joe of his Fridays when he was in yeshiva and he wished he had more time to simply walk up and down the avenue and soak up his nostalgia for Jerusalem, but he had an appointment to keep, so he gathered as much as he could before turning down 46th Street heading towards 12th Avenue.

In the middle of the block he found the address, a two-family semi-attached square house smack in the middle of a whole row of similarly built houses. He walked up the few steps to the porch where a gas barbecue grill and four plastic chairs were locked to the railing with a serious metal chain. Two doors were at the right of the exterior wall and the doorbell under the right one had a named taped under it: "Rosenzweig." Joe rang the bell and as he waited, he straightened the lapel of his coat, smoothed his pants, all the while looking over his shoulder as if he was already being scrutinized by her neighbors. After about fifteen seconds he heard footsteps and the door opened, revealing a ten-year old girl staring up at him with a puzzled face.

"Is this Rosenzweig?" he asked, knowing full well what was taped under the doorbell. The girl nodded. "I think I have a meeting with your mother."

Then the girl yelled up the stairs as loud as she could, "Mommy!"

A voice called to her, asking, "Who is it? Is it Joseph?"

Joe answered the question by calling up, "Yes."

"Shoshanna, tell him to come up."

The girl motioned to him and he walked up the stairs and found himself entering a large living room with parquet floors and off-white leather couches along the walls. To his right the room opened to a dining area with a large table with the kitchen off to the side behind it. Leading towards the back of the house was a hallway, the first doorway connecting to the kitchen and more rooms further down. As he stepped in from the stairwell he could hear something bubbling in a pot on the stove, and after that the matchmaker's voice: "Joseph, please sit and make yourself comfortable."

Joe ignored her suggestion. He padded towards the big window that looked onto the street, but a large maple tree blocked the view. Thrusting his hands into his pockets, he strolled towards the bookshelf, casually reading the titles of the seforim. Just next to the door, the wall was lined from floor to ceiling with carefully arranged books of all types: kids' books, Jewish books in both English and Hebrew, two shelves of photo albums, and an open shelf with black-and-white photos of their previous generations. After a minute he realized he was being watched by a boy of about six, who was shyly tottering by the back of one of the chairs. Joe smiled but the boy continued watching.

Mrs. Rosenzweig emerged from the kitchen wiping her hands on a dish towel. She was dressed conservatively, a styled short wig covering her hair. Joe guessed her age to be approaching fifty. She was taller than he imagined but not broad. While still drying her hands she scolded her son. "Shloimie, don't stare. Go say hello to Joseph." Shloimie smiled briefly at Joe before hiding in his mother's skirts. "He's a bit shy," she was saying to Joe.

"It's fine," said Joe.

"So, you work for Stadler & Klein?" she asked. "You look rather young."

Joe felt his cheeks warm. "I finished college after three years."

"Oh," she said with a nod. Then she motioned towards the table. "Please take a seat. Any chair is fine."

He walked over to one of the side chairs while Mrs. Rosenzweig went into the kitchen. It then hit him that he was actually doing this and the shock nearly made him miss the seat as he sat down. He didn't know why he was so scared; he convinced himself that all he was doing was meeting a woman who might suggest to him a girl that he might meet and then might agree to marry. There were too many maybes before anything serious to be worrying this much. He was tapping on the table with his fingers as she returned with a pad of paper, a glasses case and a plastic box sized for index cards. Sitting on the end of the table, she removed the glasses from their holder and put them on, prompting Joe to sit rigidly in his chair to get himself ready for an interrogation.

"OK," she started, looking down as she wrote. "What is your full name?"

"Joseph Charnoff," he stated.

"Hebrew name?"

"Yosef." Joe quickly glanced over at the hallway, convinced that someone was watching him.

"Are you a Cohen?"

The question puzzled him. "Does it matter?"

She looked up. "Only if you are."

"Oh. No, no I'm not."

She resumed her writing. "OK…where were you born?"

"Where was I born? Or where was I raised?"

She looked up at him and smiled. "Relax, dear. I'm not the FBI." He smiled nervously. "You could tell me both."

"I was born in Chicago but raised in Potomac, Maryland, from age six."

"I haven't heard of Potomac," she said absently. "Are there Jews there?"

Joe understood that "Jews" meant frum Jews. "There are a few shuls, but most Orthodox kids get bused to Rockville or Silver Spring."

"Did you go to a Jewish school?"

"Yes." He loosened his shoulders. "I attended Jewish Day School in Rockville through high school."

"I see," she said, resuming her writing. "Where did you learn after that?"

"Learn?" Joe glanced at the hallway and thought he saw the back of a head dart into a room. "Like, college?"

"More like yeshiva."

"I spent a summer in yeshiva before college. I was in college for three years, and now I learn nights and alternate days at Ohr Eliyahu in Flatbush."

"Alternate days?" she repeated.

He blinked rapidly. "I'm in graduate school and I only work part-time."

Then she remembered. "Oh, that's right, for Marty." Joe assumed that she was referring to Mr. Siegel, whom Joe thought was named Moshe. "So what do you consider yourself—Modern, Hassidish, Yeshivish, Yekkish?"

Joe took a deep breath and started scratching his chin. "My parents are traditional—Conservative, you know, that's how I was raised. I became a *ba'al teshuva* in Israel. I guess I'm more yeshivish, but can't really say I spent enough time in yeshiva to fit the bill. I really don't like labels so much," he admitted.

"I understand. We're all Jews, right?" She raised her eyebrows and then smiled. "I wish. Anyway, what about your parents? What are their names?"

He started tapping his cheek with his fingers. He was finding it strange how long she was continuing to look down at her writing. "Robert and Linda."

"Hebrew names?"

"Dov Reuven and Leah."

"What do they do?"

He leaned back in his seat. "My father is an accountant and my mother is a tour guide at the Holocaust Museum."

"Do you have any siblings?"

Joe quickly turned and looked down the hallway, this time catching the little boy peeking from behind the breakfront. Joe smiled widely, which the little boy reciprocated before skipping into a room. "One older sister," Joe answered. "She's married and lives in Baltimore."

Mrs. Rosenzweig continued to look down as she wrote. "How old are you?"

"Twenty-two."

"How tall?"

"How tall?" he repeated. *What does this matter?* "5-10, if I remember correctly."

"That's fine. So," she announced, lifting her head and removing her glasses. Looking straight at Joe, she asked, "What are you looking for?"

Joe was stumped. He was starting to think that all of her questions would be similarly straight-forward inquiries. He scratched his head with his kippah. "What do you mean?"

"What kind of girl are you looking for?" she repeated herself.

Widening his eyes, he shrugged. "To be honest, I really haven't thought about it."

"Well," she said pleasantly, putting down her pen, "I need some hint so that I don't suggest someone completely wrong for you. You probably wouldn't want to marry a girl who's six-foot-six."

"I guess that's true," he conceded.

"So you have some criteria. Some guys might be all right with a girl who's tall or big or whatever. I'll give you a few minutes to think about it. What time is it?" She glanced at her watch and did a double take. "Gosh! Excuse me for a moment." She stood up and started walking towards the hallway. After a few steps she stopped and turned back to Joe and smacked her forehead lightly. "Where is my head? I'm not being a great host. Shoshanna!" she called out. When the little girl popped up from the couch, Mrs. Rosenzweig told her, "Bring our guest some of the *babka* from Shabbos." She then went into a back room and closed the door.

The obedient daughter went to the kitchen and brought Joe a large chunk of pastry and a glass of orange juice. He thanked the girl, who watched him as he made his bracha and then skipped off. He thought about what sort of girl he was interested in meeting while he was eating but didn't arrive at any answers. *How can I generalize what preferences I have? Why reject someone because of a trivial characteristic that won't matter in the long run? Sure, I don't want someone too different, but how different is too different?*

The shadchan returned shortly after. "Isn't it delicious? So moist! Better than any bakery. What a daughter-in-law I got. So, what did you come up with?"

Joe drank from his juice to cleanse his palate. "I'm sorry," he said, "but you're going to have to be more specific."

"Look, to be honest with you," she said as she returned to her seat, "I already had a girl in mind once you called and told me that you worked with Marty. But if it doesn't work out, then I'll have your details and won't schlep you back here. It isn't too complicated. For example, do you want a girl from a big family?"

"It really doesn't matter," he replied as he took a forkful of babka.

"Should she have gone to college?"

He swallowed before answering. "I guess that would be more compatible."

"What about seminary?"

He furrowed his brow and leaned forward. "What does that matter?"

She looked away. "Some people think it's a good experience…"

Mrs. Rosenzweig tapped her pen on the pad as she waited for him to answer. He shook his head uncertainly. "I really don't know."

"It's fine," she said shortly. "I can tell that you're just looking for a good girl that you can talk to, who's similar in *hashkafah* and will accept your background. You don't care where she's from or what her family is like or whether she'll support you. Am I more or less correct?"

"More or less," he agreed with a nod.

"No, seriously, don't just humor me." Joe felt his face freeze up; he hadn't expected her to scold him so. "I'm trying to help find the right girl for you. Some of these things are major details. Do you want to learn or are you particular about working?"

"I work now," he said, moving around the crumbs on his plate. "I'm finishing a Master's degree. I don't have experience sitting and learning, so I can't say for sure that I could. I enjoy learning, but all day…"

She cut him off. "That's fine. I've heard enough." She opened the index card box and started shuffling, focusing on one and taking it out. "So I have a girl who might be *matim*. She just turned twenty-three, so she's not too much older, graduated from Stern, living in Washington Heights and working for a school in the city. She's from St. Louis originally, but she boarded here since high school."

Joe glanced at the card and noticed a small picture at the bottom corner of the index card. "You have a picture?" he asked her.

"I have a picture of every one of my clients," she replied, turning it away from him, "which is for my purposes only. I'm going to take yours shortly with my new digital camera, which my son Mendy will shrink and copy for me, because I am completely lost with this machine. Anyway, I think it might be a good shidduch, but in the end I don't make that decision. Now," she handed him an empty card, save for his name at the top. "Please write down your references at the bottom, how to reach them and what relationship you have with them."

"References?"

"Yes. The family will want to know more about you than just what I can tell them. Put down people who know you best. Three is enough."

Three? Thinking who he wouldn't mind knowing he did this, he anxiously put down Mr. Gruberman, Rabbi Josh, head of the morning program at Ohr Eliyahu, and the rabbi at NYU whom he still saw occasionally. He thought to put down Mr. Siegel, but opted not to. Then he gave the card to Mrs. Rosenzweig, who read the names and put the card at the front of her box.

"Now," she was saying, "I will give these names to Rachel's parents—her name is Rachel Rosen, like half of my name—and they will get back to me if they are interested. Here," she showed him a list of names and phone numbers. "These are her references. Do you have anything to write them on?"

When Joe shook his head, she flipped to a clean sheet from her notepad, tore it off and handed it to him. Since she was expecting him to do something with them he might as well have them. After he wrote them in silence, he looked up to see her smiling pleasantly.

"That's it?" he asked.

She nodded slowly. "That's all we can do. The rest is up to you and Hashem."

"Right." Joe bit his lip before asking, "How much do I owe?"

"Owe?" She chuckled. "No, dear. I don't collect any fees until you close a shidduch."

He looked at the table. "How much will that be?"

She inhaled quickly. "There's a standard amount that all shadchanim take. Discuss it with your rabbi if it becomes relevant."

"Oh," Joe said as he stood up. He breathed deeply. "Well, thank you then for meeting me on such short notice."

"It's better this way. We don't push off *mitzvos*. Besides, I'm kidding myself about all this rush to pack. The truth is that it isn't like when we used to go up. I got two kids married and now it's just five of us up there, but we still seem to bring up just as much!"

Joe laughed and stepped towards the door. "Don't forget an after-bracha, sweetie," she reminded him.

He sat back down slowly and quietly murmured his bracha. "Thank you twice," he said with a blush.

"My pleasure," she said. "Shoshanna, go see Joseph out. Do you prefer Joseph? What should I call you?"

"Joseph is fine," he decided.

"Great. Bye," she said, walking into the kitchen. Joe was already halfway down the stairs before she called him back. "Wait, I need your picture!"

Chapter Eight

Sharon

AROUND 7 PM ON WEDNESDAY night, Sharon found herself in her apartment very bored. She had done little that day, really for the last few days, and needed a change of scenery. Sure, there was the increasing pile of clothing in her bedroom to organize, but with no particular plans for tomorrow she pushed it off. Even escaping into cyberspace provided little release. She checked her friends' Facebook pages, commented on a few posts, and uploaded some photos. Even Joe, who she wanted to be sure wasn't throwing in the towel on women, hadn't yet answered her calls all week. Just as Sharon was about to forage her cabinets for snack foods, she received a Whats App message from Esther.

Esther Jacob: HEY SHARON, IT'S ESTHER. WANNA COME OUT? BUNCHA PPL.

Sharon: WHAT DOING?

Esther Jacob: MAYB SUSHI...DON' NO. COME HERE.

Sharon didn't need too much convincing. She quickly threw on a skirt and her vintage T-shirt over a half-sleeve. She went to the bathroom and washed her face, sprayed her neck and wrists with perfume and put on just enough make-up to appear both spontaneous but together. Grabbing her 'out' bag from behind her door, she looked at the unfinished piles of papers on the vanity and her clothes from Shabbat still draped on the back of her desk chair and sighed. *Tomorrow* she thought as she stuffed the bag with her lip gloss and keys and debit card, as she could find no real money. She'd go to an ATM on the way.

Stepping outdoors for the first time in more than a day, the coolness of the evening excited her and she walked jauntily. Still, she was cautious enough to call Joe so that she wouldn't be walking alone.

"Hello Sharon," she heard him say after a sigh.

"Hey Joey. Where've you been all week?" she inquired.

He was slow to answer. "I've been busy. Work, you know."

"Too busy to answer? Or even to call back?"

"I think I saw your voice mails. I was underground when you called and only saw them after. What's up?"

A doctor who lived on her floor was passing, with whom she exchanged a slight nod. "I'm going out for sushi and didn't want to walk alone."

"Where is there to get sushi?"

"Everywhere. They probably have sushi at Dunkin Donuts."

"Murray's doesn't make sushi...neither does the bagel place, to tell the truth."

"You're funny. I don't know; if we're staying local then we'll probably end up at Estihana."

"Didn't we go there once?"

Sharon rolled her eyes. "I *tried* to take you there once, but you bounced with one look at the menu."

"Oh right. Who pays $15 for sushi?"

"It wasn't that much," she countered. "Whatever, my friend Esther invited me. It's going to be a bunch of people…I don't know."

"Well, I'm making dinner, so can I play you a recording of my voice?"

"Making dinner?" she exclaimed. "At this hour? Where'd you go after work?"

"Out," he replied quickly. "Food shopping, then learning."

"I see," she said blankly. She didn't believe him. "Are you still angry from Shabbat?"

"What? Oh, no. I'm over it."

"Good. You didn't seem so happy when we hung up Saturday night."

"I'll be fine," he said unconvincingly. "Don't worry."

She had reached the well-lit ATM of the HSBC bank. She took out her card and opened the door with her phone held only by her shoulder. "But I do worry. That's what friends are for."

He coughed. "I think I read a Hallmark card like that."

"Ha ha. Seriously though…"

"It's fine," he said quickly. "I got some sleep that night and calmed down."

Something was strange about the way Joe was answering so tersely. She put in her PIN and withdrew $100. "Well, I'm home for Shabbat this week. You can sort yourself out?"

"What do you think?" he exclaimed suddenly. "Why do you think I'm so helpless?"

Sharon clenched her teeth. "I don't. I was just asking."

He coughed. "I'm sorry. It's not you."

"OK," she said slowly. "Look, I'm finished at the ATM, and Esther's building is only a block away. I'll let you go."

"Thank you," he said in a scratchy voice. "Bye."

She hung up and wrinkled her nose. This wasn't the Joe she knew, to be all hysterical and tense. She didn't dwell on it, though. He was hungry and perhaps really was overworked. Before she left the bank she called Esther, who said she was already coming down.

They greeted with a big hug. "Hey, great to see you," Esther said. She was wearing a red plaid blouse and a knee skirt, much more casual than the evening gown from Shabbat.

"We're meeting the guys at Estihana, but we'll see if we stay there. You remember Andy? He suggested that I call you..." Hearing that, Sharon smiled slyly, inwardly congratulating herself on wearing her vintage T.

Chapter Nine

Joe

JOE HAD ACTUALLY BEEN sitting on the steps to his basement apartment when Sharon called, his head buried in his hands. So much had happened since he met Mrs. Rosenzweig that he didn't have the guts to refuse her call. He had hoped that talking to Sharon would help calm his inner frenzy, but it didn't.

The day after he went to Borough Park, Joe tried to find Mr. Siegel at work but wasn't successful. He wanted to tell him that he met Mrs. Rosenzweig and to thank him, but his secretary didn't know where he was. It wasn't out of the ordinary for him to disappear; he was the head of acquisitions and had to be out acquiring. Joe did have his cell phone number, but he didn't feel right calling him on a non-work-related issue and texting felt too casual.

On Tuesday he woke up at 7:30 to *daven* with the *yeshiva*. He got on his $20 bicycle purchased from a friend who moved to Jerusalem after graduation and rode to the yeshiva building housed in an old Colonial-looking two-story house with a big sign on the front that said, "Zichron Mordechai," the name of the boy's school downstairs. On the second floor was the *beis medrash* of Ohr

Eliyahu, which had formerly been Rabbi Yoni's home before he inherited a house in Seagate, with its own entrance on the side. The old kitchen doubled as the lunchroom where free food was served every morning and night as an incentive to come learn, and two bedrooms in the back were designated as the rabbis' offices. The big main room was well-lit and filled with foldable tables and plastic chairs, bookshelves on the walls and a metal combination-lock *Aron Kodesh* on the east wall. Rabbi Tzvi Aaronson, effectively the dean but called "the *mashgiach*," always said that as long as guys don't bring more friends or find sponsors, they'd remain in temporary quarters.

Joe arrived so early the door was still locked, but after two minutes one of the regular guys who knew the combination showed up. Upstairs they turned on the lights and Joe put on his *tefillin*. By the appointed time of 7:50 their minyan came, but remained only ten men. After davening a spread of cereals, random pastries, coffee, juice, and some wrinkled apples was laid out in the kitchen. Joe joined their predominantly silent breakfast; these guys were the serious ones who wanted to learn and didn't come to joke.

At 8:45 Rabbi Tzvi arrived, bringing with him a contagious enthusiasm that immediately changed the mood.

"Good morning everybody!" he exclaimed. Looking around the kitchen, he asked, "What's with the gloom? Not only do you get free food, but you get the constant smile of Rabbi Josh. Nu, Ricky, it was worth getting up just for Rabbi Josh's smile, eh?"

He gave high-fives, handshakes or shoulder pats to each guy, reaching Joe last, smacking him lightly with the newspaper he was carrying. "Yosef! How's the new schedule treating you?"

"It's great," he replied, putting down his spoon.

"Benji's a good guy to learn with, no?"

"Yeah, we're doing well…I didn't see him yet today."

Rabbi Tzvi made a sweeping inspection of the guys. "Hmm, well then come to the back when you're done, all right?"

Before Joe could ask why, the Rabbi had already turned to address the table. "OK, enough time spent reading the recipe for Rice Krispie Treats. Get to your Gemaras already."

After the rabbi left the room, Joe finished his cereal with unease. He had no clue why Rabbi Tzvi would want to speak to him privately. Besides for a "how's it going?" or the occasional "how's the *havrusa* working out?" he didn't have much to do with Joe, his hands full with the guys who came for the hangout but rarely sat for more than ten minutes at a time. Joe was so absorbed in his thoughts that he forgot to make an after-bracha as he stood up, eliciting curious glances from the other guys as he smacked his forehead with his open palm.

Joe knocked on the bedroom that was Rabbi Tzvi's office, which he shared with Rabbi Yoni who came once a week and dealt with the administration issues. In the back corner was Rabbi Yoni's completely empty, spotless desk, while directly behind the door Rabbi Tzvi was already sitting at his chair.

"Come and sit," he told Joe as he perused the open newspaper.

A single folding chair was leaning against the wall, which Joe figured was as good as any other. He unfolded it and sat opposite Rabbi Tzvi, who spared no time in jumping to the point.

"I got an interesting phone call last night," he said. "A mother from St. Louis asking questions about a Joseph Charnoff in our yeshiva. Do you know anything about it?"

Joe wanted to crawl into the filing cabinet and hide. He shrugged and replied meekly, "I don't know why anyone would call you, Rabbi—"

"Did you give my name as a reference for a shidduch?"

Joe shook his head vigorously. "No, I didn't give your name." *I gave Rabbi Josh's name.*

He turned a page in his newspaper. "Well, somehow she called me. Was it a mistake? Are you dating?"

"Who at my age isn't?" Joe tried joking, but the Rabbi wasn't amused.

He looked up from the newspaper and stared into Joe's eyes. "No, I want to know, because I didn't know what to say. I have no problem with my guys dating; I just want to know about it."

Joe stalled, chewing on his fingernail. "Look, my boss at work gave me the number of a shadchan and I met with her on Sunday. She asked where I learned and I mentioned Ohr Eliyahu, so she must have traced you that way. I can't really say that I'm dating."

Rabbi Tzvi inhaled half the air in the room and leaned back in his chair. "Is this your first time meeting a shadchan?" Joe nodded. "Can I ask why you decided to call her now?"

Joe looked down at the floor. He didn't feel enough of a rapport to explain his predicament, but he had already said enough and Rabbi Tzvi was involved, however unwillingly. "I don't know exactly. I feel pretty frustrated with girls and wanted to try something else and getting her phone number was just, I guess, good timing."

He looked up to find the Rabbi nodding pensively. After a short silence, Rabbi Tzvi broke into a smile. "Well, good," he said. "Much better place to turn to than where some guys in that situation might turn. How old are you?"

"Twenty-two," Joe answered quickly.

"You have a way to support yourself?"

"Like, a job?" The rabbi nodded. "Is that necessary?"

The rabbi widened his eyes. "It certainly helps. I mean, you could have some farmland in Kentucky and raise your own grain and dairy, but most women in today's age live urban lifestyles where the necessary items of life are purchased with money."

Joe laughed. "I thought you meant if I have a job now. I'm a paid intern for a research firm and I'm finishing a Masters, but I don't have a full-time position."

Rabbi Tzvi put up his hand. "That's fine. I'm just making sure you're not expecting to be supported your whole life. Not that there aren't women out there willing to do so, I just didn't know your situation." He turned a page in the newspaper and sighed. "So give me her references and I'll see what I can do."

"What do you mean?" Joe asked.

"You probably need someone to check her references for you." Rabbi Tzvi looked up. "I'll assume that your parents weren't involved in your decision, correct?"

"Correct."

"Nor should they be, necessarily, for a guy in your situation. You look puzzled."

"You don't have to bother. I never wanted to burden you in the first place."

The Rabbi leaned forward and rested his elbows on the desk. "Well, who's going to do it for you?"

Joe stammered. "I don't really see the need. I mean, I'm perfectly capable —"

The rabbi interrupted him. "Hold on, Yosef. I'm sensing that you might not know exactly what you got yourself into. You see, a shadchan doesn't just act as a headhunter of sorts, merely pairing up potential couples and leaving them to their own devices. Shidduchim is much more than that."

Joe leaned forward. "How so?"

"I'll tell you," he said as he heaved himself out of his chair. "But I need a coffee. Do you also want?"

Joe shook his head. "I had."

"You only drink one a morning? *Kol HaKavod*. I'll be right back." He opened the door and stood for a moment, listening to the sound of Torah argued at high volume. "Come, we'll talk in the kitchen and see if Benji arrived."

Joe stood up slowly. "In front of everyone?"

"We'll be quiet," he assured him. Still, when Joe joined him in the hallway, the Rabbi spoke in a hushed tone. "Shidduchim is an entire framework of matchmaking that follows a potential couple from the suggestion through to the engagement. It doesn't just abandon two strangers, hoping everything works out. Certain…precautions, for lack of a better word, are taken to smooth the initial awkwardness that comes with two unfamiliar people trying to start a marriage."

Joe wasn't buying it. He stopped walking. "Come on, rabbi. She's a matchmaker, not a mediator."

"I would say that she's more like a facilitator," he clarified, gently nudging Joe towards the kitchen. "Look, any relationship has the potential to be a disaster if it doesn't start on the right foot. All the more so with a marriage, which is meant to last forever. We have very solid traditions about how to carefully guide a couple in those initial stages, and the whole shidduch works to follow those steps. In particular, though, the shadchan works as the objective third-party who listens to each side and either moves things along or acts as the buffer in the event the suggestion is a no-go." They reached the kitchen and Rabbi Tzvi started opening up the top cabinets, asking out loud, "Where's the Sanka supposed to be?"

"Behind the cereal," Joe replied, leaning on the countertop. "It gets stuffed back there. Most of us drink from the coffee maker."

"And don't leave any for me," Rabbi Tzvi commented as he took out the jar of Sanka and shook some of the crystals into a paper cup. "Is Benji here?"

Joe poked his head into the *beis medrash*. "Not yet. So what's the big deal with phone numbers? It sounds like everything starts with the first date."

The Rabbi chuckled. "A suggestion is not prophesy. She does her best to make a match, but it has to be checked to the particular needs of the man or the woman." Rabbi Tzvi then filled the fast-pot boiler and turned it on. "That's really the job for what I call the agent."

"The agent?" Joe repeated.

They paused as Boruch, who opened the door for Joe in the morning, came in for a cup of water.

"Yes," he continued after Boruch left. "It's like an athlete's agent. No baseball player negotiates his own contracts with the team; he pays an agent who knows the business and deals with the franchise owners so the player can concentrate on playing ball. You're fortunate enough that I'm willing to do it for free." He smiled widely.

Joe smiled back sarcastically. "Thank you for the offer, but why must I bother you? I can make a few calls."

Rabbi Tzvi went and put his hand on Joe's shoulder. "Trust me. It's better that someone who doesn't have a personal interest in the matter hears what the references have to say."

"I can be objective," Joe declared defiantly, standing up straight.

Rabbi Tzvi took a step back and looked at him as if he was a child who had just said something cute. "Don't fool yourself. We're all victims to our subconscious preferences. Try giving an honest assessment of a woman who you don't find so attractive. She could be the sweetest, nicest, most compatible, caring… perfect for you, but it'll be very hard to look beyond your initial disappointment. Or imagine the opposite: that you're set up with the prettiest woman you've ever seen in your life but she's *terribly* wrong for you. You'll give her first chances and second chances and you'll rationalize everything—"

"You're saying that looks aren't important? The water's boiled."

"Thank you," Rabbi Tzvi turned to pour the water into his coffee cup. "Are you sure you don't want any?" Joe shook his head. "It's a shame to waste this hot water."

"Ask in the beis medrash if anyone want."

"And interrupt their learning?" The rabbi left it at that. "What were we talking about?"

"First impressions and looks."

"Right. Physical attraction is surely an important element, but it shouldn't be the first thing a man, or a woman for that matter, decides about the person he or she will build a lifetime with."

Joe crossed his arms and leaned back on the counter. "But that's going to happen the first time a couple meets on a shidduch as well."

Rabbi Tzvi's face lit up. "Yes, you are one-hundred percent correct, but in shidduchim we are prepared. Come," he walked towards the office and Joe followed. "By the time the couple meets, all the technical details have already been checked out so that no couple becomes deeply attached and suddenly discovers five months later that they disagree entirely on fundamental issues. Instead, the couple is left to discover whether there is a potential for an emotional relationship and let that be their only concern."

Joe made a face of disbelief. "How does the fact that there's a shadchan and an agent ensure that?"

"It takes away the burden of dealing with the other person's emotional needs. If you decide that the girl isn't for you, then you simply talk it out with the shadchan who protects you from the backlash of the disappointed girl, or vice versa. You also won't get strung along because you feel too bad ending it."

"But the shadchan can't be the intermediary for their entire lives."

"Don't worry," the Rabbi said, as he put his hand on Joe's shoulder. "The shidduch process isn't long enough for that. When both sides commit, a good shadchan steps down."

Joe stopped when they reached the office. "So what do I have to do now then?"

Rabbi Tzvi turned to him and smiled. "You just sit back and let me make these calls. Just don't go telling the whole world that you're getting into shidduchim. It might not seem like a big deal, but it's best to limit who knows your business. Too many opinions will overwhelm you."

He didn't understand why, but he nodded anyway. "Look, I gave Rabbi Josh as a reference, but the shadchan asked what yeshiva I learned in, and I guess they traced you."

"You already told me," Rabbi Tzvi comforted him. "Did you get her references?"

Joe reached into his wallet and pulled out the folded torn sheet from Mrs. Rosenzweig and handed it over to the rabbi.

"Good." With his open hand, he took Joe's hand and gave him a heavy shake. "*Mazal tov*."

*   *   *   *   *

Joe thought that he wouldn't hear anything back for at least a week, but Mrs. Rosenzweig called him already on Wednesday while he was about to grab lunch at a kosher pizza shop downtown.

"You spoke with my rabbi?" he asked in disbelief as he leaned against the display window. "I only spoke to him yesterday."

"I did," she replied. "A very nice man, I must say. He says that you two could meet."

He was watching the faces of the strangers passing him as Mrs. Rosenzweig's last statement registered in his psyche. Would they understand why he was smiling? Why his heart was pounding? That he was just approved as a date for a certain woman somewhere on this island? Something about that gave him a sense of pride that only he could feel. Even the loud wail of a passing ambulance sounded very distant and it was only when he discerned that Mrs. Rosenzweig was asking him something that he returned to Earth and tried to hear her by covering his other ear.

"Is tomorrow night good for you?" she was asking him.

Joe struggled to keep his voice even. "Tomorrow night?"

"Does it work for you?"

He struggled to come up with an excuse. "The thing is—"

"If it's better for you we can push it to Sunday. I don't like Saturday nights in the summer, especially because you two are traveling from so far apart."

"Great, then. Sunday is fine," Joe replied quickly. "Sunday is much better."

"All right. I thought that you two should meet in Midtown. Can you think of anywhere?"

Joe was glad that no one was looking at his face. Wasn't this something the shadchan should decide? He only knew the kosher fast food places near Penn Station, nothing worthy of a date. "I don't really know…"

"How about the Marriot in Times Square? It's quiet and usually unoccupied. How does five sound?"

He was ready to agree to anything. "Sure, fine with me."

"So meet at the Marriot. It's a little hard to find the elevator to the lobby, but you're smart enough. It's on the eighth floor. How will she know it's you?"

"Isn't there some central location?"

"Trust me, it's better to have something to indicate you so she doesn't end up meeting Joseph Charnofsky and marrying him and leaving you crying. It doesn't have to be too much, but something."

The only ostentatious thing in Joe's closet that he could figure wearing on a date was his orange tie. It was a dull orange with white diagonal stripes that matched an orange shirt that he used to wear during his more 'fashionable' days at NYU. "I have this orange tie."

"Orange tie it is," she repeated. "I'll let Rachel know and I'll call you back to confirm."

"I didn't necessarily mean that," he retracted hastily, drawing strange looks from a passing elderly woman. Joe smiled to assure her that he was sane, but she glared nonetheless before turning and continuing down the sidewalk. "I mean, you think that an orange tie won't make a bad impression?"

"What do I know? You should see what some of the boys on my block are wearing."

"Wait." He was confused. "I don't have to call her?"

"No, you won't be getting her number. Not while I'm in charge of this *shidduch*. I'll get back to confirm." She hung up without any further explanation.

Somehow he went inside, ordered his lunch, sat down and ate it, but the whole time his mind was occupied with several phases of inner dialogue:

I'm not ready to go on a date with a stranger – It's
been checked out, so she can't be that bad – They
didn't check out how she looks – There's no
obligation to marry her just because you meet her
once – I'm not even really ready to get married – Who
says I'll marry the first girl I meet? – Who says I
won't? Most people date for a long time before getting
married – Who says I'll be like most people?– I want
to remain single forever? – No, but I don't have the
money, and I'm not done with school, and I don't
really know why I did this in the first place – But I
did, which means that I have the guts to see it through
– Maybe I'm just acting on impulse – Maybe I'll
really like her though…

When he got back to his office, he told the panel of judges in his head to postpone their decision until after work, when he would try to call Rabbi Tzvi. They remained dormant until he finished his day's work and got on the train, reiterating their positions ad nausea, somehow yelling over the music coming from his mp3 player. When he emerged at Nostrand Avenue, the voices accompanied him to his basement through a thick fog that cooled the night and gave him a slight chill. After unlocking the door and heaving his bag into the table, he fell into his bed. The audible ticking of the clock in his kitchen reminded him of his learning partner, and he checked the time on his phone. With twenty minutes until he had to get on his bike and get to the yeshiva, he decided to call Rabbi Tzvi. Heaving himself off his bed, he went out to his stairs and waited four rings before loud crying pierced through the quiet night.

"Hello," Rabbi Tzvi said amidst the noise.

"Rabbi? It's Yosef Charnoff."

"How are you, Yosef? Did Mrs. Rosenzweig call you?" the Rabbi asked above the wailing in the background.

"Yes, we scheduled a date for Sunday."

"Why so late? You couldn't do tomorrow?"

Joe huffed. "How fast do you want me to get married?"

"It's just a date. How much time do you need?"

"I…I guess I don't need, but why the rush?"

Joe then heard such intense toddler screaming through the phone that he had to move the phone away from his ear. "Sorry about that," the rabbi then said. "Now isn't good."

"Can I call tomorrow?"

"Try tonight around eleven. Gotta go." He hung up.

That was when Sharon had called. Joe was going to ignore it, but how long could he snub her before she became suspicious? For about ten minutes after he hung up with her, he sat listening to his inner dialogue drive him farther from sanity:

> Why did I say that I'll wear an orange tie? What
> will she think about that? – It isn't a bad tie; but
> it definitely isn't a frum thing to do. A gray tie is
> perfectly fine – My gray ties are so bland. I also
> have to get my suit dry-cleaned. Who will have it
> ready before Shabbos? Is there even anywhere open
> now? That place by the subway? – Why did I agree
> to go to a hotel lobby? Aren't dates supposed to be
> in restaurants? – Rabbi Tzvi said that the point of

the date is to talk – I don't know the first thing about dating. I've hung out with girls before, but never with the formality of a real date – So I'll talk to Rabbi Tzvi later – No, I can't stay up so late, I'm beat...

The automatic unlock of the Grand Cherokee behind his head interrupted his thought, and soon after he heard the unmistakable husky cough of Mr. Gruberman. "Joe," his landlord addressed him from above, "How're you doing?"

"Fine," he answered, not facing him.

"What are you sitting out here for?" he asked, concerned.

Joe turned around and mustered a smile. "My cell phone doesn't get good reception inside."

"Really? Hmm. You davened yet? I'm going to Landau's now."

"I'll come," he said, the yeshiva not far from where Mr. Gruberman was going. Joe jumped up, grabbed his suit jacket from the chair and locked the door. Mr. Gruberman was already getting into the car as Joe reached the ground level and went around to the passenger side. As he opened the door, Mr. Gruberman started the ignition and turned down the volume of some Jewish pop music.

"Those girls," he grumbled as Joe put on his seatbelt and they backed onto the street. "So what's new? How's work?"

"All right," Joe answered absently. "Keeps me busy."

"You need to keep busy? What about school?"

"Grad school? I have a few weeks off."

"Oh." They were waiting for the traffic light at the end of the street, silently staring ahead and listening to very faint Jewish pop. Mr. Gruberman then joked, "Maybe you should start dating."

Joe laughed hollowly. *Mr. Gruberman never gives up.* "What makes you say that?"

"Well, if you have some time off…" Again, Joe laughed. "What's so funny?"

"Nothing," Joe lied. *Should I confide in him?* "I don't know. Dating's not for me."

"What do you mean?" Mr. Gruberman shot him a glance. "You've never been on a date?" Joe shook his head. "It's no big deal, really. Just call up a shadchan and set one up."

Joe faced the window to hide his smile. "Still, I wouldn't know what to do. There's probably all these steps and rules—"

"Nah," Mr. Gruberman waved his hand. The light changed and they dashed through the intersection. "Please. All you do is talk. No dinner, no mini-golf, no big whoop. You buy her a drink and just sit and talk with each other without being bothered."

"That's it?" Joe asked in disbelief. "I mean, aren't you supposed to ask certain questions?"

"That's for later on, after you've met two or three times. But the basic idea is to listen. Is that too much for you?"

"I guess not," Joe conceded. "I just figured a *date*," he emphasized the last word, "at least from what I gathered, is supposed to be an event of sorts."

"OK, so you dress up in a suit and comb your hair and present yourself as a gentleman, as you always should. You certainly want her to think you're something special. But a shidduch date is a short affair. Two hours or so."

"Two hours?" Joe interrupted. "How much can you find out in two hours?"

"There isn't so much to find out. It's certainly enough time to see whether you're attracted enough to hear what she has to say the next time. If you don't want to, then you aren't stuck wasting an entire night for no reason."

Joe listened to the faint music and his smile widened. His whole apprehension seemed to disappear as the entire house of cards he'd built in his head toppled with Mr. Gruberman's nonchalance. Joe breathed deep and leaned his elbow on the window. "And you did this with Mrs. Gruberman?" he asked his landlord.

Mr. Gruberman chuckled. "That was a long time ago," he said before slamming on the brakes and sending Joe's elbow flying into the front window. "Sorry, I saw a spot. So…do you want a number of a shadchan?"

Joe tried soothing his elbow with his other hand. "I'll think about it," he said.

Chapter Ten

Sharon

HOWEVER NOSTALGIC SHARON FELT seeing the front lawn of her
old high school set up as it was when she had graduated, it was bit-
tersweet. She hadn't loved high school, a place where her imperfect
figure prevented her from any real popularity. Though she was very
outgoing, always volunteering to organize school functions and
even in charge of the yearbook, her photograph only appeared in it
twice—once by her name and the other holding a havdalah candle
after a Shabbaton, surrounded by her entire grade. Academically
she excelled enough to get into NYU and while she liked a few
of her teachers, she never really embraced high school with any
particular fondness. At least she could feel good about not failing
to achieve a whole list of dreams.

She sat with her mother and two little siblings who were
absorbed in some Smartphone game and oblivious to the world
around them at the back of the audience. With wet eyes her mother
sat on the edge of her chair, listening to every word of the speech-
es. She was decked out in an elaborate outfit with her pearls and
hoop earrings, her wig curled better than Sharon could do with her
own hair. In photographs from when her parents had lived in Israel

her mother had worn very simple clothing, only adopting a gaudier wardrobe on integrating to their American community. Sharon, on the other hand, cared about enough for this event to wash her face and brush her teeth.

"I always wondered why they made the final march of the graduates in the direction of the church across the street," she noted to her mother when the head rabbi's speech ended. Her mother didn't answer, her gaze fixated on the dais. "How come some shul hasn't bought that building already? How many Catholics still live in this neighborhood?"

"You'd be surprised," her mother said. "I see them on Sunday mornings."

"Where's abba?" her sister Tehilah asked without looking up from the Smartphone.

"I don't know," her mother answered. "Oh, doesn't he look so handsome?"

Sharon turned to look at her brother sitting towards the front, all spiffed up and smiling brightly among his peers. Only she knew that the bags under his eyes were from last night's trip to Montauk Point, but she granted him the last vestiges of his carefree adolescence and didn't tattle. She would never forgive him for invading her turf when she was a few months shy of her seventh birthday, but on his graduation day she would let herself share vicariously in his special moment.

Her father still hadn't arrived when they started distributing the diplomas. "Get the camcorder ready," her mother ordered Sharon.

"Don't know how to work it," she replied.

"I do!" cried her little brother. "I know how!"

One look from their mother vetoed that option. "Turn it on and press the red button."

She acquiesced. "But don't blame me if I end up recording the heads of the people in front of us."

Eventually it ended. The little ones ran off to play with friends while Sharon's mother tried to drag her over to give her brother the embarrassing hug and kiss in front of all his friends and teachers and rabbis. He was busy giving high-fives to all his hockey buddies as they walked over, so Sharon decided to spare herself from their glances and get lost in the crowd. To her left were her old teachers, none of the ones she particularly liked, so she went to the right to stand by a tree from where she could still be seen by her mother. Suddenly, she felt a blow to her legs from a small boy not looking where he was running, who had subsequently fallen to the ground and was now crying. A woman came running to apologize for his behavior.

"I'm so sorry," she said to Sharon while looking down at the adolescent. She was dressed in the standard outfit of an Israeli *sherut-leumi* girl: flowing linen skirt, short-sleeved t-shirt over a long-sleeve t-shirt, elaborate head-covering and Naot clogs. She scooped up the child, raising her face to a position where Sharon immediately recognized her as one of her former classmates. "He's still jet-lagged and isn't sleeping well..."

"Anna!" Sharon exclaimed.

The startled woman twitched and settled her eyes on Sharon. "Sharon Gilboa! How are you?" They hugged, drawing a puzzled look from the young boy. "I didn't recognize you. You look...wow, great!"

"*Mi zot?*" the boy asked his mother.

"This is a friend of Ima's from school," she told her son, displaying Sharon with a sweep of her hand.

Sharon smiled at the boy and asked him his name in Hebrew,

but he buried his face in his mother's neck.

"He's having a tough time here," Anna explained to Sharon as she began to rock him in her arms. "English…Hebrew…he doesn't know where he is."

"You're living in Israel?" Sharon asked her, to which she nodded. "Where?"

"Elazar, you know, the Gush. I wanted to be in the Golan, but my husband works in Yerushalayim, so I'll have to just hold onto my dreams."

Sharon got distracted by the sight of an elderly woman kissing her blushing graduate granddaughter just behind Anna's head. "I didn't even know you were in Israel," she said.

Anna became wispy-eyed. "Yeah, I guess I never left after seminary. I can't believe that you aren't in Israel...I mean, you're Israeli."

Sharon shrugged. "I guess I'm waiting for a real Israeli guy to sweep me off my feet and take me there."

"Do you still live in the Five Towns?" Anna asked.

"Oh no," Sharon assured her. "I live in the city."

"And what do you do?"

"Nothing too interesting," she said, looking down and noticing dirt on her shoes. "A lot of little things. What did you come in for?"

She put down her son, who began running around her while holding her hands. "Well, besides for Jeremy's graduation, my younger sister is getting married."

"Dinah?"

Anna lifted a shoulder and nodded. "Yep."

Sharon frowned. "How old is she, like, twenty?"

"Twenty-one," Anna corrected her before getting pulled down

by the boy. "Ima's talking with her friend now," she reminded him as she straightened her back. "She's marrying some yeshivish guy from Staten Island. Come," she grabbed Sharon's hand. "Come say hello. She'll be so excited to see you."

"What? She's here?" Sharon gently tried to free herself but Anna was already tugging her. "Doesn't she have what to do before her wedding?"

"Come, Avishai!" Anna called over her shoulder, still holding Sharon's hand. "I thought it would be good for her to get out, you know. This week is her Shabbat Kallah. You should come, if you're in the area. It'll be at my parents' house."

"Sounds great," Sharon tried to say without committing. Avishai ran ahead and took his mother's other hand, which made Sharon feel as if Anna was leading her and the boy off to bed. The three of them made their way through the crowd of graduates and their families posing for photos and sharing congratulatory hugs. Smack in the middle of the lawn they slowed down when they saw Dinah smiling brightly and talking enthusiastically to a red-haired woman facing away from them.

"Deen," Anna called to her sister. "Guess who I ran into!"

Dinah addressed Sharon with the same smile she was giving the red-haired woman, making no indication that she knew Sharon. "Hi," she said with vague enthusiasm.

"Dinah, don't you remember Sharon from the yearbook?"

The red-haired woman turned around and Sharon immediately detected the face. She couldn't believe her eyes. "Erica Warren?"

Erica made a small curtsy. "Sharon!"

The two girls emitted high-toned gasps and hugged tightly. However uncool Sharon thought she had been in high school, she at least wasn't as bad as Erica. Everyone thought she was weird—

quoting Shakespeare, wearing mismatched clothing and covering her forever-frizzy mass of red hair with an awful French beret. She followed Sharon to the Village, scoring a coveted spot at the exclusive Fine Arts program at Cooper Union but transferring out halfway to learn fashion design in LA. Now she looked completely different: her red hair exploded in thick curls, her face tanned to a toasty glow, and her white linen outfit suggested that somewhere on the West Coast she took an interest in how she dressed.

"I thought I recognized that shade of red," Sharon then said. "But wow…Erica! How long has it been?"

"Two years," Erica remarked.

"So, what are you doing here? You came in for Michal's graduation?"

"Yes, but I'm back." She threw her head back like a model. "The Coast is not for me."

"You know," Sharon leaned in, as if to whisper, "I never really pictured you there. But I see that you did well. I love your…outfit." She gave a nod of approval.

"Thanks," Erica demurred, sighing. "Wow, Sharon."

"Yeah, Sharon," Anna interjected. "I'm glad you got to see Dinah before her wedding."

"Me too!" Sharon gushed, turning to Dinah and reaching out to give her a light hug. "I'm so excited for you."

"Thank you," Dinah said politely, hugging back.

"I told Sharon about the Shabbat Kallah," Anna told her sister.

"Great," Dinah said through a smile before turning to chase after Avishai playfully.

"You'll be around on Shabbat?" Erica asked Sharon. "You live here?"

"Oh no," Sharon said, shaking her head vigorously. "I live uptown, on the West Side."

"Really?" Erica asked. "How do you like it up there? I hear it's a cool place to live."

She rested her hands on her hips and glared at Erica. "How so?"

"You know," she rolled her hand, "social life, plenty of singles."

Sharon shrugged and made a face. "Sure, if you're approaching forty and don't plan on marrying."

Erica frowned disappointedly. "Really?"

"No, I'm being cynical. Many different people live up there. You just have to find your niche."

"Have you?"

Sharon grimaced. "I know people. I wouldn't say that I have a niche."

"Oh." Erica tossed her head and let her curls fall down to her shoulders. "Well, it would be nice to visit."

"Sure," Sharon said immediately. Then her eyes lit up. "Hey! Come for the aufruf. You remember Rob Heller? From the Caf?"

Erica had to think before she nodded. "I think so. When is it?"

"Next week, I believe. He's having a whole thing Shabbat afternoon. You'll be my guest and surprise everybody."

"Great. So I'll call you before. You still have the same number?"

Sharon looked at her in disbelief. "You still have it?"

Erica rolled her eyes. "Yep, my parents left my room exactly as I left it. All my address books and calendars are still on my shelves."

"Tell me about it," Sharon agreed, reaching over and touching Erica's shoulder. "Except that my little sister threw everything to the top of the closet."

Erica laughed. "I took one look at my closet when I got back and felt like some Goth demon was screaming out at me." She stretched out her arms like a mummy towards Sharon. "'Why have you forsaken me!'?"

Sharon laughed so hard she was scared she would fall over. When she composed herself, she wiped away the tears from her eyes and breathed deeply. She looked up and saw her little brother not far away, inspecting people's faces, probably looking for her. "Well, I think I should get back to my brother. It's his day."

"Right, we too," Anna then said. "It was great seeing you, Sharon. We'd love to see you on Shabbat."

"Me too," she said, pivoting her feet to turn away. "It was great seeing you, Anna. You too, Erica. Really, call me and come. You'll see everybody."

"Thanks," Erica said. "It was great to see you again, Sharon."

Sharon smiled. "Anna, tell Dinah mazal tov again for me."

"Will do," she said as she scanned around for her son. "Oh, Sharon, we'll probably take in Shabbat early to get the kids to sleep," Anna informed her. "So don't come too late."

"Kids?" Sharon was walking away but stood in place. "You have another?"

"Yeah, Talia is sleeping away in the stroller," Anna pointed behind her. "She's really adjusted to the time change very well—"

"That's great, really great. Bye!" Sharon walked away quickly until she ran into her brother.

"Ima wants you," he said simply.

"Lead the way," she told him with a smile.

Chapter Eleven

Joe

BY SUNDAY AFTERNOON, Joe was bouncing off the walls from cabin fever. Though he had been entertained by a lively meal at Rabbi Josh's house on Friday night, he was effectively barred indoors all Shabbos by heavy rains that persisted throughout the holy day and through Saturday night. After sitting through Shabbos davening with his socks and the lower half of his suit pants soaking wet and the air conditioning in the shul on full blast, he took his afternoon lightly when he felt the beginnings of a cold tingling behind his eyes. The rains diminished to a light drizzle on Sunday morning, but Joe was sneezing and so he lounged around, reading an essay on statistical methods and saving his strength for his date.

As he was ironing the suit pants that lost their crease in the rain, he called his parents.

"Hello," his older sister answered the phone.

"Ellen?"

"Hello Joe," she said enthusiastically, then to someone else, probably his mother, "It's Joe."

"What are you doing there?"

"We came for Shabbat and stayed the night. Michael didn't

want to drive home in the rain. Did it rain by you yesterday?"

"All day." He coughed. "I think I caught something."

"I'm sorry to hear that. What's going on with you, anyway? Found yourself a wife yet?"

He stammered. "What? No…why would you think that?"

"Come on, you're a twenty-two-year-old religious guy in New York. You didn't think that we'd expect you to be dating already?"

"But…"

"So, what's her name?"

He couldn't help laughing at the irony of his sister's inquiry. "There's no girl," he said in mock-sorrow.

"Then what's so funny?"

"Nothing."

"I don't believe you. You haven't even started dating?"

He finished with his suit pants and wanted to hang them. "Can you hold on? I want to get a hanger from the bedroom."

"Dodging the question, eh? I can't talk long; we're about to sit for brunch and I have to change Aviva."

He coughed deeply. "Ah, brunch. Family tradition."

"You don't sound so good. Go get some rest."

"I've been in all day," he explained.

"Oh. Well, we're missing you down here, Joe. Ask your rabbi to find you a date, at least. You aren't getting any younger."

"Whatever you say, Ellen. Who's there to speak?"

"Just Mom. Dad and Michael are out getting the bagels. Should I get her?"

"Sure."

He put the phone down next to the iron and ran to the bedroom before his mother came to the phone. As he reached for a hanger, he pulled out his cleanest white shirt and grimaced at its wrinkles.

When he returned to the table where he had spread a towel over to iron on, he heard his mother's voice.

"Hello? Joe?"

"Hi mom," he answered breathlessly. "I ran to get my shirt to iron."

"Iron a shirt? What's the occasion?"

He clenched his teeth over his potential slip. "I'm meeting someone in the city."

"You sound all stuffed up," she commented with motherly concern.

Joe sneezed into the towel. "I am."

"So who're you meeting? Who is she?"

He almost choked on his breath. "Why do you think it's a she?"

"Who else would you iron for?"

Laying the shirt on the towel, he checked the iron and found it out of water. "Sharon?"

"Oh Joe. You don't have to lie to me."

"What? I wouldn't iron a shirt to meet Sharon?"

"You wouldn't say that you were going to 'meet someone.'"

He laughed to himself. "Can you hold on a moment while I fill the iron with water?"

She was used to broken conversations while he was in his apartment, so he just put down the phone and went to the kitchen sink. As he filled a plastic cup with water, he started breathing deeply. *Should I tell her? Rabbi Tzvi said not to say I'm dating, but she's my mother.* He was so absorbed in his thought that the water overflowed from the cup onto his hand and onto his shirtsleeve. He took the water and refilled the iron before picking up the phone.

"OK, mom," he announced dramatically. "You caught me. I have a date tonight."

She didn't respond right away. "What did you say?" she asked after a moment. Joe's heart was beating as if he'd just completed a marathon. "I'm sorry, your father just came in the front door. Did you say something?"

He felt sweat beading on his forehead. "No. Maybe you heard the rain from the roof over here. Go eat while the bagels are hot."

"OK. How are things otherwise?"

They hung up a minute later and Joe dropped into a chair. For a few minutes he sat there, staring at the steam rising from the iron, hoping he made the right decision. He finished his ironing, ate a hearty lunch, and at 3 PM was poised to leave his apartment, giving himself two hours to both get there and to settle his nerves.

As he left his basement, he opened his umbrella to avoid the runoff from the roof as he locked the door. He had a small packet of tissues that he put into his coat pocket as he pulled out his keys. Just then, he was startled by Mrs. Gruberman's voice coming from the driveway above him.

"Good afternoon, Joe. Are you going out in this weather?" she asked.

His hand shook as he heard her, causing him to drop his keys to the ground. He bent down to search for them among the wet leaves. "At least it isn't yesterday's rain," he responded.

"That's true. Do you need to go somewhere?"

Hoping she couldn't see him in his suit from behind his umbrella, he took extra time locking his door once he found the keys. "No. I have a pretty good umbrella."

"It's no problem. Why get all wet?"

He had no real reason to fight her, so he walked up the stairs and blew his cover. "Can you bring me to the subway?"

Her eyes twinkled at the sight of his suit and tie. "Sure. Sit in the back; Aliza's coming too."

Great. He went quickly around to the passenger side and settled into the back seat as Aliza came from the front of the house. When she and Mrs. Gruberman were in the car, Aliza turned to her mother and said, "I brought the gift certificate to the Fitting Room. Do you mind if I use it for some new — ?"

"So Joe," her mother inserted quickly, speaking over Aliza. "Where are we taking you?"

Aliza turned quickly and found Joe in the back seat, her eyes darting directly at his tie. All he could grant her was a forced smile. "Whichever subway station is on your way."

They dropped Joe at Avenue J, where he got on a Q train and spent the whole ride into Manhattan going nuts. He tried to convince himself of the lack of significance this event would have in the grand scheme of his life but it wasn't working very well. *We're only getting together to chat; I'm not obligated to marry her just because we meet once.* His chest was pounding and he felt the urge to pace the length of the car, but he and the other passengers were following the strict etiquette of the Metropolitan Transit Authority to avoid all eye contact and sit as motionless as possible, so he instead suppressed his inner frenzy, occasionally blowing his nose. He became acutely aware of the noise of the car as it sped through the underground tunnels, a subtle nuance of his frequent train travels that he was usually able to ignore.

By the time he reached Times Square he was breathing normally, but still conscious of all the traffic noises set behind a background of a low rumbling vibration in his ears. It was raining still but not enough to clear the sidewalks of its normally thick mass of pedestrians. As Mrs. Rosenzweig had warned him, Joe had some difficulty finding the entrance, even though he had studied the picture on Google Maps. It was situated somewhat off Broadway, beyond a taxi driveway and very well hidden. Walking through the maze of umbrella-toting tourists in Times Square set him back, arriving at the Marriot only ten minutes early, the rumbling still echoing in his head at full intensity. Looking through the doors he found no lobby, only a small sign on a velvet-enveloped stand pointing to a vestibule and informing him that the lobby was on the eighth floor. He rode up alone, catching a quick glimpse of banquet and dining halls through the glass windows of the elevator.

At the eighth floor the elevator stopped at what looked like a large ballroom with a high ceiling. It was lit with plenty of lights, suspended from the sky it seemed, yet remained dim. Joe stepped into the lobby with his neck craning upwards to try and figure out where the ceiling for this humongous room was. The entire hotel seemed to surround the open air of the lobby as he could see all the hallways with the suite doors extending all the way up to an indeterminable ceiling. He was walking around the perimeter gazing at the lights, which he observed were actually shining from the room hallways of the floors above, when he felt as if he was being scrutinized and looked down to see a religious-looking girl sitting on a couch. She appeared to be rather young, perhaps twenty, but she was dressed nicely and though Joe was pretty sure that she was too young to be Rachel, she was cute enough that he wouldn't mind if it was her. As he came nearer she stood up and looked right at him.

"Reuven?" she asked him. He was so startled that he jumped back a bit.

"No," he told her apologetically. She returned to her seat with a huff. Joe went to find a place to sit far from her, eventually settling at an armchair with a two-seat couch opposite it. He sank into the seat and blew his nose. Then he thought he should stand by the elevators to meet her, but looking around and finding very few other people he figured she could find him. Besides the other Jewish girl there was an older man reading a newspaper and at the far end of the lobby was the hotel check-in, however inconvenient it appeared to be. There was a small shop where Joe thought to buy her a drink, as Mr. Gruberman had advised him, but all of a sudden he put his plan on hold.

From behind Joe heard a light cough that meant someone was calling for his attention. He spun around to find a female hovering a few feet away from where he was sitting. In one second he surmised that it was probably his date. She had a thin face, touched-up but not made-up heavily, and he could tell that she had thick curly hair put up in some way; more than that he didn't have the time to register because his mind was already processing the fact that she was speaking to him. "Are you Joseph?" she asked.

"Yes," he answered. "I guess you're Rachel."

She nodded. "Your tie stood out."

He looked down at the tie. "It did its job."

"Yeah," she said, still standing in the aisle. It then occurred to Joe that she was waiting for him to invite her to sit.

"Oh, please sit down," he motioned towards the couch. She accepted, settling into the two-seater and removing her coat. Joe watched her as she placed her coat over the arm of the couch and her umbrella next to her. She looked at Joe and smiled politely. There was a silence of about three seconds until Joe realized that the burden of conversation was on him. He began with whatever came to his mind.

"You're coming from Manhattan?" he asked. "I mean, you live here in Manhattan?"

"Yes," she said. "I live in Washington Heights."

He leaned back in the chair and scratched his chin. "Did it take a long time to get here?"

"Not really. I travel downtown every day so I don't even feel it."

"It was raining up there, too?"

She didn't answer right away. "Yes, it is," she said slowly.

Then he remembered her umbrella. "Right," he laughed nervously. "So, where do you work...if I may ask?"

"I work in a Jewish day school doing administrative tasks." She grimaced. "It's work."

Joe felt the urge to sneeze, but he held back. "It's not what you want to be doing?" He thought he sounded like a journalist.

She shrugged. "Let's say that it isn't what I expected to be doing."

He reached into his coat pocket to grab a tissue but didn't pull it out before he sneezed into his forearm. "Sometimes we have to start out and get our feet wet before diving in."

"Bless you," she said, offering him a concerned frown. "Do you have a cold?"

He brushed off her question with a shake of his head. "I did yesterday."

Rachel hummed, granting him an elongated glance before looking around vaguely. Joe noticed behind her that a flustered Reuven had finally arrived.

"Do you like living in Manhattan?" Joe asked, folding his arms across his chest.

She thought about it. "I guess so. I've been living here for a while."

"Since college?"

"Yes. You also went to college in the city, no?"

"I went to NYU," Joe explained. "Downtown is a whole other world."

"I hear that," she said. There was another pause, in which Joe felt he should elaborate.

"I mean, downtown isn't so Jewish. We had one minyan at school and there was a Young Israel in the area, but there wasn't so much to eat out or anything."

"I know. I went to Stern. There wasn't much in Murray Hill either."

He coughed lightly. "It's different for you. You didn't have to go find a shul three times a day, *davka* in the early morning and at the most inconvenient times in the afternoon."

"I guess so," she said. Her eyes followed a trio of women walking past.

"Plus you always had all those restaurants on Broadway."

She folded her legs. "I don't know. We certainly thought that there wasn't much."

The elevator chimed and a family of obvious tourists entered the lobby. They were conversing loudly, drawing Rachel's attention. "Do you understand what they're saying?" Joe asked her.

"No," she answered, giving him a puzzled look. "Why?"

"Does it sound like they're talking French?"

She shrugged. "I don't know."

"Maybe Manhattan is like that," he commented, leaning forward.

"What do you mean?"

"Like, I had a thought once that nowhere in Manhattan can feel very Jewish because there's so much else going on to overshadow it."

She thought for a moment. "Perhaps."

There was a silence of a few moments while Joe chewed on his tongue. Somehow he could talk for hours with Sharon or with girls from school, and yet nothing was coming to him. He at least detected a lack of interest in discussing Manhattan. "So I hear you come from St. Louis."

"Born and raised," she answered.

"How did a Jewish family end up there?" Now he thought he really sounded like a journalist.

"We've been in St. Louis for a few generations," she stated proudly.

His eyes caught Reuven get up and walk towards the gift shop. *Right, I'm supposed to buy her a drink.* The French tourists stared at Reuven as he passed them. "That's great. I don't know anything about St. Louis. Is it a small community?"

"Everything is small compared to New York," she said with slight disdain. "But there are a number of shuls, if that indicates a Jewish community's size."

"It might be," Joe said. "I come from the suburbs of DC, and in our town there's a big Orthodox shul and a not-so-big one, and that's about it."

Rachel made another humming sound and began to look around again. She was sitting up very straight, her lips slightly pursed and her eyes squinting. Joe wasn't sure whether she was genuinely uninterested or whether his conversation wasn't engaging enough. She appeared to have something to say, only that Joe hadn't gotten her to open up yet. Was she supposed to on a first date? Mr. Gruberman told him to be a mentch and to just talk, so he would try more. It wasn't over just yet.

"What do you enjoy doing?" he asked her as he pulled out a tissue to blow his nose.

She gave him a puzzled look. "What would I like to do, like for a job?"

"No, like," he rolled his hand, "What would you do on a day off…if you weren't occupied with some other obligation?"

"That's an interesting way of asking," she said, amused. Joe inwardly congratulated himself. "Um, I enjoy running along the river, drawing, reading. I enjoy cooking; I cook for Shabbos a lot because my roommates have to stay at work 'till late on Fridays."

"That's nice of you," Joe complimented. His face froze, scared he crossed some line by complimenting her, but she carried on.

"Well, I've been doing it for a long time. When I was boarding during high school I lived with a family and the mother would make everything from scratch. She didn't work; her husband was a cardiologist."

Joe was watching her face but caught her uncross her legs and then cross the other.

"But I really learned the most in Israel. Our seminary didn't organize Shabbos for us, so if we didn't want to invite ourselves to random families from the list, we had to make Shabbos ourselves," she paused and when she realized he was looking at her, she added, "which I didn't mind."

As she talked, Joe watched her face relax. She widened her eyes, fluttered her lashes, made broad hand motions as she talked, which he enjoyed seeing. When he saw Reuven returning with two bottles of soda, the urge to do the same returned but he didn't want to interrupt her. "You got a real Israel experience."

"Oh, I loved it there. I learned so much."

"Did you have a hard time coming back? I know I did."

She moved towards the arm of the loveseat, resting her arm on it. "Yeah." She made a face. "You can imagine coming from

Yerushalayim and being dropped in St. Louis."

He shrugged. "Actually, I can't."

"Did you learn in Israel?" she asked.

He leaned back in the chair. "I was in yeshiva for a summer *zman*, but I was there for a total of seven months."

"What else did you do?"

He coughed into a tissue. "I went to this funny high school that graduates its seniors in January and then goes to Israel for the rest of the year and tours and volunteers."

She lifted her eyebrows. "That sounds fun."

"It was," he said shortly.

"How did you get to yeshiva then?"

"Oh, that's a long story," Joe said. He looked at Rachel and read in her expression that she was waiting for him to tell it. The realization that she might actually be interested in what he had to say shook him a bit, but he composed himself. Then he remembered that there was something he was supposed to do. "I'm sorry. I haven't been a gentleman. Would you like something to drink?"

Chapter Twelve

Sharon

SOMETIME ON SUNDAY MORNING, Sharon was startled from her sleep by a sharp feeling that she was being watched. At first she thought that it was the end of some strange dream, but looking around she saw her younger sister in the middle of her room, standing perfectly straight and staring at her. She was still young enough to be excused for such odd behavior and so Sharon waved to her while stretching and saying *Modeh Ani*. "What time is it Tehilah?"

"Ima told me to wake you," she said.

"OK. But what time is it?"

"I don't know," she replied in a childish way before turning and skipping out of the room. Sharon sat in her bed for a few minutes and admired the cleanliness of the room that was never this tidy when it was exclusively hers. Then she dragged herself down to the kitchen where her mother was listening to a small clock radio suspended above the counter where the family ate its quick meals. Her mother was dressed well, drinking coffee and eating an Israeli salad with pita.

"A very healthy breakfast," Sharon noted to her mother. "Ethnic too."

Immediately her mother shushed her. "I want to hear the traffic report," she explained.

Sharon raised her arms in a way that said 'I'll stay out of your way' and poured herself a glass of calcium orange juice from the fridge. Sitting at a stool, she waited for her mother's attention to return to the room.

"Your grandmother isn't doing well," she eventually said, looking out the sliding doors at the side patio. "We should go visit her."

Sharon knew that *we should* really meant *you're coming, so get dressed.* "You're going today?" Her mother hummed an affirmation. "I was planning on returning to the city a little earlier—"

"I can bring you to a train station in Jersey," her mother offered, though Sharon wasn't sure whether it was in response to what she had said. She didn't pursue the matter when she felt she was being insensitive.

After a makeshift breakfast, she chose an outfit that wouldn't be too ostentatious for visiting a nursing home and packed whatever she absolutely needed into a single shoulder bag in the event she had to meet Andy straight from the train. Everything else would have to sit in a duffel bag in the car to be retrieved the next time she would be persuaded to visit home.

Sharon, her mother, and her sister left the house around 10:30 AM, arriving in Lakewood at 12:00. When they got there her grandmother was awake and very happy to see them. She clutched at Sharon's hand for a long time, smiling faintly and looking at her with glossy eyes as she quietly answered Sharon's mother's questions about how she was being treated. Sharon's little sister mostly sat with a book in the corner and periodically came over to the bed to smile at her grandmother. After only an hour a nurse came and said that their grandmother was very tired and should be left to rest.

Her mother protested and the nurse allowed them to stay for twenty more minutes. They said their goodbyes and silently left after her grandmother had fallen asleep.

They ran through the rain to their car, buckled their seatbelts and backed out of the parking lot in heavy silence. For ten minutes nobody spoke, the silence filled by classical piano from a local college radio station. Sharon leaned her head against the window, watching the plinking of the rain against the glass. She didn't know whether her mother wanted to talk or whether she preferred not to, but when the concerto finished and the radio announcer started talking, her mother lowered the volume and tried to lift the mood in the car.

"She seems to be all right," she said pleasantly. "Your uncles don't think so but I don't see the issue."

"Does grandma not know how to talk anymore?" Tehilah asked innocently.

There was silence for another minute. "It's hard for her to talk," her mother eventually answered, glaring at Sharon in the passenger seat. She knew that the little one was not to know the full extent of the situation. They changed the subject and sped along the Garden State Parkway with little traffic.

When she got back to the apartment that her grandmother had lived in for nearly forty years, she spent a long time sitting on her bed, really her grandmother's bed, staring blankly at the bedroom furniture. She had been a strong woman, living alone in the city for more than ten years after Sharon's grandfather passed away, and seeing her in her current frail state left Sharon numbed and unable to do anything. For some reason she felt an urge to call Joe, but before she could Andy called her.

"Hello," she answered without emotion.

"Hey Sharon, it's Andy," he replied.

"Hello Andy." She shook her head to jumpstart her energy. "I'm sorry I couldn't talk earlier—"

"It's no problem. I just wanted to be sure that we're still on for this evening."

"This evening?" she repeated as she stood up and started looking through her clothing. "How late do you want to meet?"

"Sorry, whatever. I meant around 6:00, which is still evening."

"Oh, well then. I guess you have to be specific with me. I was an English major." *What am I doing this for?*

"I'll try to remember that. Shall we go for dessert? I don't feel like a whole meal."

She pulled out her denim jacket and returned it to the closet with a disapproving shake. "That's fine with me. I ate enough over Shabbat."

"So should I come to your building at 6:00, or is that too early?"

"I'll be downstairs at 6:30."

"Great. See you then."

She hung up. She had heard somewhere about hanging up first to keep him wanting more. With only three hours to prepare, she resumed scanning her wardrobe for the perfect outfit that was both casual enough for a 'dessert' date but not too casual, as if she could just as well be going out with anybody. Eventually Sharon settled on an outfit and proceeded to grooming and primping. After flattening her hair, she painted her toenails and fingernails the same color, knowing full well that she would be wearing closed shoes. Before make-up she ate a bowl of cereal and a banana. By 6:00 she was ready and with half-an-hour until she was to be downstairs she sat down on the couch and closed her eyes.

At 6:40 she was shaken awake. "Your phone has been ringing

nonstop," Tamar told her.

Sharon jumped up, ran to her room, and sprayed herself three times with Tommy Girl in three different places. With one final glimpse in the mirror, she grabbed a shoulder bag as she ran out, waving to Tamar in thanks. The elevator didn't come right away, despite her pressing the button repeatedly, but when it finally arrived she used the fifteen seconds while descending to compose herself, apply one last coating of lip gloss, and breathe.

She saw him sitting on the couches as she came into the lobby. "I'm sorry for keeping you waiting," she said to the back of his head, prompting him to turn and stand.

"I was afraid that you'd forgotten," he said as he stood, coming towards her. All of her preparations had been for that moment when he looked her over, and from the fact that for a moment or two he wasn't able to speak, she knew that it was worth it. "I guess you were in the elevator or something."

"Or something," she repeated, smiling in approval of his appearance. He was wearing a dark blue Oxford shirt, black pants and a 3/4 raincoat, which she felt was appropriate. He was also holding a black umbrella. "It's raining?"

"On and off all day. It's for you."

"For me? You think I'm going to let you get wet?" Upon her skepticism, he pulled out of his coat pocket another umbrella the size of a small water bottle. "Very well prepared," she complimented.

Under their respective umbrellas they walked to the subway, which didn't bother Sharon. She wasn't spoiled enough to expect a taxi when they're at most going two or three stops on the express. She didn't care to ask where exactly they were going, letting him surprise her.

"So I don't know anything about you," he said as they waited for a train. "All I know is that you live in one of the Five Towns. Did you go to HAFTR?"

"Yes," she admitted. "How did you guess?"

"It's the only school I know there. There was a guy from HAFTR in Shalevim. Morty Shulman."

"Shulman, yeah. It figures that he would go there."

They heard the familiar beep warning of a train entering the station. "Uptown local," he blurted out.

"What?" she gave him a puzzled look. "We're on the downtown platform."

"No, it's a game," he explained. "Me and the guys bet from which direction it's coming. Quick, what do you say?"

She glanced down the tunnel and saw a reflection of headlights. "It's our train."

"Nah!" he groaned. "You looked! You cheated!"

"Oh, sorry," she pouted. "It's my first time."

"All right," he excused her. "I'll let it slide. But next time—no mercy."

"OK," she agreed, with a smile. "What were we discussing?"

"Morty Shulman. You knew him?"

"Not really. He won a lot of competitions and so his picture was all over the yearbook. He was in your year?" Andy nodded. "So I guess we're of the same year." *I thought he was much older.*

"You worked on the yearbook?" he asked before their train blew its loud horn as it entered the station. "That's kind of cool."

"No, it's not," she laughed at the suggestion. The clacking of the train was so loud she had to wait to explain herself. "No one hands in things on time and the layout people don't know what they're doing and everyone complains about how expensive it is and 'why am I only in it thirteen times?'"

He looked down. "I'm sorry."

"It's all right. I'm not that bitter."

"If you say so."

Sharon allowed him to be playful. She didn't know why she wasn't being as critical with him; the barrier she put up with other men seemed to have been forgotten somewhere along the way. When the train stopped and opened its doors, they sat down next to each other on the bench along the wall, with some space between them.

"And what about you?" she asked. "What type of Jewish name is Andy?"

"It's not my real name," he admitted. "It's says Randall on my passport, but that wasn't what I was called at my *brit*."

Sharon waited with eager eyes. "So…what's your real name?"

He paused and took a big intake of air, adding to the dramatic revelation. "Refael Yechezkel."

"Wow," was all she could say.

"I take it that Sharon isn't your real name either."

She leaned in close, as if telling a secret. In a voice only he could hear, she said, "Actually, it is. My father's a Sabra, and I'm named after his mother. Really it's Shar-*on*, but only he calls me that."

"And your mother?"

She leaned back to finish her story. "From the Bronx, of all places. She backpacked onto my father's kibbutz in the seventies and stayed until she convinced him to move here. His whole family bounced from the kibbutz at some point because they all live in Rechovot now."

"It was a religious kibbutz?"

"We drove through one time when we were in Israel and I didn't see much. I really don't know what happened."

Andy nodded. They were speeding past the 59th Street station and she noticed his eyes rapidly shifting back and forth as he tried to focus on the mosaic tiles of the walls of the station. However, the train was still traveling too fast to focus on one tile long enough before it passed from sight, and so his eyes kept trying over and over again to find a tile it could stay with to no avail.

"It's interesting how that happens," she commented, "how people's eyes move back and forth like that."

"Like what?"

"Like, they shift very quickly back and forth. It happens only when the subways are entering or leaving a station."

He hummed. "I never noticed it."

In the pause she detected the slight stubble around his face, as if he hadn't shaved since before Shabbat. She wondered how old he was, but then he said that he had been in the same year as her. "Mark Shulman was in your year at Shalevim?" she asked him.

"I don't remember him as Mark. We called him Morty but he was called to the Torah as Mordechai."

Ah, so he is older than me. "I was talking about Moshe, his younger brother."

"Who names their kids two 'M' names? It just gets confusing."

"People are into that," she said.

"Are you?" he asked.

"I never thought about it," she admitted. "Let me have a few kids and I'll see what I do."

"That's fair," he said. While she felt that it was an awkward topic to be discussing, she was glad that he ended it cleanly.

As she predicted he stood up at 42nd Street. "I always like

Times Square at night," she gushed. "The lights are much more captivating than in the daytime."

"Would you like to go on the Ferris wheel?" he offered. "It's probably the only thing to do there besides for Broadway shows or buy shoddy souvenirs."

"Ferris wheels are for children," she commented pointedly. "Besides, where is there one in Times Square?"

"In Toys R' Us."

"Ha, I told you," she said in a sing-song way. "It probably isn't running now anyway."

"But you'd be interested?" he urged her. She didn't know what he was getting at, but something about his insistence seemed genuine.

"Maybe another time," she assured him. "We came to have dessert, so let's do that."

They got off the train and walked underground as far north as they could, only to find the Broadway entrances closed. Turning back to the escalator at 42nd Street, they came onto the sidewalk to find a light mist falling from a light gray sky. Andy opened his umbrella, signaling for Sharon to follow suit, and they walked close together towards 6th Avenue.

"Let's go up Broadway," she suggested. "If we're walking through this rain anyway, we might as well be covered by the awnings."

"You don't even know where we're going," Andy reminded her.

"You're right," she conceded. "Are we going in that direction?"

He nodded, motioning for her to lead the way. Despite the overcast sky and the rain, Broadway appeared as bright as noontime as huge floodlights illuminated the billboards so that not a moment would pass without passers-by being reminded to Enjoy Coca-Cola.

People walked quickly, much to the chagrin of the peddlers who were already contemplating closing up shop as the dreary weather persisted.

As they stopped at a red light at 45th Street, Sharon looked across Broadway towards the bright neon flash of a Fuji film advertisement, and through the drizzle noticed an obvious couple on a shidduch date. The girl wore an open beige coat over a simple cardigan and a black skirt that reached just above her ankles while the guy wore a dark suit with a dull orange tie. "Look over there," she pointed to Andy. "Tough luck to have a shidduch in this weather. His umbrella doesn't even look big enough for both of them."

"How can you tell?" he squinted. "They're, like, 500 feet away."

"Come on, what else would a couple dressed like that be doing on Sunday afternoon in Times Square?"

"Coming out of a Broadway matinee," Andy offered.

"With a kippah like his?" Sharon countered.

"You can see under that umbrella?"

Sharon turned back and caught them leaping over a puddle as they entered the crosswalk heading south, and for some reason she thought that she recognized that particular tie pattern from somewhere. "Maybe you're right," she conceded.

Her eyes were still following them when Andy's hand passed in front of her eyes. "I think we can cross now."

Chapter Thirteen

Joe

LATER THAT WEEK, on Thursday morning, Joe found himself struggling to remain focused on what he was learning with Benji at Ohr Eliyahu. It was after twelve and Rabbi Tzvi still hadn't shown up, even though he told Joe the night before that he would be around to talk with him. While Joe knew not to expect punctuality from Rabbi Tzvi, this time he had pressing matters to discuss.

> It's been two dates and I don't know what I'm
> supposed to feel – I like talking to her and she's cute,
> but isn't there more to a shidduch than this? – I've
> been told to see if I have a good time with her, and I
> do. What else is there? It can't be that I'm just meant
> to hang out with her. Aren't there signs that it's a good
> match? Where is Rabbi Tzvi when I need him?

"Are you saying that the Rashi is agreeing?" Benji was asking Joe, who had just turned his gaze towards the steps. "This line doesn't seem to match what Rashi is saying." Benji looked up.

"Hey, Yosef!"

Joe quickly returned his gaze to his havrusa. "Ignore that line and look at their answer to the second question."

"That's not how Rashi holds," Benji retorted. "Rashi says that it's *deoraisa*."

"Where does he say that?" Joe asked as he noticed that Rabbi Tzvi had in fact come up the stairs. Joe then became very interested in his Gemara. "He doesn't say it explicitly."

"It's certainly what Rashi means. Look here…"

All of a sudden Rabbi Tzvi was hovering over them. "Yosef," he said breathless, startling them. They stood up from their chairs, Joe nearly pushing his into the table behind him. "I'm sorry to interrupt, Benji," he said, then turned to Joe, "But I'm in an incredible rush and have to speak to Yosef right now."

"No problem, Rabbi," Benji said.

Joe closed his Gemara and followed Rabbi Tzvi back to the office. When he arrived he saw that Rabbi Tzvi had already turned on the light and dropped into the seat behind his desk. "Sit," he told Joe as he started opening drawers, apparently looking for something.

Joe remembered that the Rabbi had been preparing to go to the Catskills 'any day now.' "When are you leaving?"

"After I speak with you," he answered, adding a smile. "I only got out of the house because there's a particular binder that I need to take with me."

"Thank you," Joe said automatically.

"So then let's cut to the chase. How are you?"

"Fine, thank G-d," Joe answered again automatically. The Rabbi took a break from his search and stared blankly at Joe.

"I guess I have to be more specific," he said. "How are things progressing with your shidduch? How many dates have you been on?"

"Two," Joe answered. The Rabbi then became preoccupied with refilling a stapler, so Joe continued. "She's very nice, and we're going out again tomorrow."

"Three dates, Yosef!" Rabbi Tzvi beamed. Joe braced himself for a whack on the shoulder from across the desk. "How come this is the first time we're meeting?"

Joe shrugged. "You're busy, I'm busy…"

"Excuses. So, what are you feeling? Do you find her pretty?"

He didn't know how to answer. "I mean, yeah. She's pretty."

The Rabbi gave him a suspicious stare. "Let me guess, you're not…smitten by her?"

"Not really," he admitted with a chuckle, his anxiety defused by the Rabbi's choice of word.

"But she's cute?"

Joe nodded. "Yeah. This is a little awkward to be talking about."

"I know, but it's important. If there's no attraction, however compatible you two might be, it's like multiplying by zero. But it isn't everything either. So don't think that it's over if you're not 'wowed'. That's another word you didn't think a frum-looking rabbi like me knew, eh?" Joe couldn't help but laugh. "So, what else are you feeling?"

Joe looked at the desk. "I mean, what am I supposed to be feeling?"

"What?" Rabbi Tzvi exclaimed, his smile disappearing. "Did you ask what you're supposed to be feeling?"

Joe was taken aback by the sudden change of mood. "You told me to go and have a good time, and I am. Isn't there more? Aren't there specific feelings I should be looking for?"

"Oh, that's what you're asking." Rabbi Tzvi wiped his forehead. "I just have a pet peeve against blind following and it sounded like you were heading there. Well, look, how you feel about her is your department. But if you want to know what to look for, just answer this: what else do you need to know to get engaged?"

Joe did a double take. "Engaged? I don't know anything."

"Sure you do," Rabbi Tzvi countered as he stood up and opened the file cabinet. "You talked about the news on your two dates?"

Joe clicked his tongue in exasperation. "No, but it wasn't enough."

"Great," the Rabbi declared as he slammed the drawer shut. He then addressed Joe as he leaned on the closed cabinet. "So now it's time to get serious. What do you need to know about her to decide whether you'll marry her?"

Joe halted the conversation with his open hands. "Whoa. How did we jump from engagement to marriage in twenty seconds? I've only met her twice."

"And our forefather Yitzchak married Rivka when they first met. You at least have an advantage."

Joe almost got hysterical. "This is silly. You told me to just go out and talk with Rachel and I did, and now when I ask you what the next stage of dating is about you ask me if I'm ready to marry her?"

They stared at each other for extended moment until Rabbi Tzvi broke into a smile. "I'm just trying to get a point across. Instead of thinking that you're just spending time together to eventually fall into marriage, know that every date you go on has a serious purpose."

Joe continued staring, waiting for the answer. "Which is?"

"To find out what you need to know in order to decide to marry

her. Once you meet the shadchan, everything afterwards is intended-
ed to get you to the wedding, and so once you two have met and
are both willing find out more, don't waste any time! We Jews are
very particular about contact between men and women, through all
stages of life, and though it's completely permitted to spend time
with and converse with and get to know a woman that you might
not marry, only what's necessary."

"But what are those things? What's important in forming a Jewish marriage?"

Rabbi Tzvi excitedly clapped his hands. "Yes, that's what I've
been waiting for. Great question."

Joe blushed. The rabbi's chair squeaked as he settled into it.
"Well, there are standard qualities you want to find out about her,
such as her kindness and her seriousness towards halacha and how
she handles stress, but also things that you specifically might be
looking for, you know, if she's musical or organized or whatever is
important to you—but *really* important to you. Not just someone to
be your tennis double or who can name all the state capitals. You
have to think about what you *really* find important and isn't just a
passing preference. Get the idea?"

Joe took a quick breath. "Yeah, but we could square that away
in one more date. After that might not be what you called 'more
than necessary,' but I still might not feel ready to get married just
because she passed an interrogation." Joe caught the Rabbi glance
down at his watch. "You have to go?"

Rabbi Tzvi then sat in his chair and leaned back. "I have all the
time in the world."

Joe was ready to get up. "Seriously, if you have to go."

"I'm serious," he said with a straight face. "OK, your question.
Well, little do you know, but you haven't just been going out to

schmooze and chat." He lowered his voice. "You've also been secretly developing a relationship." He put a lone index finger to his lips. "Look, a shidduch isn't a square, dry meeting. You're also getting to know someone, albeit under a pretext of knowing enough to decide to get married, but it might take more time to feel comfortable with her than just the amount of time necessary to answer your list of questions. That's supposed to be assessed after each date, but—" he crossed his eyes back and forth, hinting to Joe.

Joe laughed and pointed at Rabbi Tzvi. "Hey, you're going away."

"Not to Africa," he countered.

"Wait," Joe halted him. "Didn't you just say that we're very particular about unnecessary dates?"

Rabbi Tzvi exhaled deeply. "Yes, you found the paradox. How do we both limit the number of meetings but give the relationship the space to develop?" He threw up his hands. "What can I say? We try our best to be normal, knowing what we're up against."

At that moment, Rabbi Tzvi's cell phone began to rotate as it vibrated on his desk. He reached for his phone and put it to his ear. "Can you hold on a moment?" he said into the receiver as he started writing on a scrap of paper. "So off you go. Take my number in the country," he told Joe as he tore the number off and handed it to Joe. "We'll be in and out of the bungalow but leave a message and I'll try to call at nights. Your next date is Monday?" Joe nodded. "Where are you for Shabbos?"

"I have an aufruf for a friend on the Upper West Side," he stated.

Rabbi Tzvi stroked his chin. "Who?"

"A friend from college."

Rabbi Tzvi shrugged. "Well, maybe you'll come up some time

this summer. It'll help you calm down."

Joe stood up, extending his hand. "Thank you for coming in, I really appreciate it."

Rabbi Tzvi stood up also. "Call me if you need anything. I'm rooting for you."

Joe smiled. "Have a good trip."

"Thank you," he said. Joe was at the door when the Rabbi suddenly banged on the desk. Joe turned to see him flailing a stapled bunch of papers and announcing into the phone, "It's always right under your nose!"

Chapter Fourteen

Sharon

ON FRIDAY, Sharon met up with Erica in SoHo and shopped with money she didn't have for clothing she didn't need. Neither of them was looking for anything specific and so they spent most of the afternoon perusing the tiny boutiques and giggling at the prices. After entering and exiting every clothing store between West Broadway and Lafayette, their hunger overwhelmed them and sent them uptown to Jerusalem Café for a light lunch. It was relatively crowded, even for a Friday, with pizzas still flying out of the ovens every minute or so and the cash register chiming. There was enough white noise to make conversation somewhat difficult, but they nonetheless spoke loudly over the din of the dining room as they waited for their turn at the salad buffet.

"Did you see the face on that redhead when I asked her for an application?" Sharon asked Erica. "She looked as if I'd asked to buy her dog."

"Hey, I'm a redhead!" Erica returned in mock offense.

"I'm not saying anything about her hair," Sharon defended herself. "I just wouldn't want to meet her evil eye in a dark alley."

"You offended her expertise. Not everybody has the training to smoke cigarettes all day while protecting a dozen $1,000 dresses from the proletariat."

Despite the solemnity of the business lunch crowd, they were unabashedly laughing and playing like two best friends who had just met up after two years. Sharon was overjoyed to have a girl-friend to gush with, especially one who wasn't married or working ten-hour days.

They got their salads and settled at a booth in the back of the seating area, sitting side-by-side to people-watch.

"I don't believe that you haven't prepared anything for Shab-bat," Erica remarked. "It's almost 2:00 already."

"We aren't in Cedarhurst," Sharon reminded her. "All the su-permarkets uptown sell everything we need. Besides, Shabbat only comes in at, like, 8:00."

"Still," Erica began, then gave up. She took a bite of salad and while chewing, she indicated to Sharon to look up. Sharon com-plied and saw a young man in a starched pink shirt with slicked-back hair quickly turn his gaze away from them as he placed his tray at a table and sat down. "I caught him."

Sharon shrugged it off. "I don't pay attention anymore."

"It was way too long."

"Eh."

Just then Sharon's phone chimed. She pulled it from her purse and unlocked it. "It's Andy."

"Who?"

"Just a guy I'm...seeing." She thought for a moment. "Do we still use that term?"

"Seeing? I understood. Not exactly 'going out,' but something more than friends."

"Exactly. He's asking about Shabbat."

"So bring him over. I'll stay out of your way, chill with your roommate."

"If she's around. But Shabbat's a whole new level."

"Have you gone out with him? Like, really gone out?"

She replied with a nod. "Sunday."

Erica hummed. "You've spoken with him since?"

"Sure. He texts me all day." She corrected herself with a roll of her hands. "Not all day, but a few times a day."

"So go for it," Erica assured her.

Sharon twisted her lips. "Are you sure? What about you?"

Erica attempted to stab a cherry tomato with her plastic fork with little success. "I'll be fine."

Sharon frowned and thought for a moment, then snapped when the idea came to her head. "I know. I'll get Joey to come over. You remember Joey Charnoff?"

Erica became all wispy. "You mean Joe? Of course I remember Joe."

Then Sharon recalled how much Erica liked him. "Oh, Joey would be delighted to see you. He's really doing well. He's getting his Master's and he's got a job on Wall Street. We talked about you last week, even."

Erica smiled widely. "Really?"

"Yeah. I'll tell Rob to send him over for Friday night." She unlocked her phone and dialed a number. "He's going nuts trying to find places for everyone."

"That's nice of him." Then, in a whisper, Erica said, "he's looking again."

Sharon placed down her phone dramatically and stood up. "Do you want me to tell him off?"

"No!" Erica cried as she pulled Sharon down. She gave a nervous smile to those who in the dining room who turned their heads at the commotion. "Sharon!" she whispered in humored exasperation.

"So stop looking," she suggested.

Sharon shifted in her seat and again dialed Rob's number. Through the corner of her eyes Sharon peeked over at Erica as she abstractly looked around the dining room. For a moment she doubted whether she should have told Erica about Joe, what with his current funk about girls and his overall weirdness of late. But the moment passed.

Chapter Fifteen

Joe

JOE STAYED AT WORK on Friday later than usual, catching up on his entire backlog and then loafing on his computer. By the time he realized it was nearly 5:00 PM, he stood up from his chair, rubbed his eyes and yawned loudly. He had never heard the office this quiet, and began to worry that he would have to somehow turn off the lights and lock up for the weekend. As he poked his head into the cubicles in search of someone to assist him, he saw Mr. Siegel's secretary walking towards the elevators, bobbing her head to music from tiny headphones and stuffing another bridal magazine into her shoulder tote. She was about to walk right by him had he not stepped directly into her path, eliciting from her an annoyed glare.

"Do you know how to lock up?" Joe asked her. "Is anyone else here?"

"Someone's here," she said quickly and resumed her walk to the elevator. Joe stood in his place, unsure whether to seek out that someone or to take her word. He then heard a distant phone ring and a voice answer it, so he followed the secretary's lead and made his way to the elevators, where she was waiting and still bobbing her head to her music.

For a minute, he glanced up at the floor indicator above the elevator doors while he watched her through the corner of his eye. Seeing her in the hallway reminded him that he hadn't run into Mr. Siegel since he suggested the shadchan nearly two weeks ago. Whether she knew she was being observed or not, she maintained a perfect poker face, staring at the closed elevator doors until the music stopped and she reached into her bag to change albums. Joe turned in her direction and opened his mouth, prompting her to slowly lower one of her headphones and await his question.

"Do you know what's up with Mr. Siegel?" he asked her in one breath. "I haven't seen him in a few weeks."

She shrugged. "Me neither."

"So…what do you do when he isn't around?"

"I have what to do," she assured him curtly, returning her headphone to her ear. Joe deliberately looked away from her as they rode down the elevator in silence, save for the blaring music.

On the street he headed towards the 2 train at Wall Street amidst the usual, though somewhat thinned, downtown pedestrian traffic. Just before he got to the stairwell to the subway, he answered a call from his friend Rob. "Hey, it's the man of the hour. How's everything?"

"Pretty hectic," Rob answered quickly. "Are you on your way up here yet?"

"I just left work. Everything all right?"

"Yeah, great." He made an exhale of relief. "Just a little change in plans."

"You're still getting married, right?"

Rob laughed. "No, nothing to do with that. I almost didn't have a place for you. You were all set to stay by my father's partner, but he flew to Miami last night last minute. Sharon just called me a few minutes ago and said you could crash by her upstairs neighbors…"

Joe groaned. "Man! Why didn't you tell me sooner—"

"I didn't know. Besides, Sharon's right downstairs—"

"Yeah, but…" He stopped himself. *You can't blame people for things they don't know.* He clicked his tongue and sighed. "Right. Sorry you have to deal with all this."

"You sure?"

"If it's what there is…"

"Good, 'cause you're eating there too tonight."

Joe held the phone away from his ear and stomped his foot. "Just me and Sharon?"

"No, she said there'd be other people there. Look, I really gotta go."

"Go, Rob. Anything you need?" Joe asked, but Rob had already hung up.

Joe lowered his head and hobbled down the stairs. Going to Sharon wouldn't help his attempt to slowly break away from her, especially not after last week's phone call. He knew that he couldn't keep her as a friend, but what else could he do? He never forgot the look of venom on her face when she found out he didn't want to eat a particular *hashgacha*. "Just don't get so *frum* that you never talk to me again," she warned him coldly. It was so against her character that he never wanted to see that look in her eyes ever again, but he couldn't just continue living against what he knew was the right thing. He wouldn't ditch the aufruf over this. Who else was Sharon inviting? He hoped it was only her roommate.

When a 2 train finally pulled into the station, he squeezed into the standing space of the crowded car, using the conventional subway-theft-prevention method of nestling the bag between his

ankles. At 34th Street the car lightened its load of passengers and
Joe moved to sit down. At the end of the car he recognized Nati
and so he forfeited his potential seat. Running into him the first
time was amazing enough, but twice in a month was no less than
Providence.

"Hi Nati," Joe said after squirming through the crowded car.
"Twice in one month, eh?"

"What?" Nati asked, looking blankly at Joe.

"That I've run into you on the subway," he clarified.

"Isn't that funny?" he said absently. Nati didn't seem to share in
Joe's amazement.

"You on your way home?"

Nati nodded. "Yep. Work around here?"

"Wall Street. You?"

"Yeah, right around Madison Square."

"That's cool. Get to any games?"

Nati made an amused smile. "No, not really. You?"

"Nope."

Nati's smile waned and he turned to stare out the windows at
the dark tunnels. When the silence felt oppressive, Joe called him
on it. "You seem out of it, Nati."

He continued looking out the window at the subway tunnel.
"You could say that."

"Long week?"

"No, just…" he breathed in deeply, looking down and then up
at the lights. He breathed deeply again before staring Joe straight in
the eyes, but only for a moment. "Just kind of down, I guess. My
friend Jessica's making *aliyah*."

Joe widened his eyes. "Wow, she's moving to Israel? That's
great."

Nati huffed. "It is," he said unconvincingly. His mouth twitched before he said, "It's really great."

At 42nd the train stopped and a mass of people clotted in front of the door. Joe and Nati pressed together to make room in the already-stuffed standing space. "When is she leaving?" Joe asked.

"A month, just before August," Nati said blankly.

"That soon?" Joe exclaimed. Nati became all startled and shushed him, as if what Joe said offended the Koreans standing behind them.

The doors closed and the car became silent, save for the sound of the air conditioner. "To be fair," Nati then said as they started moving, "she only decided two weeks ago, when her job offered her a position in Tel Aviv, but I thought, of all people, she would at least tell me she was thinking about it. Out of the blue she tells me yesterday."

Nati sighed again and returned his gaze to the subway tunnel. The express train slowed down as it passed the local station at 50th Street, and Joe saw Nati's eyes rapidly shifting back and forth as they tried to focus on the tiles of the walls. It was a phenomenon he and Sharon noticed one day, and as he thought of Sharon, Joe recalled Nati's strange comment from the last time he saw him. He went out on a limb. "You don't seem too happy for her."

He continued gazing out the window, but he slowly nodded his head to the clanking of the train against the tracks. It reminded Joe of how Rebecca leaned her head against the bus window on the way to the airport. Unlike Rebecca, though, Nati turned and looked straight at Joe with sorrowful eyes.

"I am," he said simply. "It's just hard losing a friend."

Joe examined Nati's face, watching his cheekbones quiver. "How long have you known her?" Joe asked him gravely.

"Since freshman orientation," he answered, almost in a whisper. "They split the class into different groups, and we were the only religious Jews during that shift. We ate our kosher microwave meals together..." He laughed hollowly. "She was scared, you know. She was warned about college, didn't want to deal with guys. We became friends, though, because we shared that first nervous orientation." Nati bit his lip and Joe thought he was going to cry, but he didn't. "Time went on; she loosened up, got a boy-friend...then another when she broke up with the first...but I was still her friend. I had a girlfriend too for a while, but Jessica..." He paused and took a few deep breaths. "We got really close after we graduated and moved up here...now she's going."

The train slowed down as it passed another local stop, and it felt as if the entire car had silenced, pensively listening to the clacking of the train and empathizing with Nati. Joe could only think one thing: *he loves her*. He felt like giving Nati a hug, but held back. "Are you going to tell her?" Joe asked him.

Nati looked up in alarm. "Tell her what?"

Joe chose his words. "That you'll miss her."

He said nothing, then stood up straight when the conductor an-nounced the next stop. "I don't know," Nati eventually said. "I'm getting off."

"Don't get too down," Joe said hastily. "I mean, I'm sure you'll be all right."

Nati smiled for a moment. "Have fun on the West Side."

"Give me a ring if you need someone to talk to," Joe said. He reached over and gave Nati a quick hug, which was accepted but not returned.

"Thanks Joe," he said and started to go when the doors opened. Nati then stopped in the doorway and turned back. "I don't think I have your number."

"I'll get yours from Sharon," he told him, and with a nod of his head, Nati got off the train.

Chapter Sixteen

Sharon

AROUND THE SAME TIME Joe was on the train, Sharon was picking out her outfit before her pre-Shabbat shower while yelling at her mother over the phone, finding little success at either task. "I don't care. They agreed to let me watch the place while *savta* isn't around, and so it's my place. Tough luck if I'm not home."

"I'm sorry it had to happen," her mother said quickly. "Your Uncle Simon had a few hours before spending Shabbat down with savta and he decided to check out the apartment and when nobody answered he used his key. Had you been home I know you certainly would have let him in."

She was standing in front of her grandmother's bureau, shaking her head at the constraint her clothing had to share with her grandmother's, most of it still in plastic coverings from the dry cleaners. "Tamar had just come out of the shower and he scared her half to death."

"Yes, he told me. He didn't seem so happy to hear that she lived there..."

"Well, I asked you and you told me that bringing her in wasn't a problem."

"I know, but they have a right to change their mind."

"If you even asked," Sharon muttered under her breath.

Her mother was still speaking. "I know you're upset but listen. When your grandmother had her first attack and had to be checked-in, your uncles agreed that you could move in while she was recovering. We all thought that she would only need a few months there at most, but then…" She sighed. "What happened today got me thinking and…"

After a few seconds of silence, Sharon checked her phone to make sure they hadn't lost the connection. When the silence per-sisted, she threw the shirt she was trying to extract from its hanger onto the bed and tossed her head to the ceiling in exasperation. "And…?"

"And I think that you should bring some of your things here, in case the situation gets more unsettled. I don't want you in the middle."

She dropped onto her bed and stared up at the paint-drip motif on the ceiling. Sharon wasn't picking up and moving back home because of her mother's unfounded worrying, but her uncles were another story. She let out a dramatic sigh, and then realized that her mother had said nothing for some time. "I'm with you Ima."

Only then she heard her mother crying. "The doctors don't know what to do."

Suddenly, the computer chimed, "*You've got mail!*" at full volume. Sharon jumped up and started randomly pressing keys to lower it. She understood from the title of the e-mail that a monu-mental once-a-year sale at Gap Online was on and deserved her undivided attention. She asked, "How long?"

Her mother was slow in responding, answering brokenly, "They don't know." She continued more composed. "That's why Uncle Simon came in. Mendy is coming next week; maybe the week after that."

Sharon shook her head. "But we just saw her—what was it, last week? She seemed fine."

"I know. I don't understand either."

Sharon listened intently to her mother's heavy breathing before asking, "How are you holding together?"

"I'm all right." There was a pause. "I have to go dress your sister. Think about what I said."

"OK, Ima."

When her mother hung up, she held the phone in her hand and stared at it. Even when the screen blacked automatically she continue to stare. She couldn't remember the last time she heard her mother like this. Normally she was so put together that it was odd to see her so vulnerable. Heavily, she gathered her clothing for her shower and peeked into the living room to find Erica leaning back on the couch, reading. Just behind Erica's head was the picture of her grandmother and her mother at the Kotel, and for a moment Sharon stared at it, unable to move.

"Everything all right?" Erica asked when she caught Sharon staring.

Sharon blinked rapidly and forced a smile. "Yeah. I'm showering," she announced.

Erica turned back to the book. "Great."

While she dressed in her room afterwards, she heard Erica call out "It's open!" and the creak of the front door. Sharon was too busy watching the photo screensaver on her computer displaying captured memories of her last eight years of life at random to think anything amiss about Erica admitting someone into her grandmother's apartment without her consent. There was a shot of her braiding her sister's hair, followed by her and Elisheva Ashkenazi in front of the fountain in the middle of Washington Square Park, followed by Joe modeling $10 sunglasses he bought from a newsstand on Fifth Avenue. The thrill of not knowing what would pop up next glued her eyes to the screen, so much so that she didn't notice how long Erica was talking to the unknown deep voice in the other room. Only when she heard Erica exclaim, "What a small world!" did she surmise that Joe had arrived and quickly finished getting dressed.

Already from the hallway she could see him rigidly leaning on the bookshelf, a duffel bag still on his shoulder and a shopping bag from Dagostino in his hand. He was staring in the direction of the couch with his mouth slightly open.

"Hello Joey," she said as she came closer, startling him. He turned to Sharon with frightened eyes, as if he had seen a ghost. She pointed towards the couch. "You remember Erica."

He turned back to Erica and blinked rapidly. "Erica…Warren."

"Right," Erica said with a smile. Turning to Sharon, "We've been getting reacquainted."

"Very nice. Erica just got back from two years in LA."

"She told me," he said with a shaky smile. He dropped his bags with a strained moan. "Is anybody upstairs?"

Sharon walked over and picked up the Dag Bag. "What'd you bring me, Joey?"

"Uh, bring…" He tried to grasp the bag, but Sharon was already pulling something out.

"You got me Snapple?" she cried. "How sweet!"

Joe shook his head. "Uh, actually…"

Sharon turned to Erica, "Joey's very thoughtful."

"I see," Erica said with a smile.

Joe quickly smiled. "I couldn't think of anything else," he asserted as he grabbed the Snapple and brought it into the kitchen. "I'll go put it in the fridge."

Sharon gave a puzzled glance at Erica before following Joe into the kitchen.

"Everything all right?" Sharon asked him from behind. "What was that about?"

With strained eyes, Joe whispered, "I didn't recognize her."

"Isn't she gorgeous?" Sharon beamed. "I ran into her last week and I invited her to the aufruf."

"What?" he exclaimed. "She's here the whole Shabbos?"

Sharon nodded rapidly. "She's eating here tonight, so be on your best behavior. She just arrived from LA and you get first dibs. Thank me later."

"No, I will not thank you. I'm not…" he trailed off, pouting like a spoiled child. Gravely, he added, "I don't like surprises, Sharon."

"So I'm sorry," she said quickly. "But don't ruin your chance."

She went to take the Snapple bottle from him, but Joe snatched it away. "Sharon!" he hissed.

"What's gotten into you?" she demanded. He didn't answer, instead glaring at her with piercing eyes and pursed lips that were quivering from him grinding his teeth. "I have no idea what's the big deal." He opened his mouth to speak but quickly shut it when they heard skipping footsteps from the living room. "Lighten up, OK? I did this for you."

"For me?" he asked incredulously, but before he could continue, Erica walked in.

"I guess you can't sit still," Sharon said to her.

"No," she replied cheerfully. "Is there anything I can do to help?"

"I have all the help I need," Sharon said, motioning towards Joe. "He's the most helpful guy I've ever met." With Joe's guard down, she pulled the Snapple from his hands and displayed the bottle as if it were a trophy. "And he brings me my favorite flavor! Thank you, Joey!"

"Wow," Erica marveled. Joe turned red and mustered a smile.

"Is anybody upstairs now?" he asked.

Chapter Seventeen

Joe

Joe slouched in his seat at Sharon's table, nursing his sorbet and watching Sharon and Erica chattering away, oblivious to his disdain. From the moment he realized why Sharon had called Rob and rearranged his evening, a sour coating had formed on his tongue, spoiling his appetite and ruining the taste of her cooking that Joe always enjoyed. He was mostly angry at himself; Sharon couldn't be faulted for trying to set him up when she didn't know he was in the middle of a shidduch. But he resented being used as a "wingman" while Sharon devoted her attention to some guy she also invited, who Joe was finding to be nice but dull. So he mostly sat quietly in his seat, eating with no appetite, responding when spoken to, and counting the minutes until he could go to sleep.

"I still can't get over your apartment," Erica said to Sharon. "It has so much potential if you just get rid of all the 70s furniture."

"You find me a storage space around here that isn't an arm and a leg," said Sharon. She asked Andy, "How much do they go for anyway?"

"I can tell you how much a parking space goes for," Andy offered as he reached for a piece of melon. "Much more than that."

"Well, nobody asked that," Sharon said to him jokingly and flashing him with a funny face.

"No, this room needs an earth-tone motif," Erica said, looking around inquisitively. "Or something Southwestern."

Sharon then said, "You know, Joey, Erica is a designer."

Joe hadn't heard a thing and was instead giving much attention to his inner dialogue:

> Fine, she's incredibly pretty, but she isn't Rachel – What's so special about Rachel? I've only met her twice – There's a rapport, we haven't had a stuffy conversation since the first date, and she's been checked out – Erica's a friend of Sharon, and she even liked me in college, so what could be wrong with her? – That was two years ago, but Erica isn't on the table right now. The question is whether to continue dating Rachel, not whether Erica is an option – But why miss the opportunity if I'm already in doubt about Rachel? – What doubt? Just because I've never sat so close to such a beautiful woman in my life I'm going to throw away the whole shidduch? – Aren't I meant to find out through dating whether a girl, who already makes sense, also feels right, otherwise why meet her? – No, there's gotta be more to it than just that. Besides, I do like Rachel – Really? So why am I staring at Erica? – Because I'm stuck here for the next few hours and don't want to tip Sharon off to something amiss – Why do I care about Sharon's feelings? Look what she got me into? – But staring…

"Joey!"

Amidst his ponderings, he discerned that he was being called from across the table. He shook his head and found everyone staring at him.

"Sorry," he murmured with a dramatic yawn. He took a big spoon from his ice cream. "Brain freeze."

Sharon glared at him and squinted suspiciously. "I just said that Erica works in fashion design."

"Right, you told me." Joe blinked rapidly until he felt he could open them widely enough to appear interested. "Where did you pick up something cool like that?"

"It's not that cool," she said dismissively, looking away from him. "After I left Cooper, I learned so much about art and fashion in LA that I dumped the first and stuck with the second."

"I always thought you had it in you," Sharon declared. "I guess you had to go out there to bring it out."

"Are you saying I didn't know about fashion in high school?" Erica asked, shooting Sharon a playful glance. She grabbed a piece of melon from the tray and asked Joe, "So what's it like to move to the big city?"

He picked up his cup of Snapple and took a long gulp. "You tell me."

She shook her head. "No, it's not the same. I was going in all the time, you know, to shop and to shows. You came from Maryland. That's far out."

"I also went into DC when I was a teenager," he boasted.

"Yeah, but it's not New York."

He closed his eyes and opened them again. "So your real question was 'what's it like to move from Maryland to Manhattan?' Am I correct?"

"Don't get all Gemara on me!" Erica cried. "Just answer the question!"

He raised his cup to his lips, hiding a feigned smile as Erica laughed unabashedly at her last comment. Through the corner of his eye, Joe caught Sharon mouthing something to Andy, who tilted his head towards the door. She stood up, raised her eyes to Erica and grabbed the remaining plastic plates as she walked towards the kitchen. Before Andy could escape the table to join her, Joe grabbed his attention.

"So Andy, where are you from again?" he asked.

Andy shifted in his seat. "Teaneck. Just across the river."

"Yeah? Can you see your house from here?"

He laughed. "No, not that close. Like, ten minutes from the bridge."

"Oh." Joe nodded, which Andy mirrored.

After a moment, Andy stood up. "I'll help clean."

"Thanks," Joe said, not looking up. When he left the room, Erica dropped her elbow onto the table and leaned towards Joe.

"I've been wondering this all evening," she started, "if you don't mind me asking."

He blinked quickly, his heart racing. He could smell the scent of raspberry body spray wafting in his direction. "Go ahead," he tried to say coolly, his voice cracking nonetheless.

She licked her lips, and stared directly into his eyes. He was ready to admit anything, everything, when she asked him in a lowered voice, "Everyone calls you Joe, but Sharon calls you Joey. Which is it?"

"Oh, that," Joe said, leaning back in his seat. "You gotta ask her."

"You don't know?" Erica asked in amazement.

"I do, but she tells it better." He added a hasty smile.

Erica wrinkled her nose and smiled. She leaned back and shook her shoulders playfully as she finished her melon. Joe figured he should add something.

"I'm pretty tired," he explained, heavily drooping his eyes. "I usually make Shabbos early."

"I understand," she said softly. "We still have all day tomorrow."

Joe was relieved that Erica turned her head when they heard footsteps and didn't see his frown. When Sharon came into the room, Erica immediately turned to her. "He told me I have to ask you why you call him Joey."

She looked at Joe and asked him, "What, you're too tired or something?"

Joe gazed back at her tiredly. "Maybe. You tell it better anyway."

"Well, Andy's falling asleep so I'm going to walk him halfway." When everyone turned to him, he closed his eyes and wilted his head against the wall.

"Well, I could use a walk," Erica said as she jumped up. "I'll be your company for the way back."

"So, then why don't you come too, Joey?" Sharon asked quickly. "We can tell Erica the story on the way."

Joe looked up at Sharon and in so many motions, detectable only to Joe, she made it clear that she wanted to walk with Andy and didn't want Erica to be a third-wheel. For a second he made the face he'd wear to tell Sharon he didn't appreciate her nagging, but then a moment later he stood up with a jerk, inhaled deeply and started to sing, "*Shir Ha'ma'alos...*"

*   *   *   *   *

Joe got out of the elevator on Saturday night on the twelfth floor and dragged himself over to the apartment at the end of the hallway. He was clammy and exhausted and only wanted to sit down. He knocked on the door and leaned against the mantle as he waited. Pressing his ear against the door, he heard nothing from the other side. *Someone better be home*, he thought hopefully. He waited a minute before knocking louder and falling to the floor. As he sat in the still quiet of the hallway, he became aware of the sounds of a televised baseball game from the adjacent apartment. The third time he pounded the door with his fist, the reverberations carrying down the hallway. Only when he started drumming a marching-band rhythm did the door unlock and Avi Glass appeared in the doorway.

"I was in the bathroom," he explained lethargically. He looked all around before finding Joe on the floor. "How long have you been sitting here?"

"Who's counting?" Joe exhaled, hoisting himself up.

"Sorry," Avi said, wrapping his arm around Joe to help him in. Avi was one of Sharon's upstairs neighbors, a tall, lanky guy with curly brown hair and thick glasses. He was already dressed down in shorts and a T-shirt that had the San Antonio Spurs logo under Hebrew letters spelling the name of the team. "We already made havdalah."

"I heard it in shul," Joe explained as he gently pushed away Avi's hand and hobbled into the apartment, loosening his tie.

"Which shul?" Joe told him the name. "You were all the way over there?"

Joe stood in place and sighed. "Don't ask. We were walking back after the whole aufruf meal when we saw some people going to the park, so we went to the park," he sighed again, "and then it was late so we rushed to the closest shul where they had this whole spread for shalosh seudos, so…yeah."

"Who's the redhead?" Avi asked.

Joe dragged the closest chair from the dining table and, as if suddenly relieved of a tremendous burden, fell into it and rested his head between his outstretched arms on the table. "Erica. Sharon knows her from high school, but I knew her from NYU…I mean, she went to Cooper Union, but…" After a sigh, he continued, "I basically chaperoned while Sharon entertained her boyfriend."

"You must've hit it off with her," Avi then said.

The statement wasn't well received by Joe, who slowly turned his face to show Avi a sneer. "What makes you say that?"

Avi leaned against an arm of a couch. "I don't know anything about anything, but judging by when you returned last night, I can't imagine you were an unwilling chaperone all that time."

Joe straightened and nodded in reluctant agreement. He slid his suit jacket off his shoulders and folded it over the back of the chair. "You're going to play now?" he asked Avi.

"Every Saturday night. It keeps me in shape."

"I hear." Avi was still standing around, apparently waiting for a confirmation to his observation. "Yeah, it looks that way, doesn't it?"

"What looks that way?"

"That I had a good time with Erica."

"Only looks like?"

"Brilliant deduction, Watson," Joe said cynically. Rubbing his eyes, he confessed, "I'm kind of dating someone at the moment."

Nothing was said for a few moments, until Eitan made an elated cheer from his room. "He's watching the game," Avi explained. "What do you mean 'kind of'?"

"I've been on two dates and am going out again tomorrow."

"It's a shidduch?" Joe nodded. "So what's with Erica—?"

"There's nothing," interrupted Joe. He laughed a bit. "I knew all along."

"Just say you're uninterested."

"It's not so simple."

Another few silent moments passed. Each had found a spot in the room to stare and were both absorbed in their thoughts. Joe had no idea what would make Avi so pensive, but he accepted the empathy.

"What do you think," Joe started to ask. "You have a minute, Avi?"

"Yeah," he said, dropping into the couch. "A minute."

Joe tapped his fingers against his cheek. "I mean, I'm not going to throw away a shidduch because of one pretty girl…you saw her, right?"

Avi nodded and winked. "Whew!"

Joe smiled and exhaled. "I know. But I'm worried that I won't be able to continue dating with the same…without comparing. You hear what I'm getting at?"

Avi stretched his arms. "If you aren't excited by the girl you're dating—"

"But a shidduch's more than that. You aren't just sizing up your attraction level after each date. It develops over time."

"OK." Avi gave him a blank look. "So?"

"So how can I be objective when I'm knocked out by a pretty girl?"

Eitan made a loud groan from the other room. "What happened?" Avi screamed down the hallway.

"Caught at the wall," Eitan called back. "Mets had three on base."

"Sorry," Avi said, laughing to himself. He turned back to Joe. "What were you saying? Oh yeah. Is there nothing else to this redhead? Nothing else you liked?"

Joe propped up his head with his hand as he thought. "Why?" he eventually asked.

Just then Avi's phone began to ring in the other room. "I don't know how a shidduch works," he said as he stood up, "but it's never good to have feelings for two girls. Choose one and forget all others. My father told me that."

As he left the room, Joe dropped his head onto the table and sighed. Behind the backdrop of a clicking clock he heard a car alarm blare for seven seconds before being silenced, then the flush of a toilet from the floor above.

When Avi returned, Joe didn't pick up his head but opened one eye. Avi had a backpack on his shoulder. "That's my cue," he said. "Go home and sleep on this. Don't get any more confused."

"Don't worry. I don't know if I'll be back here ever again."

"Never say never," Avi asserted. "My father taught me that too."

Joe silently agreed. "Thank you, Avi. For Shabbos, for the advice."

Avi simply smiled. "Eitan is still here, so he'll lock up."

"By the way," Joe added. "Don't tell anyone about, well, about anything."

"You got it," he promised Joe, "but I don't talk to anyone anyway."

When the door closed, Joe rested his head between his outstretched arms on the table, remaining motionless for what felt like a long time. In his state of doubt he preferred sulking over the past rather than contemplating the future.

He somehow carried himself over to the room that he had

occupied and turned on the light. He fell onto the bed in his clothing and reached over to grab his phone from the desk. He saw a missed call and a voice message. It was from Mrs. Rosenzweig:

"*Gut voch* Joseph, this is Penina Rosenzweig. I spoke with Rachel just before Shabbos and didn't have a chance to get back to you sooner, but she wanted to push your meeting tomorrow to an earlier time, perhaps noon. Please get back to me this evening, thank you. *Kol tuv*."

Joe closed the phone and threw it in the direction of Steven's paper garbage bin. He remained motionless for some time, stirring when he heard the baseball game turn off and Eitan open the door to his room.

"Hey Joe," Eitan called into the hall. "You still here?"

"Yeah," Joe murmured quietly, then with more volume, "Yeah, I'm here."

Eitan, Avi's second roommate, came to the doorway and saw Joe spread out on the bed. He was dressed in a black collared shirt with black wool pants and black leather slip-ons. "I'm going out for a while. Do you want my key or will you be leaving tonight?"

Joe didn't move at first, but then forced himself to sit up. "Let me get my things and I'll leave with you."

"OK, but it's gotta be now, like..." he looked at his watch, "right now."

"Even better," Joe told him.

Eitan took a step towards the bed. "Is everything all right? You look as if you've been whacked by a baseball bat."

"Just reality," Joe admitted. Eitan nodded, perhaps understanding, and then returned to his room. Joe didn't have much to pack, but he still set Steven's room quickly and two minutes later was standing by the door with his duffel bag on his shoulder and his phone in his hand.

"I'm ready," he called to Eitan.

"What's the rush?" Eitan asked as he came towards him. "Not hanging out with Sharon tonight?"

"No," Joe said decisively, catching a strong gust of Cool Water as Eitan stood to lock the door. "I have to get back to Brooklyn."

"You like living there?" Eitan asked him as they walked towards the elevator. "It's mostly families, no?"

That isn't necessarily a bad thing. "I rent a cheap basement, it's an easy commute to work and school, and it's a nice community."

"If you like it," Eitan commented. "I have family who live by Avenue I and Bedford."

"That's not far from me."

"Really? You live in a mansion too?"

Joe shook his head vigorously. "Just in the basement."

"I couldn't see myself living there."

"It's not for everybody," Joe admitted. "Neither is this community."

Eitan agreed with a nod of his head. The elevator came and they got in. Just then Eitan smacked his head. "I forgot my Metrocard. Will you hold the elevator?"

As he waited alone in the silent hallway, he could hear his heart pounding. He had never done anything so sneaky to Sharon, fleeing without telling her, and he could only imagine what her face would look like if he was caught. But she wasn't his most favorite person at the moment. After a minute Eitan returned and they went down and parted at the lobby.

Even as he walked the streets towards the subway Joe still felt apprehensive, waiting for the dreaded call. As a distraction, he flipped open his phone and called Mrs. Rosenzweig. Her young daughter answered.

"*Shavua tov*," he said. "Is your mother at home?"

"No," she said. There were feminine voices in the background.

He was shooting a look at every dark corner, scared Sharon would pop out like the monsters in an amusement park haunted house. "Do you know when she'll be home?" he asked.

He heard someone say from afar, "Shoshanna, who's on the phone?" to which the girl said, "I don't know." Then the voice came closer, saying, "Give me the phone and go to sleep," then to Joe, "Hello."

"Is Mrs. Rosenzweig in?"

"Who's calling?"

"Joe…seph Charnoff," he answered. He didn't know whether he had to maintain privacy with everybody, but he had to explain why he was calling. "Mrs. Rosenzweig told me to call her."

"Is this about a shidduch? She stepped out. Can she call you back later?"

He was relieved that she broke the ice. "Sure. She has my number."

"Yosef Charnoff, you said?"

"Joseph, whatever. But I'm going to the train—"

Whether she heard him or not, she quickly said, "OK, bye." She hung up.

His next call was to Rabbi Tzvi, who didn't answer. He had already reached Broadway and was crossing the downtown direction, waiting for the light at a median with a few benches and enough space to pace as he left the Rabbi a harried message. In the middle, Joe felt the pulsating vibration of another call. It was Sharon. Suddenly incredible pangs of guilt caused him to halt in midstride. He walked over to a bench and sat down, in order to ground himself for the shock.

"Hello," he said dryly into the phone.

"Where are you?" Sharon demanded. "We've been pounding on the door for five minutes."

"I had to run," he answered. "I need to get back to Brooklyn right away."

"Is everything all right?" she sounded worried. "You couldn't stop downstairs to tell us?"

"Eitan wanted to lock up and I guess I was distracted in the elevator. I'm sorry that I had to run like this."

"What's going on, Joey? Really."

He breathed out through his nostrils. "What do you want me to say, Sharon?"

"The truth, perhaps?"

"Is Erica there?"

"She's in the other room."

As they talked, he watched the flashing of the traffic lights. They were synchronized all the way up Broadway, so that when the lights changed from green to yellow, the effect of all of them switching in succession simultaneously appeared like a runway lighting up, preparing for an oncoming airplane to takeoff. He had nothing to say to Sharon because she had done nothing wrong, but the lingering bitterness in his mouth told him that Sharon wouldn't understand even if he tried to explain himself.

"I don't appreciate surprises," he said simply.

"Ugh," she scoffed into the phone. "You're always doing this—never growing up. This is why you're alone."

Exactly the opposite! He didn't respond for a moment. "That was below the belt."

"Wait," she began automatically, "I didn't mean that—"

"Yes, you did. Don't lie."

"No, Joey, I'm sorry."

"No, maybe you're right."

"Come on, I'm sorry—"

"I've gotta go. We'll talk." He hung up, knowing that Sharon wouldn't bother him about Erica ever again. With a heavy sigh, he lifted himself off the bench and ran towards the station.

Chapter Eighteen

Sharon

A FEW DAYS LATER, on Wednesday afternoon, the sun was still high in the sky as Sharon walked towards Riverside Park. She had been trying to complete a translation of a will so that she'd have nothing on her mind the whole July 4th weekend tomorrow. She looked up from her computer at 4:00 PM and realized she hadn't seen daylight all day. Forty minutes later, with the translation complete, she laced on her sneakers, threw on a loose skirt over her legwarmers, and went for her semi-weekly jog. The park paralleled the northbound side of the West Side Highway, but there was a section of the bike path that ran right along the river and she hoped that there would be some breeze to relieve her from the summer afternoon heat.

There were more joggers on the path than usual, probably because of the upcoming holiday. While she was aware that physical activity lent itself to a certain ease in modest attire, she was surprised at how little the other female joggers wore. Sharon, on the other hand, felt a certain pride in choosing to hide her body behind a loose T-shirt and skirt, however content she was with her figure. Since that summer when she lost nearly thirty pounds and began exercising regularly and toning, she always felt a selfish urge to get back some of the attention she never got in high school. Still, her religious education had instilled in her not to sacrifice her modesty for such urges.

Her upbringing didn't, though, bring her to cut off all contact with guys. Joe had tried many times to convince her to join his no-touching initiative, but she just couldn't make such a statement of abstention, however much truth he espoused. Perhaps she relished the attention she got and feared that it would cease once she declared herself off-limits. Whatever the case, she wasn't publicizing her preferences, something she hoped Andy would respect until their exact status was clearer. He had invited her to join his friends on their traditional trip downtown to the Statue of Liberty for the fireworks display, and was hoping to gage the future of their relationship, if she could find an opportunity with his friends around.

Once Joe entered her mind, she thought of calling him. They hadn't talked since she scolded him on Saturday night and she couldn't dreg up the energy to apologize. Besides, she had no idea what prompted him to act so strangely and run away like that, without even telling them he was going. What was wrong with Erica? She thought that he would be ecstatic to be handed such a girl—one who was even showing signs of interest. There was always something amiss with him and girls but Sharon couldn't put her finger on exactly what it was.

Towards the end of her jog, when she saw it was 5:40 and he was certainly out of work, she decided to call him. Finding a bench with a direct view of the skyscrapers along the New Jersey side of the river's edge, she sat down to drink and dialed his number. As she took a long gulp from her hip flask it connected immediately, though Joe gave no greeting.

"Hello Joey," she said into the phone. Still there was no answer, only the distinct sound of street traffic. "Hello? Joey?"

"Hello?" he then asked, suspiciously. A different voice murmured something.

"Joey? What's going on?"

"Who is this?" he asked confusedly.

Doesn't he see my number on Caller ID? "Joey, it's me," Sharon replied, and then the call ended. *Weird.* She checked the display screen; her battery was nearly full and the reception at peak performance. When she called again, his calls went straight to voice-mail, meaning that he had either lost reception, or turned his phone off. Brushing off the possibility of the latter, she resolved to call him later and stood up to jog home.

Chapter Nineteen

Joe

A FEW HOURS BEFORE Sharon's jog, at 12:28 PM, Joe was leaning on a wooden railing that separated him from what looked like
a replica of a pirate ship. His neck was craned up as he tried to see
up to the deck of the immense boat docked at Pier 17, but he could
see nothing besides the side of the hull bobbing up and down from
the movement of the water below. He had walked up here from
his office building with a hope that there would be a breeze from
the river but found none, just less shade from the strong sun that
he would have to endure with the noise from tourist groups lining
up for boat tours of lower Manhattan. Looking at his phone for the
time—12:29—he sighed and started tapping his feet on the dock.
He scratched at his chin, turned to his left and his right to ensure
no one was within earshot, and at the exact moment the minute
changed he called Rabbi Tzvi.

"Good afternoon, Yosef," the Rabbi answered pleasantly.
"Punctual, I see."

"You told me to call now," Joe reminded him. "I only have an
hour for lunch."

"What's up?"

Joe laughed to himself; all morning he had tried working out exactly how he would answer that question. After two more dates and another scheduled for later that day, he still didn't know exactly what he was looking for on these dates. Sure, Rachel was pretty, and he was finding himself smiling more naturally, and there were long spans of conversation that didn't feel forced, but what was he to do about Erica? Not her, exactly, but the lingering question from Shabbos whether he could still like another girl despite being in a shidduch. Was that an indication that Rachel wasn't…it? How would he ask that to Rabbi Tzvi?

"What's up?" Joe repeated. "Well, I have Date #5 scheduled for tonight—"

"What?" interrupted the Rabbi. "Last Thursday you'd only gone out twice."

"Right."

"So what's with the rush?"

Joe took a quick breath. "Well, Mrs. Rosenzweig told me on Sunday that Rachel was finished with work for the summer and had some free time, so we picked up the pace."

"Why wasn't I informed?"

Joe started tapping his foot rapidly. "You once asked why our dates were so spaced apart, so I thought that it wouldn't be a big deal to bunch them."

"That's with the first dates," he clarified. "The later dates have a whole different purpose, and you can't just rush through them. You're poised to go on a fifth date and we haven't even discussed the last two."

A sudden breeze whisked by and carried with it a distinct smell of raw fish. "I'm sorry," Joe said automatically, turning away from the odor.

"You don't have to be sorry all the time. Don't think you're do-ing me a service by not calling. I might be out-of-town, but I'm not off the planet."

Joe smiled. "OK."

"So, how were the last dates?"

"Pretty good," he said, clicking his tongue. "She has a lot to say."

"You like that?"

"She asks these deep questions, like, 'who would I want to meet, dead or alive,' or 'what was the pivotal moment of my life, up to now?'"

"That's nice. Are you finding out anything about her?"

Joe was pacing the pier, looking at the ground as he talked, once or twice narrowly avoiding passers-by. "Sure. We're talking the whole time. I just find her questions interesting."

"Great. How are you feeling towards her?"

Joe stopped in mid-stride. He quickly glanced around to see if anyone was watching him, but all the tourists were too absorbed in their tour guide's oration to notice.

"Well, that's what I wanted to know," he struggled to find the right word, "like, how attracted I'm supposed to be."

"How attracted?" he repeated.

"Yeah. How…not necessarily after four dates, but, overall, where are we aiming to get?"

"Didn't we talk about this already?" Rabbi Tzvi asked.

"Maybe," Joe said quickly, "but, do the dates end when there's this overwhelming attraction, or is the decision based on other things?"

There was a pause, which drove Joe mad. He never knew

whether Rabbi Tzvi was actually thinking about an answer or just distracted with any of a thousand things going on around him. After an audible inhale, the Rabbi said: "The short answer is yes and no. It isn't a prerequisite to getting engaged, but it helps. I don't like the term 'attraction' but for lack of a substitute…look, shidduchim isn't the Jewish version of the Hollywood romance— the climax of the relationship being the engagement and after that a sharp drop in the excitement. If a person looks at everything together after a number of dates and finds himself really drawn to her, then it's a good sign, but it isn't the determining factor."

The tour group had moved on and Joe's gaze was fixed on the overdressed senior ladies struggling to step onto the boat's gangplank. He ran his hand through his short hair and replaced his *kippah* to its spot just behind his bangs. "But even if she is pretty, attraction is usually accompanied by feelings. We're talking about it as if it's another trait, like speaking the same language."

"I think that you still have this romantic idea in your head. Shidduchim is totally different from what you're used to, if not the opposite of what you thought about mating and dating. What they believe to be the 'beginning of a beautiful friendship' we stay far away from. We don't subject our teenagers to the domination of their hormones, and we don't even let boys and girls become close friends, all in order to spare them the potential emotional damage of misplaced attraction. So it wouldn't make sense for romantic attraction to be the sign to proceed."

What did he say about friends? Joe heard the words, but didn't understand the context. He didn't have much time, so with no other choice, he spoke bluntly. "What if I don't find her as attractive as other women I know?"

He never thought that Rabbi Tzvi would laugh. "That took some guts to admit, no?"

Joe almost laughed also. "Yeah," he answered curtly.

"I can hear the dilemma, but you really can't compare a woman you've met through shidduchim with one you met without any checks to your attraction. Why do you like this other woman? Is it an emotional connection? A physical one? Are you taking into consideration all her character flaws and still finding her more attractive? Don't answer for me, but you see how it isn't equal."

Sweat was beading on Joe's forehead as he leaned on the railing by the big ship. Wiping it away with the back of his hand, he sighed. "I hear, rabbi. I thought this was different. I went away for Shabbos and this girl popped in and I was just...wowed, you know? I know that it was just that, but I was scared it undermined the shidduch. That's what I'm trying to determine."

The tour boat blew a loud horn, startling Joe. "If you're being honest," said Rabbi Tzvi, "and you're sure that it was 'just that,' then you're better off continuing with your shidduch. It sounds like you're having a good time. Get back to me after your next date with an answer to this question: what else do you need to know?"

"I'll try," he agreed.

He breathed deeply, inhaling a cloud of steam. Shortly after they hung up Joe ran back to his office to catch mincha. He wasn't able to fully review the whole conversation as he was too busy running through the crowded lunch-hour pedestrian traffic to think about it, and then there was mincha, and after that his boss met with him about his next project...

At exactly 5 PM he left the office and took the subway uptown. By 5:20 he was in Rockefeller Center, which he had chosen as their meeting spot because of something Rachel had said on a previous date. Many people swarmed around the plaza, heading home from work or out to dinner, and Joe felt a certain camaraderie knowing that he could share in their eager anticipation. After sorting out his particular quandary with Rabbi Tzvi, he was looking forward to an unencumbered date with Rachel. Mrs. Rosenzweig suggested that they "raise things" and go out to dinner, but Joe felt odd dictating which restaurant, so he prepared a list of possibilities. On the spot where a gargantuan evergreen spent the winter months he waited, eventually moving towards the railing overlooking the skating rink, providing outdoor seating to the restaurant on the mezzanine level during the summer. After a few minutes, he heard a feminine voice from his right.

"Saying hi to the reclining statue?" He spun around to find Rachel, her soft smile captivating him for a suspended moment. She wore what Joe could best describe as a summery outfit: a pastel-pink button-down collared shirt, a light khaki linen skirt and brown Mary Janes.

"You startled me," he told her. "I thought your voice came in with the breeze."

"I'm sorry," she said sincerely. "I didn't want to take you out of your conversation with the idol."

He bent his neck as if to stretch it. "I got tired of looking up at my memory of the tree, so I tried to count the seats at the restaurant occupying your skating rink."

"My rink? Did you say 'my rink'?" She stepped towards him and gave him an accusatory glare. "Did we meet here because I mentioned it the other day?"

"No," Joe tried to deny. "It's a central location." He cracked when she started squinting at him in a humorous mock-suspicion. Raising his shoulders, he said, "You got me."

"You've been listening to what I say," she said, amused. "I'll have to watch my words. Where are we going, by the way?"

Joe explained his dilemma. "I didn't think to pick a restaurant without you."

"Oh," she said surprised. "I specifically stayed pareve."

"Even still," Joe continued slowly, "I brought a list of places in the vicinity. Can I tell you the options?"

As he reached for the list in his jacket pocket, he saw her wrinkle her nose, albeit unconsciously, and Joe felt his jaw clench. He immediately ascertained that she had probably enjoyed the mystery of not knowing where they would be going. In an act of bravery, he looked at his list and then quickly folded it back up. "You know, let's go to a café," he said. "Simple food, plenty of coffee choices…if you like coffee."

"You remember my rink but you don't remember whether I like coffee?" she asked playfully. She seemed relieved. Joe felt his shoulders loosen.

The kosher café was a few blocks away and so in the summer evening they strolled while he answered her question about what he was learning in yeshiva. When he sensed she was interested he got a bit carried away and started explaining to her the whole Gemara, thumb motions and all. It was only at Fifth Avenue, when they were waiting for the light to change, that he realized she had patiently allowed him to ramble for nearly five minutes.

"I'm sorry," he said with a shrug. "You asked."

"No, it was great. I got to see a glimpse of something that excites you."

Joe looked over to gage her sarcasm and found none. He took a breath and noted that he actually felt the air enter his lungs and spread throughout his body. "OK, so I'll let you now go off on a tangent," he offered. "Anything you want."

"No," she frowned. "I don't believe in revenge."

They crossed the street and walked down 48th Street, looking up at the marquises to find Café K but to no avail. They nearly passed it before Joe doubled back upon seeing the name on the door. "It's here," he called to Rachel, who was already in front of the next storefront.

"This place is also kosher," she observed about the adjacent restaurant. "Wolf and Lamb."

"I saw that on the list, but I figured that they only serve heavy game meat, like venison or bison."

She walked towards him and stood exactly in front of the wall dividing the two restaurants. "I think you can only get kosher bison in Chicago. This looks like a regular steakhouse. Maybe the name is taken from the verse about when Moshiach will come."

Joe stood next to her and the two of them looked back and forth at the two eateries. Then they caught each other's gaze, and Rachel made a face of indecision. "I can't choose," she said.

"I already decided," he declared, pointing to the café.

"Splendid," she said, stepping to the right and opening the door. "It's just funny that two kosher restaurants are side by side like this, especially one meat and one dairy."

"We had that downtown," Joe said as he stepped towards her. "There were two restaurants on First Avenue, one meat and one dairy, and—"

Two things caused him to stop in mid-sentence. One was that he recalled how he and Sharon had frequented those restaurants so much that they started referring to them as "the spot," a memory he didn't want to elaborate on with Rachel. The second was that he felt his phone vibrating against his leg. He made an embarrassed grab for it, pulling it out of his pocket to turn it off, but when he did he must've answered it, because he heard a voice emitting from the speaker.

Rachel stopped and turned back to him. "Is everything all right?" she asked him.

He was so flustered by the thought that she might think he answered the call, he figured he had to cover himself. "Hello?" he asked suspiciously into the phone.

"Do you want to take this and I'll get us a table?" Rachel asked him.

He told her to wait by raising a finger, clenching his teeth when he heard Sharon's voice demand, "Joey? What's going on?"

His blood started pumping faster. "Who is this?" he played dumb.

Rachel was within earshot when Sharon then said, loudly and audibly, "Joey, it's me." For a moment he wore a face of worry, but before Rachel detected it, he pulled the phone away from his ear and hung up quickly. With a shrug, he said shakily, "Wrong number. I forgot to turn it off. Shall we go in?"

Chapter Twenty

Sharon

"I KNOW YOU DON'T want to hear this again," David started to say to Zeke.

"So then don't say it," Zeke told him.

"But if you want to get anything from your bosses," David continued, oblivious to Zeke's suggestion, "You have to go to him on a Monday morning, before the higher-ups have berated him for not meeting quotas or whatever sadism they thrive on."

"Could you let me enjoy my day off and not discuss work?" Zeke asked him. "We don't want the lady to think we have nothing better to talk about."

Sharon smiled as a gesture of thanks for being mentioned. She was accompanying Andy, Zeke, and David on their traditional July 4th trip to see the fireworks by the Statue of Liberty, squished into a downtown 2 train. She was the only one of the four sitting while the others hovered over her, hanging onto the bar. The train had been traveling slowly since filling up at 34th Street and the weary strap-hangers were looking irate as the air conditioners barely alleviated the car of the additional warmth from the body heat of so many holiday travelers. Andy, in particular, looked beat, or in the least preoccupied, silently staring above the heads in the crowded subway car, once in a while offering a statement of arbitration between the bickering David and Zeke. Still, he did dress up for the occasion, sporting a multi-colored striped collared Oxford, dark denim and brown yachting shoes, contrasting with Zeke's T-shirt and khakis and David's polo and jeans. Sharon had no idea how they could all be friends.

"We have to get off at Chambers," David was telling her, "because the 2 train turns eastward after Chambers. We'll have to walk a bit, but it's better than transferring to the N-R. There's a bridge by Stuyvesant. That's where the park begins."

"Will we be able to see the fireworks from there?" she asked, looking at Andy.

David answered her question with a shake of his head. "We'll have to walk down to the Financial Center, maybe even to the Holocaust Museum."

"Is that far?" she asked politely.

David shrugged. "It's not a very long walk, but it depends on the crowd. I see that you have semi-comfortable shoes. That helps."

She wondered what else of her outfit he had noticed. Though she had spent two hours deciding exactly what to wear, she didn't need the whole world to appreciate the effort she had taken to look as if she was going to an out-of-town country club on a Sunday afternoon. She was still swooning from Andy's simple comment of "very elegant" when they met at the train station.

Sharon wanted to nudge him to get his attention, but held back, having never touched him once in the month or so of knowing him. After their Shabbat together and another light dinner on Tuesday night, Andy must've felt confident with where they were standing to invite her to intrude upon his group's ritual trip to Battery Park.

"Are you feeling all right?" she asked him.

He nodded his head slightly. "Yeah, I'm fine," he assured her, returning his gaze to the station they were approaching. She watched his eyes as they shifted back and forth rapidly as the train was slowing down. Her feminine instinct understood that he was distracted, but she wasn't going to prod.

She started a new subject. "I'm worried about Joey," she said. "He completely blew us off Saturday night."

"Maybe something did come up," Andy suggested.

"It's completely not like him. I've known him for almost four years, and he's never acted this…sneaky. He's always been straight with me. OK, one time he went to Boston to meet some girl he knew from high school and I only found out days later when he came back all depressed, but otherwise…" she trailed off with a shrug and a sigh. Andy looked at her and shrugged too.

"One more stop," David sang. Andy thanked him.

"I thought Erica was perfect for him," Sharon continued. "They seemed to be getting along so well. I mean, Joey even came to the park."

Andy hummed. Absently, he asked, "have you spoken to him since?"

Sharon clicked her tongue. "That's even weirder. He hasn't been answering his phone, and the one time I caught him he got off really quickly."

"Weird," Andy agreed. "Maybe he didn't really like Erica and he's scared to tell you."

"I don't think so. You saw the way he was acting with her. It reminded me of how he would be with other girls he's liked."

Andy pouted. "He doesn't seem like the type to be into meeting girls like that."

"He never had much experience." Lowering her voice, she added, "He was kind of dorky in high school. I've tried to help him, but he just never got the confidence."

"Maybe he should meet a shadchan."

"Oh please," Sharon scoffed. "He doesn't need to waste his money on something that he could do if he got his act together. He'll get there someday."

Before Andy could respond, they were at Chambers Street and exiting. Sharon kept close to him as they followed David up to the street level and towards the river. Zeke was asking Andy about something baseball related, so Sharon silently tried to keep pace with the men as they hustled. After crossing a footbridge over the West Side Highway, they passed a large high school and entered the park by descending a rounded stone staircase with a dry fountain at the base. Like a tour guide David described the park's features as they headed towards the river. They walked around a large lawn where small groups had placed picnic blankets down and in anticipation of the fireworks.

"We should've brought a blanket," cried Sharon. "Made a picnic, too."

Zeke crushed her dream with a shake of his head. "By the time the fireworks start the crowd is so thick you don't see anything, unless you're standing by the barriers." She pouted, prompting Andy to say: "I thought it was a nice idea."

With his compliment she warmed up, trotting along with new energy as she imagined how she would cater their fantasy picnic. They had reached a path along the river where many people were already congregating, their attention turned towards the river. Finding an empty spot along the railing she broke off from the party and nudged through the crowd to her spot and leaned slightly over the railing to see the water. The high-tide waves crashed against the barrier and Sharon could feel a few cold drops splash against her cheeks. Andy came and stood alongside her and the wind was blowing hard enough for him to have to hold his kippah.

"We're going further," he yelled to her over the noise of nature.

"How much?" she asked him, squinting in the wind.

"This path ends at the marina about five minutes ahead, but we normally go around it and continue down."

She was nervous to take their relationship to a new level, but she figured that someone had to. She leaned over the railing, as if trying to see the marina. As hoped, Andy asked, "Do you want to stay here?"

"Will I be ruining your evening?" she asked coyly. "Will we still see the fireworks?"

"Sure," he said expressionless.

"So go ask them," she requested, adding, "we can also meet up later, if they want to keep going…"

Without responding he disappeared, leaving Sharon to enjoy the breeze. She was relieved that he had passed the test of loyalty, however minor it might have been. It wasn't as if she was seeking a boyfriend who would submit to her demands, if she could even call him a boyfriend at this point. Still, it was nice that someone was considerate enough to fulfill her whim.

He returned alone. "Yeah, they're going on," he said out-of-breath.

She gave him the nicest thanks she could muster. "I didn't expect this much walking," she explained. "It was really thoughtful of you."

"Don't think anything of it," he replied. "I wanted to spend some time with you anyway."

I would hope so. "How much longer?"

"They wait until it's totally dark."

"Do they turn off all the park lights?"

Andy laughed. "That would make the fireworks much better, but no."

"Do you like the dark?" she then asked him. "Like, were you afraid of the dark when you were a kid?"

He looked at her interestedly. "Why do you ask?"

"Just curious." She stared into his eyes to the point that he seemed overwhelmed with her directness.

"Uh, I guess it's a bit weird," Andy admitted. "I've heard of too many axe murderers in the woods to sit comfortably in my parents' house late at night anymore."

"What do you think will happen?" Sharon asked. A tall blond girl nudged into her. She promptly raised her hand in apology, muttering something in an unfamiliar language. "It's so crowded. Good thing we got a spot here."

"Yeah. I don't think that it's a realistic fear. Why, you like the dark?"

"Not necessarily, but I did the day all the power went out. Were you here then?"

He shook his head sullenly. "I was a counselor in a sleep-away camp in the Poconos. Once the sun set, it got pitch dark and the campers got scared. We put them to sleep early and when my flashlight died after ten minutes, I went to bed early too. Not that much of a story."

She frowned sympathetically. "I'm sorry."

"Don't worry," he assured her. "I won't need therapy."

She smiled. "Well, I was in Manhattan Beach, which is strangely enough at the southern edge of Brooklyn, about as far away from Manhattan as one can get while still in the city." She caught his eyes closing, then opening wide as he woke himself. "Whatever. I had slept over at my cousin's house the night before and we were all set to go shopping at 4 PM and we walked all the way to the train station and found that there was no power."

"You didn't notice the traffic lights?"

She tilted her head, as if it helped her think. "We did see them out as we passed through Sheepshead Bay, but we thought it was just a local problem. My uncle made a barbecue that night on their gas grill, because what else could we eat?"

Andy nodded. "Same here. In the morning the cook barbecued all the meat for Shabbat."

"What I remember most though," she said over him, "were the stars. My cousins lived on a dead end and there was a path to the rocks by the water and from the light of the moon we climbed to a spot where we just sat. It was the first time I saw the stars—hundreds of them. Like, really saw them. There was no light to block them out. I just sat there, amazed at how I'd lived under the sky for so many years and never really knew what was up there." She paused. "I remember it being very quiet too."

"All the air conditioners were off," he yawned.

"Yeah, but there was a breeze from the ocean. It was fantastic."

"I take it that you like the water."

Sharon looked out at the Hudson River in the thickening twilight and could only hear the water as it collided with the concrete retaining wall. She was a long time answering, the din of the crowd filling in the silence between them. "I guess so. It's not like I have any fond memories of water specifically. Maybe it was just that one time."

"I hear that people who live by the water never get tired of it."

She looked at him incredulously. "What, and someone with a view of the Alps will find it boring?"

He held his hands up in defense. "Hey, I'm just telling you what I hear."

She smiled widely. "Don't worry," she assured him.

They were both leaning their arms on the railing and shared an extended glance. They both inhaled deeply and Andy opened his mouth to speak. Then, all of a sudden they heard the first explosions coming from their left. Sharon turned her gaze in the direction of the fireworks, catching the streaming tail of the first redness as it cascaded in the sky. The already dense mass of people hovering behind them started to come closer and someone was pushed into her from behind, pressing her against the railing. Then the Scandinavian girl on her side squealed as she lost her balance and toppled onto Sharon. She was much taller and almost knocked Sharon back before an arm from behind grabbed the railing and helped the girl balance herself. People were shouting to stop the pushing, but the jostling continued for about twenty seconds while Sharon was in effect shielded by the figure behind her, until he was also pushed and collided into her from behind.

Eventually the crowd settled but her protector was still directly behind her, wrapping his arm around her waist. "Andy?" she asked nervously, but he didn't respond. She looked down at the arm and when the lit up sky allowed her to make out the same pattern as Andy's striped shirt, she was startled, then pleasantly content, then strangely terrified. A sensation passed through her body as if she was going to start shaking all over and suddenly her private space was hers again and the arm disappeared. She didn't immediately turn, but continued to watch the fireworks intently until they finished. When finally the crowd started to dissipate, she slowly turned to see Andy behind her, standing very straight and staring down at the marina, pensively avoiding her gaze.

"I really enjoyed the fireworks," she said, her mouth suddenly very dry.

He didn't look down at her. "I'm glad," he replied blankly. "Let's go. The guys are probably looking for us."

Chapter Twenty-One

Joe

JOE MADE THE OBLIGATORY phone call to Rabbi Tzvi after his date on Wednesday, but another gnawing issue kept him from discussing the progress of his shidduch. After he stumbled over his words for about a minute, he took a deep breath but was interrupted before he could begin.

"I think you need some fresh air," the Rabbi posited. "Why don't you come up for Shabbos?"

Joe made a quick calculation of a boring July 4th Weekend Shabbos in Brooklyn pitted against the discomfort of a bus ride and chose the lesser of two evils. He hated buses; everything about them reminded him of the night when he and Rebecca had parted and since then he couldn't enjoy them. For four hours he stared out the window at the endless forest that ran alongside the highway, unable to find a comfortable position in the aisle seat, and so when the driver announced their arrival at "The Four Corners," Joe jumped up and got off the bus with gusto, happy to be on solid ground, even in a completely foreign place.

As the bus drove away and Joe glanced around, he couldn't

determine why this particular junction deserved such acclaim. Save
for a modern-looking post office and an auto mechanic, the dilapi-
dated Main Street storefronts were abandoned, their windows thick
with the dust of years of neglect. Behind the post office the road
crossed a river with a short causeway bridge. He walked over and
discovered that it ran over a significant stream with white-water
pools and a noisy waterfall that drowned out the noise of the passing cars. When he got bored of watching a trio of teenagers jumping into the pool at the bottom of the waterfall, he walked to the
mini-mart servicing a gas station called Stewards, bought a drink
and waited at one of the wooden tables outside.

His raspberry Snapple made him think about Sharon, just as he
had been thinking about her the whole ride up and for the last two
days since he abruptly hung up on her. He could only explain his
erratic behavior as coming from the realization that two worlds
were suddenly colliding. His time with Rachel almost existed in a
bubble; a few hours every other night where the two of them met
and shut out the world while they probed their feelings to sow the
seeds of a potential very-long-term relationship. Sharon's call sent
a shock that woke him up to the reality that he hadn't divorced
himself from his old life, reigniting communication with her despite the need to fizzle it out. Still, he could only blame himself; he
had made that call that Saturday night and brought upon himself
the whole Erica fiasco. Though he wanted to just delete Sharon's
number from his phone and never answer her calls again, he just
couldn't do it, and that made him wonder why.

After calling Rabbi Tzvi to come get him, he decided to at least
straighten things out with Sharon. Since running out on Saturday
night, he knew he'd have to answer to her at some point, and he
figured he might as well come into Shabbos with a clean slate.

When the call went through, he heard a few seconds of heavy breathing before she said his name in an astonished way.

"Hello Sharon," he said remorsefully.

"That's all you have to say? 'Hello Sharon?'" she asked, panting. Street traffic was obvious in the background.

She wastes no time. "Yeah, I know. What's going on?"

"What's going on? That's all you have to say?"

"You asked me that already," he said cynically.

"Joey," she said in a scolding way, as if he were a child who had just broken a vase. She was still breathing very heavily. "Wait a second while I drink."

"Is everything all right? Where are you?"

"I went jogging," she explained between breaths. "The sun...'s very strong."

"So let's talk later, OK? I've...wanted to call you back."

"Wait...don't go. Where have you been?... Last week..."

"I know," he began, but he noticed a car had pulled up next to the park bench and stopped. A thin, young-looking Hassidic man got out and started to walk to the mini-mart. He noticed Joe and gave a short nod, which Joe returned. The Hassid then stopped and looked at Joe, indicating that he wanted to ask Joe something. "Hold on one second," Joe said into the phone, moving it away from his ear and covering the receiver with his other hand.

"Are you waiting for someone?" the Hassid asked, indicating his car with a tilt of his head as if offering a ride.

Joe smiled. "Yes. Thank you."

The Hassid raised his hand in some sort of gesture. "I'm going towards Woodbourne."

Joe shrugged. "I don't know where I'm going. I got off a bus and was told to wait here."

The Hassid turned and went into the mini-mart. Joe returned his phone to his ear. "Sorry about that."

"What?" It was Rabbi Tzvi's voice. "Sorry about what?"

Joe didn't know what was going on. "Hello? Who is this?"

"Yosef? It's Tzvi Aaronson."

"Oh, rabbi. Hi." He figured he must've pushed a button to answer with his hand without realizing.

"Yeah, my car is blocked pretty badly here," the Rabbi was saying. "I'll be a little longer than I thought. You're doing all right over there? Did you get a drink?"

"Yeah, I'm fine." Then he remembered the Hassid's offer. He jumped off the bench and ran to the mini-mart. "Wait one second."

Joe flung open the door and saw the Hassid at the counter paying.

"Are you still offering that ride?" Joe asked him.

"Sure," he replied. "Where are you going?"

Back to the phone, he said, "Rabbi, I got a ride. Where am I going?"

Joe motioned to the Hassid that he'd retrieve his bag, and as he went out he went to hang up his phone, but he saw that Sharon was still on hold. "Sharon?"

"Yeah, you put me on hold. What's going on?"

"Uh, nothing. Look, I'm really sorry, but I gotta' go."

"Come on, Joey. You called *me* and then put *me* on hold. Now you're getting off the phone?"

He felt anxious in his fingertips. "You're right."

"I was calling you to come for Shabbat. I was up all night making food—really yummy salads." She sounded desperate.

"I can't. I'm...away."

"Where?" she demanded.

The Hassid finished pumping his gas and motioned for Joe to get in the back. "I'm in the Catskills. It's a long story, but I really have to run. I'll talk to you later."

"Joey!" she yelled, causing her to cough.

"Have a good Shabbos," he said before hanging up. He had never heard Sharon that troubled, but he couldn't have that conversation with her in the car with a Hassid. After he was settled at Rabbi Tzvi's house, he would take a walk around and call her back.

He grabbed his duffel and his Snapple and got into the backseat. Another Hassid sat in the passenger seat, curling his peyos. He turned to catch a glimpse of the stranger entering the car. At that moment the driver returned and the passenger turned back around and the two conversed in Yiddish, which Joe hoped was an explanation for his presence. Then the car started and drove up the hill behind the Stewards station. They rolled down the windows and lit up cigarettes.

"You mind?" the driver asked Joe, even offering him from the pack.

Joe refused with his hand. "Go ahead."

"Where are you coming from?" the driver asked.

"Brooklyn," Joe replied.

"We are also from Brooklyn."

"Flatbush."

"Ah," the passenger said, nodding.

"What brings you to the Mountains?"

"My rabbi invited me."

"Who's your rabbi?"

"Rabbi Tzvi Aaronson."

The driver shook his head. "Don't know him. Is he the Rov of a shul?"

"A yeshiva. Ohr Eliyahu."

"Ohr Eliyahu? Don't know it."

There was silence again. Joe looked out the window and saw a long school with athletic fields around it, followed by woods on all sides. It seemed to Joe that for the entire trip up as he looked out the window, except for shopping malls all he saw were forests of green trees to the backdrop of a light blue sky.

"Have you been to the *mikveh* yet?" the driver then asked Joe. "We're on our way now."

The last time he had been to the mikveh was on Erev Yom Kippur and though he had no qualms about it, he was in a strange car in an unfamiliar place. "I probably should get to my hosts before Shabbos," Joe said politely.

"There's almost three hours before *licht bentching*," the driver said. "It's five minutes from your bungalow."

Joe didn't want Rabbi Tzvi to worry, but then he thought he should take the opportunity while he had it. He had already gone out of himself by getting on the bus and coming here, he might as well. Sharon wasn't taking in Shabbos just yet. "I think that they'll be all right without me for a bit longer," he told the driver. "But I don't have a towel."

The passenger laughed. "Neither do we," he said.

At around 6:15 PM, after his new friends had taken Joe to the skuzziest mikveh ever, they dropped Joe off by his rabbi's bungalow colony. Joe assured them that they could leave because he saw Rabbi Tzvi's car blocked three deep in the parking lot. Before letting him go, his new friends gave Joe their number in case he ever wanted to go to Williamsburg for Shabbos. He walked into the gate and saw a row of bungalows situated around a big grassy lawn. Between the bungalows and the lawn was a thin concrete walkway where a boy who looked too big to be riding a Big Wheels rode up to Joe and stared at him.

"Where is the Aaronson bungalow?" Joe asked him. The boy made an odd face before turning around and riding off.

Joe looked around and saw that all the bungalows were the same white-washed wood with a strip of green painted on the outlines of the windowsills, the gutters and the pillars holding up the roofs of the patios. He walked up to the first bungalow by the gate and knocked on the screen door.

"One second," a female voice called. An older woman in an apron was holding a soapy ladle. "Yes?"

"Hello," Joe said. "Can you help me find the Aaronson bungalow?"

"Aaronson? I don't know if we have an Aaronson here."

Joe was sure that it was the same silver Dodge Caravan he always saw parked in front of the yeshiva. "This is Woodside Cottages, right?"

"Yes, yes. But Aaronson doesn't sound familiar. Dovid?" she called behind her. "Is there an Aaronson on colony?"

A slightly hunched older man in a gray suit and a beige Fedora came to the door. Tucked under his arm was a velvet *tallis* bag in its heavy plastic cover.

"Who?" he asked the woman.

"This young man here is looking for Aaronson. Could that be who took over Goldman?"

"No, that's Altman." He had already passed the threshold and was walking towards the lawn. He stopped at the thin path before the grass and motioned his hand as if telling Joe to join him. "We're davening mincha now, so he might as well come."

"We'll sort you out afterwards," the woman said to Joe. "You can leave your bag here."

Joe started to calculate how many silver Dodge Caravans there could be in the Catskills. "Maybe I should call my rabbi…"

"Don't worry," the matron assured him. "You're in the right place. But there won't be another minyan."

Joe figured that he could add another uncertain situation to his list of accomplishments for the day. As he was dumping the contents of his pockets into his bag, he hesitated for a moment when he saw his phone. *There'll still be time after mincha*, he resigned reluctantly before tossing it too into his bag. "Where should I put this?" he asked the woman.

"Is he coming or not?" the older man called from the lawn. "I'm starting."

"Just leave it by the door and I'll find a place for it," the woman told Joe.

He turned and hurried after the older man, who was walking surprisingly fast. When Joe got on side with him, he asked Joe, "Where are you coming from?"

"Brooklyn. My rabbi invited me for Shabbos."

"Very nice. Well, we'll find him, don't worry, and if we don't, we'll find you somewhere to sleep. Our place is pretty small, but we like it."

They crossed the lawn until they came to a building that looked no different from the other bungalows except that it was three times the size. Joe's escort placed his tallis bag on a bench that was under a covered porch and pointed towards the door. "In there is the shul," he said as he walked around the building. Joe walked up to the screen door and peeked inside; about six men in Shabbos suits waited silently. One of the men caught Joe's eye from through the door and called him in.

"Nu, we want to catch *plag*!" he called to him. "Call another few in, just for mincha at least."

"Uh, does anybody know where the Aaronson bungalow is?" Joe asked the voice.

"Where have you been, Yosef?" he heard a familiar voice ask from behind him. Rabbi Tzvi was crossing the lawn, also already dressed in his Shabbos suit. "What took so long?"

"I got taken to the mikveh by some hassidim," Joe explained.

"Ah, some *tahara* in our midst! Come, daven mincha with us and then I'll tell you where to drop your things. Where are your things?"

"I asked someone where your bungalow was and they didn't know that you were even here."

"Nobody really knows us yet. It's actually my in-laws' bungalow, but they retired to Florida and this is the first summer they didn't come up."

Just then a man and his bar-mitzvah walked into the shul. Joe heard the same voice from before say, "We got our minyan. Come in you two!"

Rabbi Tzvi turned to Joe and said, "You heard the man. You'll get your stuff after mincha," and they went into the shul.

Chapter Twenty-Two

Sharon

"WHAT IS ALL THIS?" Esther said as she opened her door. "I thought you said that you made a few things."

"Seven can also be a few," Sharon said as she handed Esther a bag of containers. "Thank you so much for squeezing me in."

"I don't know why you even hesitated," Esther said as she took Sharon's Tupperware into her apartment. "You have no idea how much you've saved me. My sister Sara's been planning to come for months. Her husband's gone with his father and brothers on some men's retreat and it has to be this week I get sick and couldn't make a thing."

"I hope it lives up to your Sephardic standards," Sharon said as she walked in and plopped onto the couch. "It's my first time making them."

"Please! I was ready to buy Sabra before you called. And besides, we're Persian. Our cooking is not so salad-based."

"Where is your sister, anyway?"

Esther sighed. "She went to Carlebach. That's really why she came; she got turned onto it when she was in Israel for seminary. You can also go if you want. They're probably still on the first *Mizmor*."

"No, I'm beat," Sharon said as stretched horizontally and rested her head on the armrest. "I went to bed at 5 AM."

"You're nuts. Why were you up so late?"

Sharon exhaled deeply. "I couldn't sleep so I went to Fairway and got lost in the vegetable section."

"Better than the ice cream section. And you didn't want to make a meal?"

"No one wanted to come," Sharon said sorrowfully.

Esther then came to the table and placed a package of plastic plates with her flatware on top. She sat on the armrest of the couch, right next to Sharon's head, and put her hand on Sharon's shoulder. "I'm sorry."

Sharon closed her eyes. "It's all right. What can I expect for seeking guests a few hours before Shabbat?"

With her hand still on Sharon's shoulder, Esther asked, "What about Andy? He isn't doing anything tonight."

"You spoke to him today?"

"No, but David called and wanted to know if I was hosting. Like, haven't I told them 100 times I don't do meals anymore?!" She threw back her head in exasperation. "These guys think they can make their plans after work on Friday and for the small price of a bottle of Moscato get treated to a three-course meal." She stood up and crossed her arms. "I think he also mentioned Andy."

"I wouldn't know. He didn't say anything about Shabbat yesterday."

"Ah." Esther took her hand away and grabbed the pile of flatware. "Their annual trip."

Sharon opened her eyes and looked up at Esther. "You know about it?"

"They've tried to drag me down there. I'm not getting anywhere near that number of people being held above the river by a few wooden pillars."

"Well, I went and it was…it was exactly that. Right when the fireworks started the crowd crunched and things got a bit…close."

"Creepy." She started to put forks onto folded napkins.

"Leave them here for me to set," Sharon offered, sitting up and reaching for the bundle of utensils, but Esther quickly pulled her hand away from Sharon's grasp.

"You don't have to get up," she said sweetly but with a stern face. "But it's nice that you went. I take it that you two are…" Esther trailed off as she went to the kitchen.

Sharon said "I guess so" in a gushing way but a nanosecond too late. Esther immediately picked up on it.

"What's wrong?" she asked, bringing glasses to the table. "Were his friends a bit too much?"

"No, they're fine. No, he's a great guy."

Esther placed down a glass heavily. "Yeah, but…"

"But what? He's very sweet."

"Yeah, but…"

Sharon was too tired to fight. "I can't explain it to you. It's complicated. I don't even know if I can explain it to myself."

Esther walked over and looked straight into Sharon's eyes in a way that made Sharon feel permeated. "You don't feel 'it' with him?"

Sharon looked away. "No, I do. He's wonderful, I like him, whatever you want to hear. I just…"

Esther straightened up and held up her hand. "You don't have to explain," she said, like a mother. "It's your business."

Sharon sat herself up on her elbow. "It's not like that. Don't think that—"

"I don't think anything at all," she reassured Sharon. "Didn't you tell me about someone else…what's his name? Joe? That has to be the funniest name for a religious guy."

Sharon sighed, falling back into the couch. "He's a whole other story. I have no idea what's up with him. Tell me what you think: last week he was here for this aufruf and I kind of set him up with this girl we knew from college who just came back from LA. Well, they totally hit it off—and I could tell that he was enjoying himself, you know? Anyway, we planned to go out Saturday night and when we're all ready, we go upstairs to find him and he's ditched us, giving no excuse why and then doesn't answer my calls all week, hanging up right away when I finally reach him, what, two days ago. Then today he calls *me*, puts *me* on hold and then comes back after five minutes to tell me that *he's* getting off and that he's in the Catskills for Shabbat. I mean, what am I supposed to make of that?"

Esther became pensive, or at least appeared to be. "Is it like him to do that?"

"Not at all. I mean, he's been weird for the last few weeks, but he's otherwise very honest with me."

"You've known him for how long?"

"Joey? Four years...why?"

"Has your friendship ever been anything…" she rolled her hand, "more?"

Sharon knew what Esther was insinuating. "No," Sharon stated definitively. "Not with Joey."

Esther wasn't convinced. "What makes you so sure? Maybe

he ran away last week because he didn't want you to think he was interested in your friend more than he is in you? Of course you'll say, 'no way, not Joey!' But guys are strange. They'll act like really good friends and always seek your advice and be super nice and friendly to your boyfriends…" Esther lowered her voice, "when they're just waiting for the most opportune moment—just when your boyfriend breaks up with you—to jump up and admit to being totally in love with you."

Sharon glanced over at Esther. "It sounds like you have experience."

Esther straightened her back and posed like a statue. "You know Andy's one of a quartet, not just a trio, right?"

Sharon nodded in agreement. "Yeah. You know, it did seem strange to me that they're always talking about Aharon—"

"Roni," Esther said simultaneously with Sharon. She pulled out a seat from the table and placed it next to where Sharon was reclining. "He's how I know Andy and their whole crew. A friend from home told me to look him up when I first moved up here. We were friends, you know, nothing more. He had a girlfriend when I met him, I had guys I was interested in—he never made any comments or acted jealous. We'd take walks, go to the same Shabbat meals. We even had a weekly dinner Monday nights—he hated Mondays and needed to 'brighten them up,' he'd always say." She sighed. "He was, maybe, the best friend I ever had. I could talk to him about anything, and we did; we talked sometimes for hours. I told him things that I didn't even tell my sisters. But we were just friends; there was no potential there at all." She paused and stared at the floor for a moment. Sharon caught Esther's closed eyes quivering as she continued. "Well, right when I had this hard break-up with this Persian guy, Roni drops the bomb—how he's been in love with me for as long as we've known each other, and that he feels so close to me…" She breathed deeply, wiping her eyes with her fingers. "I'm telling you, I had *no* idea. None. There was no hint of anything…"

Sharon just sat there, watching Esther. The room felt stuffy, as if Esther's pain was permeating the walls and stifling the air. For Sharon, the story was a double shock—not only that Esther was duped but that she was just as vulnerable as Sharon. "I'm sorry," was all Sharon could think to say.

"I'm also sorry," Esther said. "He was so embarrassed when I told him I didn't want to be friends anymore that he moved to Boston."

Sharon remained silent for a moment out of respect. Finally she shook her head and said, "Not Joey. I know, I know…but I have a pretty good feeling about him." Sharon hesitated. "One summer I went on this dieting binge and lost a lot of weight and when I came back to school all the guys suddenly wanted a lot of my attention. Joey was the only guy who didn't behave any different towards me."

Esther didn't reply, giving Sharon a look that didn't say anything particularly encouraging before standing up and going into the kitchen. For a long time Sharon lay silently on the couch, the clanking of spoons and the opening of her Tupperware containers the only sounds in the small apartment. Perhaps Sharon had finally been able to catch Esther without a response, though it wasn't making Sharon feel any more settled. Sure there were times that Sharon caught Joe looking at her funny, but she brushed it off as the nature of guys. She also knew that there was the time when Hannah Jaffe had told her that Joe had said he had 'feelings' for Sharon, whatever that was supposed to mean. Though she afterwards watched

Joe to see if he acted the slightest bit different, she never detected anything. It was Joe's second semester as a freshman and he had told her that he was interested in Elisheva Ashkenazi, so Sharon had figured that either Hannah had been wrong or that Joe had redefined his 'feelings.' For a moment Esther's story caused Sharon to think differently about Joe, but only for a moment.

Just when Sharon was about to get up and sympathize with Esther, the sister walked in and that particular conversation was put on hold.

Chapter Twenty-Three

Joe

FROM WHERE JOE WAS sitting at the Aaronson's Shabbos table, he could see the last vestiges of orange in the dark sky settling for the night as he slowly picked at his piece of ice cream cake, oblivious to the conversation around him. He had spent most of the meal in similar absorption, brooding over how he had left things with Sharon and hadn't had the chance to call her back. But he was a guest, and had shown as much appreciation as he could muster, hoping that Rabbi Tzvi hadn't noticed his demeanor.

"I still can't believe that Mrs. Kelleher didn't know our name," Mrs. Aaronson was saying. "She was at our wedding."

"That doesn't mean anything," Rabbi Tzvi objected. "People go to weddings to fulfill some social obligation or to fress at the shmorg. They have no clue that the whole purpose is to bring joy to the bride and groom."

"I think that one can share in the simcha just being there," his wife countered.

"Maybe, but it doesn't fulfill the mitzvah," the rabbi concluded, looking in Joe's direction. "You ever learned the Gemara in Kesubos?"

"I don't think so," Joe said.

"Smack in the middle of a great sugya is this whole Gemara about the mitzvah of bringing joy to the chosson and kallah. Maybe we'll look at it tomorrow."

"Great," Joe asserted. "This ice cream cake is also great. It doesn't taste pareve at all."

"Thank you," Mrs. Aaronson replied. "It's Sholomie and Hadassah's treat for being so helpful keeping themselves occupied today."

"The miracle of Rich's Whip," Rabbi Tzvi inserted. "Is it yummy, Hadassah?"

The well-behaved little girl, almost four years old, smiled widely. "I squeez'd in the choc-late."

"Very good. Afterwards it's off to bed for you two."

"But it's only nine," objected seven-year-old Shlomie.

"That's still pretty late. Your brother didn't even make it past eight."

"That's because he played football in the sun," Shlomie said. To Joe, he boasted, "I swept the floors."

Joe nodded, wide-eyed. "Very clean."

"I'll let you read one book before bed," his father interjected.

"Me too!" Hadassah cried. "Mommy said I was help-ful!"

"You're also much younger," her mother told her. "I'll tell you a story in bed. Tzvi, can we *bentch*?"

"Sure, we have no mezuman. You should've brought a friend, Yosef, then we'd have a mezuman."

"Next time," Joe said.

"I don't know if that'll help our mezuman," the rabbi commented, "but we'll be happy nonetheless." Then there was a knock at the screen door. "Come in."

The screen door opened and immediately Hadassah jumped from her chair.

"Rikki!" she exclaimed as she ran towards the teenage girl standing in the doorway, who Joe couldn't help staring at. She was the spitting image of Sharon, or what Sharon must've looked like at fifteen. She even smiled like Sharon, her joy at seeing the little girl so expressive that Joe assumed she must've been her cousin, or at least of some relation to the Aaronson family. Joe amused himself as he tried to picture what Sharon would look like wearing a similar burgundy Shabbos robe. When he felt Rabbi Tzvi watching him, he became very interested in trying to finish the remaining drops of melted ice cream in his dessert dish.

"Good Shabbos Hadassi," Rikki said in a high voice. "Your mommy and daddy let you stay up this late?"

Hadassah nodded. "And I have ice cream cake," she added.

"Wow, how nice!"

"How did your cake come out in the end?" the mother asked.

"I don't know yet," Rikki answered. "We're just reaching dessert and we found tons of ants in the sugar." Joe turned his head when she mentioned the ants because she shuddered in disgust, amusing the little girl. "We don't have any other sweetener and my *zeidi* needs his tea to be sweet."

"You can make the tea sweet when you brew it," Mrs. Aaronson was saying as she handed Rikki an unmarked jar. "It also solves many Shabbos issues."

"No amount we would put in would be enough for my zeidi. He likes to put it in himself. Thank you very much."

"With pleasure. Enjoy."

"Don't go," Hadassah whined as Rikki let the little girl down. "Stay and read me."

"Rikki is still in the middle of her meal," Mrs. Aaronson reminded her daughter.

"And it's time for bed," the rabbi added. "Goodnight Rikki."

"I'll come by in the morning," Rikki assured the little girl. "We can go to shul together. OK?"

Hadassah was appeased. She spun on her toes and returned to her ice cream. "Bye Rikki."

"Bye. Thanks again," Rikki said before she turned and left. Joe was watching her disappear from under the porch light outside when the rabbi tapped him on his shoulder, passing him a *bentcher*.

"We're holding up bedtime," he told Joe.

After *bentching*, Joe went outside to the front porch to give the family some alone time. It was a small square of a wooden frame, separating the screen door from the lawn, one step up from the path around the colony and surrounded by high bushes perfect for children's hideouts. The porch was covered and served as the family's dining space when the kitchen was too warm and when they wanted to feel the coolness of the rain without getting wet. A few folding chairs were lined up on the low walls, and Joe opened what turned out to be a lounge chair and lay down in it. He was reminded of his backyard in Potomac, where he would sometimes go late at night when he finished his homework and lie on his deck listening to the silence. He closed his eyes and savored the harmonious overlapping of the various insects chirping in the woods until the screen door opened and he jerked upright to see Rabbi Tzvi emerge and block the light from inside with his figure. Joe began to sit up but the Rabbi motioned to him that he didn't need to.

"Enjoy," he said. "I brought you up here to let you relax. Is it working?"

"Pretty much," Joe answered automatically. "It's really

something else here."

"Worth the three-hour bus trip?" he asked as unfolded a chair that was leaning behind the door.

"Four hours, but yeah."

The Rabbi settled into the chair and emitted an exhausted grunt. "We never had our own place...my family. My father always joked that we had too many of us to fit into a bungalow." He laughed to himself and was silent for a moment. "We would visit cousins, or family friends, and I came up with yeshiva when I was a bochur. I always liked it up here."

"I guess I'm spoiled," Joe said bashfully. "I lived in the suburbs all my life."

Rabbi Tzvi coughed. "It's not the same. It's the break from the routine, from the nonstop action of the city. Here I have time to think, like the great rabbonim who used to walk in the forests. I have a great view of the sunset from this porch."

"Yeah, I saw glimpses of it during the meal."

"When do I have the time to see a sunset in Brooklyn?" he complained. "It's an amazing thing...the sunset. The same sky that shows nothing but constant blue all day suddenly gets painted with oranges and yellows and reds, all those colors of high intensity—or high frequency, I forget which—only at the horizon and only right before sunset. The rest of the sky doesn't get all feminine with its colors, though; it remains very blue, even a darker blue than the rest of the day. The sun continues to set deeper beyond the horizon and the reds and oranges fade and the blue becomes so dark that it becomes black as night with no remnant of the day that just was."

Joe almost laughed. "I didn't know rabbis were so into aesthetics."

"What?" Rabbi Tzvi exclaimed. "The greatest of artists are

rabbis. They know how to view the world for the purpose that it's meant to be viewed: as a vehicle to arrive at knowledge of Hashem. As for me, once in a while I get tossed a bone. I think the sky is a parable to the ebb and flow of life. We wish for our lives to be as pleasant as the daytime: clear, constant, and obvious. However, sometimes things need to undergo change, even to a time when everything is dark and bleak, and the transition can be intense and scary. And all throughout the blue is only getting thicker—that very consistency we trusted is what eventually becomes the darkness."

"That doesn't sound too promising," Joe noted.

"You are right, but what happens when the night ends? Again the thick blue resurfaces from the bitter darkness, slowly becoming lighter and lighter as the sun approaches the eastern horizon. As it does, what also accompanies this slow fade to light? The same pinks and yellows of the sunset, but this time it heralds a clear day with comfortable blue for hours and hours. So inasmuch as the difficulties that come with any change indicate a gloomy period of night ahead, they just as much signal their eventual end." He paused, probably to allow Joe to swallow the message. "Sounds good?"

"It does," he said immediately. "You thought of it on your own?"

"I get one thought a year," he said sheepishly.

Joe was silent for a moment before he asked innocently, "But what about the green?"

The rabbi asked surprised, "The what?"

"The green. Every light spectrum must pass through all the colors, and you haven't taken into account the green between the yellow and the blue."

Rabbi Tzvi shifted in his seat. "Really?"

"That's what I learned in Earth Science."

They heard the sound of a door inside closing, causing the Rabbi to turn and motion something to the lone figure behind the screen door. "Well, I didn't have to pass any Regents in Earth Science and I certainly have never seen any green in the sky. You can sit out here all night and try and find it if you want, but davening begins at nine."

"OK," Joe said.

"So before you get lost in the stars, do you want to talk about what was going on the other night on the phone?"

Joe started breathing heavily, blinking rapidly. He had no reason to hide his feelings. "Something…came up…"

The screen door opened and Joe didn't say anything else. He looked up to see Mrs. Aaronson passing two bottles of Coors Light to her husband.

"Do you want a beer?" the Rabbi offered. Joe hesitated, never having understood the appeal of beer and never liking the taste. The Rabbi twisted off the top of one and made a strained sound as he passed the open bottle to Joe. "Don't make me drink them both."

Joe took the bottle, which turned out to be freezing cold, and thanked the Rabbi.

"Thank you, Miri," Rabbi Tzvi said to his wife, who smiled and went back into the bungalow, the screen door banging against the doorframe as it closed.

"I'm going to bed," she told him quietly. He nodded and opened his beer.

Joe made a bracha and took a sip, surprised at enjoying it. "It's pretty good."

"You gave me an excuse to get some. My wife doesn't let me

drink in front of the kids. She didn't grow up with it."

Joe lifted his eyebrows. "And you did?"

The Rabbi made a bracha and took a deep gulp. "No, but in my line of work…"

They both laughed. Joe took another sip.

"So what's going on?" the Rabbi asked.

Joe leaned back into the chair and stretched out his legs. "Things are great. We're having a really good time."

"We? You can read her feelings?"

Joe clicked his tongue. "No, I mean that I am."

"You're discussing your plans for the future?"

Joe raised an eyebrow. "Like, *our* plans?"

"Where you want to live, what you want to do, things like that?"

"Shouldn't we first decide if we want to get married?"

"You should be speaking out your individual feelings on the future, so that she won't surprise you by wanting to live in Brazil or work on the moon or something that doesn't work for you."

"Oh." Joe took a long sip. "Yeah, we've talked about that. She seems fine with living in New York, at least away from St. Louis."

The Rabbi coughed. "What's wrong with St. Louis?"

"Nothing. She just said she doesn't need to live near her family. She's flexible."

"How did it come up? You asked her?"

"Not exactly. She's been away from home for so many years and I asked her if she ever wanted to move back. She said no."

"Great. It sounds like your shidduch's moving forward."

Joe felt a sudden pressure on his chest. "That's what it sounds like," Joe eventually conceded.

But the Rabbi replied, almost coldly, "That's not a good response."

Joe sat up and looked at Rabbi Tzvi in alarm. "Why not?"

"Look, if I were to tell you, for example, that you want to buy a stereo, and you go and look into the different options and you come to a conclusion that you're going with one particular model, and you find the store that sells it at a good price with all the guarantees and warrantees, if I asked you if you're going to buy it, you wouldn't say 'that's what it looks like.' You get what I mean?"

Joe felt the weight on his chest tighten, as if he'd been pushed. "Yeah, I get it. It's just…'engaged' sounds so oppressive."

"Perhaps," Rabbi Tzvi conceded. Then he leaned forward. "But I don't feel that that's what's really bothering you. Am I right?"

A baby cried nearby and Joe turned his head in its direction. He scratched his chin, still smooth from his shave that morning, and closed his eyes. "It isn't her," he admitted. "I enjoy the time we spend together, I look forward to our dates, we agree on many things—"

"What do you disagree about?" the Rabbi asked suddenly.

"Disagree about?" Joe repeated.

"Yes. Do you have any disagreements or do you two see eye-to-eye on everything?"

"No, we've had, nothing major. There was something she said once about the Internet that I didn't like hearing."

The Rabbi was in mid-sip when he asked, "How did she take your response?"

Joe looked up. "I didn't respond. I changed the subject."

Rabbi Tzvi coughed again. "But you have to deal with things like that. She has her own opinions, so don't think she'll just accept everything you say once you get married…if ever."

Joe rolled his eyes. "I know that—"

"More than knowing that, Yosef. Be prepared to accept her and be happy with her as she is now. Whatever you disagree on will have to be dealt with, either through acceptance or compromise, but it mustn't stop you from celebrating her."

"What do you mean by 'celebrating'?" Joe asked curiously.

"Her faults can't ruin your image of her; they're obstacles, sure, but you can still enjoy her without letting them get in your way. You might even find that they'll work themselves out."

Joe swept his arms out in exasperation, splashing his beer. "What, like I'm supposed to enjoy a wife who spends too much money or constantly burns our dinners?"

The Rabbi shushed him. "Try and be a little bit quieter, OK? Not everyone might be asleep yet."

"Sorry," Joe said, lowering his voice.

He laughed nervously. "It's not a secret or anything, but you can enjoy her without enjoying her bad traits. If it's detrimental to the relationship, that's another story, but some bad traits stem from poor self-image, and your love could reverse that and bring out her best. You might have to think creatively sometimes…"

The Rabbi didn't finish his sentence, and the two sat in silence until Joe felt that he better make some sign of acknowledgment. "I hear."

"I'm telling you this because it's bound to come up, even to the best of us." He coughed. "Have you told your parents?"

Joe exhaled audibly. "I think they know by now."

"That you're this far?"

He felt his stomach acid churning. "No."

"Are they…hostile to your lifestyle?"

"No, they're accepting."

"Then they'll probably be fine with an engagement. So then what's the problem?"

Joe was conscious of his breathing for a few moments before he stood up and leaned against the wooden banister, his back to the Rabbi. He was close enough to smell the woody scent of pine from the bushes below. He closed his eyes and the image of the young girl who came in during the meal flashed in his mind. "There's a girl I know from college..."

The Rabbi nodded understandingly. "How close are you?"

Pause. "Not so close, but we have history."

"An ex-girlfriend?"

He turned around. "No, never. But—"

The Rabbi looked directly at him. "Are you sure?"

"Sure of what?"

"That she wasn't a girlfriend?"

Joe made a face. "I would know a thing like that."

"Are you sure?" he asked again, taking a drink from his beer. "It isn't uncommon for a friend to hold in her true feelings with the hope of an eventual relationship."

Joe shook his head again. "That doesn't mean she was a girl-friend."

The Rabbi jumped to his feet. "What's in a name? What would you say about a friend who doesn't show her true feelings, acts incredibly friendly and supportive to your new wife—all the while secretly resenting her and waiting for the day for cracks in your marriage to surface, and just when things get rocky will spring on you her years-long crush and put you in a major emotional dilem-ma?"

Joe watched the Rabbi's soliloquy with folded arms. "That sounds a little exaggerated. Not all life is like a soap opera."

"You're correct," said the Rabbi, stepping back and leaning on the other side of the porch. "But you have no guarantee that that *isn't* the case. I once heard a rabbi put it this way: if you knew that behind one of 1,000 doors there was a ferocious dog ready to tear you to bits, you wouldn't open any of them, no matter how much pleasure is behind all the other 999."

"I don't see the connection."

"It basically shows that you wouldn't knowingly enter into a situation that has even a thousand-to-one chance of being terribly painful against being incredibly pleasurable. In this case, it's even smaller than twenty-to-one."

Joe started pacing the small porch. "I wouldn't say it was that small. And anyway, people know how they feel about their friends, especially those they know for a long time. They know whether they're attracted to them, and they also know how the other feels."

"You'd be surprised," Rabbi Tzvi countered. "Maybe today they know, but who's to say things don't change? The longer two people know each other, they find different qualities that they didn't see before, and feelings that weren't apparent in the beginning start to surface."

"Or the opposite," Joe countered. "Look, I might have liked her once in four years, but certainly not now. I can't read her thoughts, you're right, but I know her. I know that there are no feelings there."

He turned to find Rabbi Tzvi looking directly at him, unfazed. "Just ask yourself something," he said quietly. "You know everything about her: what outfits she wears, on which days, where she bought them, what she likes to eat and what she doesn't, the names of her parents and every one of her siblings, what makes her laugh, what makes her scared, secrets she's never told anyone. You share memories of dinners, outings, evenings doing nothing. You think about her when she isn't around, you care about how she will react to what you say, what you do, news you have to share with her…I'm just guessing, because you haven't told me anything, but tell me if *even one* of that isn't indicative of a deep emotional relationship. Forget about feelings; you can 'feel' nothing and yet still be connected to someone without even being aware how deep a connection you have. Tell me how any girl seeking to build such a relationship with you from scratch will feel when you're already attached to someone else?"

Joe stopped pacing and took a swig of his beer. "Look, I know all this already. I don't hang out with any of the girls I knew from college anymore. It's just…one girl I got really close to, and she kept calling me. I couldn't just tell her to stop…" He trailed off, snorting before taking another long sip.

"So…then what's the problem to tell her now? You don't have to be a jerk about it."

"I know," Joe rolled his eyes and sighed. "I…I went to an aufruf last week, I told you, and the groom was overwhelmed…well, I had to eat by her Friday night, and there was another girl from school…" Joe didn't finish his thought. "I know that I have to do something. It's just…not going to be easy."

"Not at all," the Rabbi sympathized. "But I believe that a real friend is also willing to say goodbye when the time comes."

Joe was still leaning on the low wall of the porch with his arms crossed. He looked out at the small circle of orange light on the lawn in front of the porch. In the dark it reminded him of the lights on the highway as he brought Rebecca to the airport, when he didn't stand in her way. "I guess so." He sighed heavily. He couldn't stand any longer and collapsed onto the front stair, burying his chin between his knees. "You don't know, Rabbi. She taught me so much about Orthodoxy, about the city, she made me

Shabboses, she tried to set me up..."

"And so with that gratitude, you can also give her an untainted marriage. Don't you also wish for her the best possible life, without all this falsity and drama? Look, I hope I'm wrong and that there's nothing deep about your friendship and that she'll be sincerely overjoyed for you without making you feel the slightest bit she's being dumped. If not, though...you can't push it off any longer."

In the pause that ensued after the Rabbi's last statement, Joe thought that even the crickets had been quieted. He couldn't remember the last time he cried, but the hot tears in his eyes were at least a familiar feeling.

The Rabbi probably heard Joe's stifled breathing, because he then came and sat next to him on the step. "I didn't mean to be harsh," he said in a softer tone.

He sniffled. "I need to hear it, I guess."

Rabbi Tzvi placed his arm around Joe, but Joe didn't move. "I'm sorry."

Joe couldn't tell from the Rabbi's tone whether he was sorry for scolding or sorry that Joe had a hard time ahead of him. Either way, Joe felt comforted.

They sat silently for a few minutes until Rabbi Tzvi lowered his arm. "You have some time to think; it's a long day tomorrow. I can't tell you what to do, but whatever you decide, do it right."

Joe said nothing, just sat breathing through his mouth. Rabbi Tzvi stood up.

"Do you want me to wake you for davening?"

"I'll be up," Joe murmured.

"I'll knock if I don't see you."

"Thank you very much," he said automatically, looking up slowly.

Rabbi Tzvi smiled. "As we said before, the house is yours. Take what you wish, just don't leave anything out for the ants. Get some rest."

Joe mustered a weak smile as the Rabbi walked past Joe and opened the squeaky screen door and went inside. For a long time Joe remained sitting on the front step with his head resting on his knees, watching the shadows of the moths swarm around the spot of orange light on the thin walkway. While he first called Mrs. Rosenzweig to spite Sharon, he never imagined that it would lead to this.

Chapter Twenty-Four

Sharon

IT WAS SOMETIME AFTER 9 PM that Esther's sister Sara returned from the Carlebach shul flushed and energized. She turned out to be more engaging than Esther, asking Sharon about every detail of her life before expressing her advice. "How many siblings do you have?" she would ask. "I see. So then you should definitely…" Until after 11 they were still chatting, each of them wired for one reason or another: Sharon from waking up at 3 in the afternoon, Esther having been in bed for two days and Sara's first Shabbat away from her husband since their wedding nine months before. When Esther went to make everyone tea and Sara went to the bathroom, Sharon lay down on the couch and noted how surprisingly tired she actually felt.

She woke up in the morning to find both sisters still sleeping and the house miraculously set back to its immaculate state as it was when Shabbat came in. With no particular reason to go home, Sharon ended up staying through the afternoon, having to almost beg them to let her go. When she reached the streets she basked in the sunlight, fighting an urge to just go to the park and continue her revelry. She had successfully pushed both Andy and Joe from her mind for almost a whole day, enjoying a welcome bout of femininity. She hoped that it would continue with a quiet seudat shlishit with Tamar, who she hoped hadn't gotten frantic when Sharon had disappeared for nearly twenty hours.

At her building she waved to the Jamaican doorman as she was walking towards the stairwell. From her right a figure jumped up from the couch and darted towards her. "Sharon," was all she heard in a familiar voice. She turned to see Andy straightening his suit pants. He stopped just a few feet from her, close enough to see him blinking rapidly, as if he had been dozing.

"Where are you coming from?" she asked.

"I should ask you the same," he said, stretching his shoulders. "I've been waiting for you."

"Where, on the couches?" He nodded, still stretching. "For how long?"

He furrowed his brow and looked out the front windows. "I came up after davening last night, but Tamar said you were by Esther. I then knocked at Esther's after my meal but nobody answered."

"When was that?"

He shrugged. "11:30?"

Sharon pouted. "I don't know. I passed out sometime; I don't remember when. You haven't been waiting here all afternoon, right?"

"No, I ate at home."

"So when did you come back?"

"Not long ago," he said, unconvincingly.

Sharon rested her hands on her hips. "Well that's nice of you. To what honor do I owe this vigil?"

"Vigil?" he repeated. "I just…we haven't spoken since the other night."

"Yeah, it's been a crazy few days."

"Is everything…can we sit down?"

"Here?" she asked. Andy shrugged, as if he didn't have any other ideas. "No, let's go for a walk," she suggested.

They left the lobby and turned south upon Andy's cue, in what Sharon figured was the direction of his building. For half-a-minute or so they walked slowly and silently, listening to the background noises of the city in constant motion. Sharon glanced in his direction and surmised from the way he was scratching around his mouth that he was gathering his words.

"I was worried," he eventually said. "You were acting a bit strange after the fireworks."

She had suspected that he would want to clarify what made her act so strange, but was disappointed by his choice of words. While she was pretty sure that he had held her from behind during the fireworks, they hadn't spoken about it. Instead of approaching the subject openly, though, he had taken a more cowardly path, dropping on her the burden of introducing the issue. She didn't fault him for it, but she wasn't necessarily going to make things easy for him. "What do you mean?" she asked innocently.

He began to speak but quickly closed his mouth. "I don't know," he tried again, but again paused. "I mean, you were kind of silent on the way home."

"I was tired," she explained. "It had been a long day and that packed subway…"

"Oh." He was silent for a while, breathing deeply and audibly. "It wasn't because of what happened during the fireworks?"

She continued to feign ignorance, hoping that he would choose to take responsibility for broaching the subject. "What do you mean?" she asked again.

"About when, you know, the crowd got a bit...close?"

He elongated the pause before the last word a bit too long. Now she was in a pickle, because his question wasn't vague enough to be referring just to the crowd crunch but was most certainly about him lingering behind her. She didn't appreciate having to guess what he was referring to, but on the other hand she felt that perhaps he was repentant and didn't want to lower the conversation with explicit mention of his deed. Nonetheless, he was trying to keep himself on the defensive, which Sharon didn't feel was fair. If he was going to make a move, he should continue through with it.

"How did you feel about it?" she asked. Now 'it' was out in the open, and the ball was in his court. She inwardly congratulated herself.

"I'm more interested in how you felt about it," he said, standing awkwardly straight and looking southward down West End. "I don't know what it meant to you, so I was hoping that..." He laughed coarsely, probably trying to minimize the level of seriousness after realizing the weight of what he had admitted to. "I couldn't really sense your reaction afterwards...so...."

Then she turned and pivoted, which caused Andy to stop and Sharon looked up at his dark and pleading eyes. She no longer felt any romance towards him, this whole interrogation feeling childish and silly. Why couldn't they talk about what happened like adults? But wait, would that be any better? Wouldn't that also ruin the romance? This was sounding like Joe's shomer negiah rhetoric, and she felt like speaking to him before making any decisions.

"You're sweet," she reassured Andy. "I can't say that I haven't thought about it, but I really don't know what to say. Can you give me a little more time?"

"Sure," he said immediately, if not reluctantly. "No problem."

Andy walked into the crosswalk and froze a few feet later when he realized that Sharon wasn't joining him, prompting a loud honk from a turning SUV.

"I'm going back to my building." she declared. "I'm pretty tired and want to rest."

"I'll walk you."

Chapter Twenty-Five

Joe

WHILE JOE DIDN'T STAY up all night staring at the sky, he did remain sitting on the front step with his chin resting between his knees for an interminable amount of time, thinking about Sharon. He remembered the first time when he began to feel that she was more than just a nice girl being nice to him. It was the first Shabbos of Winter Break and Sharon had invited him to her house in Cedarhurst because he had a final that Friday morning and the dorms had emptied out and he wouldn't have gotten to Potomac in time for Shabbos. It began to snow that night and they had gone out to the bench on her covered patio to watch the light flakes fall through the streetlights. They were overdressed in coats and scarves and hooded sweatshirts and he remembered looking over at Sharon and seeing her cheeks so rosy from all the bundles and feeling towards her more than a friendly affection. She caught him staring and to cover he fabricated an interest in Elisheva Ashkenazi, a girl they knew who hung around the Bronfman Center at NYU. As he pondered his feelings towards Sharon afterwards, he came to the conclusion that no good would come from pursuing them. He still knew from

Rebecca that he was seeking someone to marry and the number of disagreements he and Sharon had about key issues made any future with her untenable, so he decided that it was best to leave her as a friend. He never even discussed the moment on the bench with anyone—except for one time confiding in Hannah Jaffe, who swore she wouldn't tell anyone.

But what were those feelings? He couldn't dismiss them anymore, as Rabbi Tzvi's question hung in front of him like the proverbial carrot on the stick. Was that the only reason he didn't let go of Sharon as easily as the other girls he knew? Was he keeping her around for a chance to condense those feelings into something else? It seemed so wrong, but then why else did they become so close his first years at NYU? Whenever it was that he went inside, he skipped brushing his teeth and just slumped his clothing over a chair and fell into the cot, too frustrated to ask for any linens or pillows.

Shabbos day passed faster than he wanted it to. Davening in the morning began closer to 9:20 AM, the *ba'al koreh* was slow and the kiddush afterwards was drawn out as its sponsor told long-winded stories about his mother in memory of her *yartzeit*. The meal was nice, but hurried because though they sat under the covered porch, the noontime heat was too much for the children to withstand without constant complaining, despite the promised double dessert. After the meal Joe attempted to rest, but more ad-venturous children were playing in the heat just outside his window and by the time his nap was over there was only one hour before mincha. He learned with Rabbi Tzvi until it was time for shalosh seudos, which was only a short hour before ma'ariv and the con-clusion of his Shabbos in the Catskills.

As promised, Joe was directed immediately after havdalah to

the parking lot where his ride was preparing to depart. Joe thanked the *rebbetzin* for her hospitality and with his bag on his shoulder, he walked with Rabbi Tzvi to the gate.

"Did you think over what we talked about?" Rabbi Tzvi asked him in a grave voice.

"Yeah," Joe lied. "Let's go forward."

Rabbi Tzvi glanced at Joe for an extended moment and then looked down. "So I'll get in touch with Mrs. Rosenzweig, maybe tonight, just to see what her side is saying and I'll get back to you afterwards. I could use an excuse to drive in."

"We aren't planning anything yet," Joe reminded him.

"Correct. Perhaps you'll need a shoulder to cry on if it doesn't work out, but from where you are holding some decision should be made this week. I'll be davening for you."

Joe took a heightened breath. "Thank you. For everything, really."

"With pleasure," the Rabbi said with a wink. "This is just the beginning, you know. The fun begins after the engagement, but things really begin after the hupah, and then they *really* begin…"

They had reached the gate and saw only one car with its headlights on and a young girl standing by the passenger side on a cellular phone. Rabbi Tzvi immediately addressed her. "Mazal tov," he said enthusiastically.

She nodded in thanks and pointed to her phone. "Yes, Ima," she said into the phone. "Yes, Ima."

From behind the open trunk emerged a tall young-looking man, clean-shaven with conservative glasses and a whiff of Old Spice. "Gut voch, Rabbi Aaronson," he said.

"Gut voch, Gershon," the rabbi returned. They shook hands. "How was Shabbos with the kallah?"

"I think that she's warming up to my family." He extended his hand to Joe. "You must be Yosef."

"That's right," Joe said as Gershon crushed his hand.

"And on time. Thank you for helping us out like this."

"I should thank you," Joe corrected him.

"We'll see if you thank me when I make you stay awake," Gershon said with a smile. "I'll put your bag in the trunk and you can get into the passenger seat."

"Don't you want your kallah to sit there?" Joe asked.

He looked at him as if Joe had said something in Greek. "No, she'd prefer the back seat." Then Gershon bent down and lugged a rolling suitcase into the trunk.

Joe took the opportunity to extend his hand towards the Rabbi. "Thank you again, rabbi."

"I'm glad we were able to give you some respite. I see that you needed it."

"That's what it looks like," Joe said with a smile.

The Rabbi patted him on the shoulder forcefully. "I'll let this one slide."

The trunk door slammed and they heard Gershon call, "Chana! Let's go."

Joe got into the car and adjusted himself in the seat. Chana also got into the car, her ear still attached to her phone, relieving Joe of having to introduce himself. When Gershon got in the car Joe waved goodbye to Rabbi Tzvi, who waved back and went back through the gate.

"That's a special man there," Gershon said, pointing to Rabbi Tzvi. "You have a big privilege knowing him."

"Very much so," Joe agreed.

Gershon reached over Joe's lap and opened the glove compartment, extracting a pair of CDs from inside before closing it. He put one of the CDs into the car stereo and started the car. Unfamiliar orchestral music started, transitioning into wedding music with a male singer that Joe didn't recognize. "He's going to sing at our wedding," Gershon remarked.

"Is he well-known?" Joe asked.

"Not really. This is his demo."

The car backed up onto the road and as they slowly drove past the colony Joe took one last look at it. It was a simple semi-circle of small bungalows situated around a nice great lawn, but Joe felt that it was more than just that. There was a familiarity that was created simply from the closeness of the families and the shared goal of maintaining a Jewish life while on vacation. After ten seconds they were slowly gaining speed as the lights ended and only the high beams guided them through the dark forest on both sides of the road.

"You know Rabbi Tzvi from here?" he asked his ride.

"This is his first year on colony," Gershon replied, lowering the music. "His bungalow actually belongs to his in-laws."

"Yes, I heard."

"No, he was in yeshiva with one of my brothers. He came to our *vort*."

"When is your wedding?"

"Less than a month," he said, exhaling heavily.

Joe sympathized with him. "Wow," he said with an excited face.

Gershon nodded. "Yeah, that's why we're rushing back. Chana has a whole day of appointments and tons of things that need to be done before the Three Weeks."

"I thought that we only minimize business during the Nine Days."

"You're right, but if it'll make Chana feel more calm knowing that she's prepared, then I won't argue. Chana, are you with us?"

"Yes," she said from the back seat. "I can't hear what you're talking about."

"That's OK. We're just getting acquainted. This is Yosef— what's your last name?"

"Charnoff," Joe answered.

"Are you related to the Charnoffs from Avenue L?" Chana inquired.

He shrugged. "Probably not."

"Oh." The sounds of her cell phone keys filled the silence that followed.

"How did you end up in Flatbush?" Gershon asked.

"I am in grad school at NYU and wanted to be in a more religious neighborhood than the Village, so I rent out a basement."

"Where is it?" He told them the address. "Are you planning on being there for a while?"

"I don't know," Joe said sadly. "My roommate moved out and my landlords are allowing me to stay and only pay my share, but I don't know for how long."

"We're looking for a basement," Chana said. "Maybe we'll check it out when we drop you off."

"Let's see how awake we'll be when we get to Brooklyn," Gershon told her. "And besides, I don't think that Yosef would want us moving in on his personal space."

Joe was astonished. "Your wedding is in a month and you don't have a place to live?"

Gershon took a deep breath. "Hashem is sending us on a goose chase of sorts, but it'll be sorted out."

With nothing to add, Joe opted not to respond and so for a few minutes they listened silently to the big-band wedding music. Joe recognized a tune he knew and wondered what it was doing on a Jewish wedding album, but didn't say anything. They passed by the Stewards at "The Four Corners" and when he remembered how he hung up on Sharon, his stomach churned and let up a taste of the fish from shalosh seudis. He couldn't believe how quickly everything had come about. A week ago he spent an entire Shabbos with her and now he had to tell he would never speak with her ever again? He couldn't just give up the shidduch; he had never felt this way about a girl who apparently wanted to go out with him. If they kept going, he'd have to end it with Sharon, blunt and final. But how could he just throw four years out the window? Sharon wasn't just going to accept it, but if it had to be done …

However upbeat the music was, it wasn't making him feel any bit uplifted. He leaned his forehead on the window and watched the dark forest pass by, an occasional house or two breaking the monotony. They slowed down at a traffic light and Gershon shook him lightly.

"Don't fall asleep on us," Gershon requested. "We need your presence until we at least get on the highway. You're saving us from *yichud* and where there are no other cars around, we can't be alone."

"I wasn't sleeping," Joe told them, leaning back in his seat. "I was just trying to spot deer."

"There are deer in these woods?" Gershon asked.

"Probably," he replied blankly.

Gershon hummed. "I've never seen one."

"I've lived in the suburbs all my life," Joe explained. "I've seen plenty."

"Where are you from?" he asked.

"Maryland."

"Baltimore?"

He shook his head. "No, a small suburb outside of DC."

"I think Chana has cousins that live near DC. Chana?" Gershon glanced around. "She's out."

"She's asleep?" Joe looked back to see her curled up against the door. "How could she fall asleep with the music?"

"The speakers weren't tuned to play in the back. Besides, she had a tiring Shabbos."

"Really? I felt like there were hours of free time."

"She was put in a bedroom with a baby who Chana said woke up several times during the night, and then she was dragged to the kiddush this morning. Our meal was long and then she graciously took my two-year old niece and nephew to the playground to let my sister-in-law sleep, only to find her room again occupied when she came afterwards with the mother trying to soothe the teething baby."

"Wow. How long have you known her?"

He thought about it. "We started dating before Purim, our engagement was before Pesach...four months or so? Why?"

"I find it—I'm amazed at how you're walking into marriage, just like that."

"I guess," he said after a short pause. "I mean, what's the problem?"

"It's no problem. It's just...normal. You have no qualms about dropping everything and devoting your life to a complete stranger..." Joe was nearly delirious.

Gershon smiled awkwardly. "I don't know what to tell you."

"No, I'm just...I'm trying to figure out what I'm not seeing. Like, what made you decide that she was the one?"

"The one? I mean, we met a few times and I enjoyed meeting her and after a few weeks they said that she was ready for an engagement, and so…" He finished his sentence with a shrug.

"You didn't feel coerced?"

"What do you mean?"

"Like, you didn't feel as if you couldn't say no when you found out she was expecting an engagement?"

"No, it's not like that. I could've said no, but I didn't want to."

Joe heard in Gershon's tone that he needed to explain himself. "I'm only asking because…well, I guess I can tell you. I'm involved in a shidduch that looks like it's going…it's going well."

"Really?" Gershon exclaimed. "That's great to hear."

Immediately he realized what he had just articulated and was amazed at not becoming apprehensive. Confidently, he said, "Yeah, it is."

"I see that we're not just shlepping back anybody, we're assisting in *hachnassas kallah*."

Joe held up his hands. "Well, we'll see about that."

"What's wrong? You said that it's going well. You wouldn't say that if it wasn't true."

"Correct, but...until it happens—"

"Right. No *eyin hora*."

"Not entirely. There are…other things..."

"Well, you should sort them out, because you don't want to lead her on."

"No, it's not her. She's really amazing—"

"So what's the problem?"

He certainly won't understand. "It's just me. Being able to jump into a new life. I can't get over the fact that I've only known her for two weeks."

"How many dates have you been on?"

"Five, but we met three times in the last week."

Gershon reached over and placed his hand on Joe's shoulder. "So don't feel rushed. Take how much time you need. Are you going out tomorrow?"

"All day," Joe said matter-of-factly.

Gershon slowed down as they approached a traffic light. He turned to Joe. "Then before you go out, decide what you want to see that will help you make your decision. After the date, go over and see if you found your answers."

"I know that already, but—"

"And even if you didn't," Gershon interrupted, "Ask yourself if those things that you're looking for are things that can be answered with another date. Don't expect more of her than she's capable of."

Joe thought for a minute. "I might have to think about this for a while."

"Go ahead. We're just getting on the highway."

"Where are we?" a sleepy voice asked from the back while stretching.

"Nowhere near Woodbury Commons," Gershon answered.

"Can we stop?" she asked with a stretch. "They have a great Lenox outlet."

"They're probably closed by now, but we should wait for the registry gifts anyway. Besides, Yosef wants to get back…" Gershon looked over at Joe as if asking permission to share the news with Chana. Joe mouthed to him, in so many words, in the negative. "He wants to get back to Brooklyn before Pizza Time closes."

"I don't think they're open Saturday nights in the summer," Chana said.

"Whatever's open," Joe conceded.

Just then, Joe felt his phone vibrating. He pulled it out of his pocket and saw Sharon's name on the Caller ID. With a heavy sigh, he rejected the call.

"You can take it if you want," Gershon assured him. "You don't have to entertain us."

"No, it's not that…" Joe started. Then he thought that he already shared one secret of his. "How much longer 'till Brooklyn?" he then asked.

"We can stop in Monsey if you're hungry," Gershon told him.

"No, I can wait. But how long?"

"At least two hours, if we get through Manhattan easily."

"Do you mind if I make a call?"

"I just told you that you could."

Chapter Twenty-Six

Sharon

AFTER ANDY LEFT HER at her building Sharon went up to her apartment and did everything she could not to think about him. She finished a novel that she had started months before. There was an hour left before Shabbat ended, so she made herself a salad and ate a solitary seudat shlishit while reading an article that Tamar had written. Then, to do something she never did, she went to the Carlebach shul hoping that Esther's sister would come. Even though she didn't, Sharon still enjoyed the musical havdalah, which lasted almost half-an-hour, only returning to her apartment well after 9 PM. She showered and dressed for lounging, hoping that she wouldn't have to explain to anybody why she didn't want to go out that night. With a deep breath, at 10 PM on the dot she lay down in her bed and called Joe with no expectation that he would answer. Sure enough he didn't, but a minute later he called back.

"Hello Joey," she said, as always. She spoke in her sweetest tone to see how he would respond. "So nice of you to call back."

"Yeah," was all he said. "How was Shabbos?"

"It was surprisingly good."

"Why surprisingly?"

Should I do this? Yes. "I managed to have a good time, even without you."

"I guess that's good," he replied. Nothing could be determined one way or another. "Anything special?"

She turned over and leaned up on her elbows, kicking her feet. "I went over to Esther's and had a girl's night."

"Just you two?"

"No, her sister was also there. She's very cool; they both are."

"Very nice."

She sighed. She could tell he was choosing his words. "Yeah, I fell asleep there and only came home around 4:00. But let me ask *you*, Joey. How was *your* Shabbat?"

"Fine. I guess I should explain."

"That would be nice."

"So my rabbi invited me on Thursday to his bungalow colony."

She sat up and looked over at her computer, the screen saver showing a picture of a snowman she and Joe made in Washington Square Park in her senior year. "You went to the Catskills? How did you get there?"

"I took a bus. It took a few hours, but it wasn't so bad. I was waiting for a ride where the bus dropped me off when you called, and I think I put you on hold when someone was asking me something."

"So why couldn't you tell me that?"

"What do you mean?"

"You got off the phone right after."

"Right. I caught a ride by a Hassid and couldn't really talk in his car."

Sharon didn't believe it. She would test him in another way. She made loud stretching sounds and rolled over on her back. "Whatever you say."

"You don't believe me?"

"I don't know what to believe. You disappeared for a week without calling or anything, and now you tell me that you got off the phone because you were in a car with Hassidim?"

"It sounds strange, but it's the truth."

"What's going on, Joey?" she asked him. "Where've you been all week?"

"I can't talk about it now. I'm in the car with some people."

She found the conversation going exactly where she didn't want it to. "Who? The Hassidim?"

"No, this couple from my rabbi's bungalow colony who are driving back to Brooklyn."

"You're on the highway?"

"Yeah, we're in the car now."

"So would you rather talk when you get back?"

He didn't answer for a moment. "It'll be pretty late."

"Yeah." She dropped her voice, and said with intensity, "I've been waiting to get your advice on something."

Immediately he responded, "What's it about?"

"It's about Andy."

"Is everything all right?" he asked, the first hint of any feeling in his voice.

She paused, allowing him to imagine anything and everything. It felt strange talking to him with a subtext, but she was beginning to suspect Joe's erratic behavior and wanted clarity. "Everything's fine," she assured him. "I just want your opinion."

"I'll try to call when I get home," he promised.

Chapter Twenty-Seven

Joe

JOE DID, IN FACT, want to call Sharon when he reached his house, but didn't feel right waking her if she had been asleep. After his conversation with Rabbi Tzvi, he was more receptive to the subtle undertones in Sharon's voice and thought that there was something suspicious about the way she was speaking to him, especially when she mentioned Andy. He seemed like a nice guy, but Joe wouldn't put it behind him to have hurt her, if that's what she had been insinuating. Was that what he detected in her voice? Why was he so sensitive to it?

Gershon's suggestion that they stop in Monsey appealed to Chana and so at 10:30 they turned off the highway and drove through what looked like just another suburban town until they reached a very crowded pizza shop filled with very Jewish-looking clientele. Even though they ate their pizza in the car, they still got stuck in traffic on the Brooklyn Bridge and Joe only got home around 12:30.

When his alarm started blaring at 6:40 the next morning, he rolled out of bed unfulfilled. He was going to have to find some way to stay on his best behavior for an entire day despite his lack of an adequate night's sleep. He davened at his normal 7 AM minyan and returned home, hoping that a shower and some strong coffee would help him stay alert. As he was walking out the door to go to the train, he got a call from Mrs. Rosenzweig.

"Good morning Joseph how are you?" she said in one breath. "Penina Rosenzweig."

"Good morning," he said as he inserted the key into the lock.

"I'm sorry to call you like this, but Rachel just told me that she wasn't able to get back to the city after Shabbos. Would you like to meet her in Riverdale?"

He thrust the key into the hole with force. "Riverdale?" he repeated. "Where is that?"

"It's in the Bronx," she explained, "just north of the city. You can catch a train from Grand Central and she'll meet you at the train station."

"You think this is OK?" Joe asked.

"You're meant to spend the day with her. She says there's what to do up there so you might as well."

So about an hour later, Joe found himself sitting in the back car of a Metro-North train, drinking coffee and eating a black-and-white cookie he bought from the bakery in Brooklyn as he rushed to get to Grand Central. As he waited for it to depart, he thought over Gershon's advice from the night before:

> What do I want to find out about her? I don't know anything about her! – I'm not supposed to, though. We have a whole life to build together – Do I really believe that? Or am I just saying over what I heard from Rabbi Tzvi? – I certainly am not used to thinking about dating in this way, but where did that get me? – That doesn't mean that I should go commit to a marriage

out of default – But I'm really enjoying the time we
spend together, and she seems to enjoy our time, too –
Sure, a few hours on a date isn't that hard – So I'll wait
and see how we relate after a whole day…

Just as he felt a slight jerk and the train slowly left the station, he
got a call from Mrs. Rosenzweig.

"Hello Joseph what's going on?" she asked immediately upon
answering the phone.

Since she wasted no time with formalities, he followed suit.
"I'm at Grand Central on a train bound for Riverdale."

"Great. When will you be arriving?"

He had neglected to ask that particular piece of information at
the Information desk. "That's a good question."

"So go find out and call me back," she said before hanging up.

He stood up and saw a conductor slowly punching tickets at the
end of his car. He returned to his seat, finished his ad-hoc breakfast
and waited for the conductor before calling back Mrs. Rosenzweig
with the arrival time.

"Great," she answered. "Where should she meet you?" she then
asked.

"How should I know? I've never been to Riverdale."

"So go to the very front and I'll tell her to meet you on the platform."

Joe had already settled into his seat and was ready to rest his
head on a discarded Sunday edition of the *Daily News*. "Why don't
you give me her phone number and I won't have to bother you," Joe
offered.

"That's nice of you to offer, but I really don't mind."

"It'll be better that I have it, in the event that something doesn't work out."

"I prefer," she said, somewhat coldly, "that my clients not exchange numbers until absolutely necessary."

"Why, if I may ask?"

"Having each other's number allows the disappointed to badger the other or to put unfair pressure."

"Even now?"

She sighed. "Unfortunately, it happens, but psychologically it's still comforting. Don't worry. You'll get it when you need it."

The train left on the hour and arrived exactly as scheduled. Just as Joe was beginning to enjoy the view of the river from the train the conductor announced their approach to Riverdale and Joe went to stand by the doors. He had been thinking about Rachel all morning and was almost dancing with excitement. When the train stopped and he was the only one to depart from his car, he immediately looked along all sides of the platform but found no one waiting. Beyond the railing of the platform he saw a long parking lot dotted with cars—much less occupied than he assumed it was on normal weekdays—with a thick forest of tall trees as its backdrop. A bell chimed and within ten seconds of its arrival the train was already continuing on its way northward. He walked with it, heading towards where he saw the few other people who disembarked from the train with him descending stairs that led to the parking lot. When he reached those stairs he waited, seeing as how other passengers had found their rides waiting for them at the base of the stairs; perhaps this was where he was to wait for Rachel. After the electric noise of the train dissipated with its passing, he was alone in a strange place.

For a while he sat on a metal bench and watched other passengers meet their rides. When the last car drove off, he turned his gaze across the tracks to see the calm expanse of the Hudson River rippling lightly from the wind. Beyond the river on the New Jersey side was a steep cliff of reddish-brownish rock all along the bank of the river as far north and south as he could see.

As he looked south he noticed that further down the platform were stairs leading to the overpass to the inbound side, and smack in the middle of the overpass was a solitary waving figure. It was Rachel!

"Welcome to Riverdale!" she cried cheerfully as he reached the top step.

"Thank you," he said breathlessly.

"It's so nice of you to come all this way. Were you waiting long?"

"No," he said honestly.

"I see that you found your way here pretty easily."

"Yeah," he huffed. He was catching his breath and bent over a bit. From his angle he ascertained that she was dressed less formally than she had been on their previous dates, judging by the stylish, but nonetheless sporty walking shoes on her feet. "What brings us here anyway?"

"Shabbos ended so late," she explained, "that by the time I was ready to leave it was after 11 PM. My aunt said that since we're going out for the day anyway we might as well go somewhere here."

"And what if I couldn't make it?" Joe asked.

She smiled. "I would have met you wherever."

He quickly looked away, overtaken by a warm feeling coursing through his whole body. "Well," he started, but couldn't continue. "Well, all I know is this parking lot and a large expanse of river. So unless we're going canoeing, I'm in your hands."

She laughed. "How'd you guess? Come."

For five minutes Rachel led them uphill along a thin but well-paved road through the woods Joe had noticed behind the parking lot. It appeared to be a residential neighborhood, but the houses were spread out with large lawns and much property between them. On the left was a very large school that Rachel indicated was a Jewish day school. It was a quiet Sunday. Only the sound of their footsteps, cicadas buzzing, and a distant leaf blower broke the summer morning calm. Rachel was carrying what looked like a lunch bag over her shoulder, which Joe offered to carry.

"Whew, what's in here?" he asked as she passed it to him.

"Just some water and fruit."

"What, watermelons?"

"Maybe. I figured that you've eaten already."

"I did."

"So then we'll eat something more substantial later. There are a few kosher places in town."

He squinted in the sun. "Where are we going, anyway? Does this residential jungle ever end?"

"You'll see," was all Rachel said.

They walked for a few moments, the rhythm of their footsteps falling in line with each other.

"Had I known that we would've been walking this much," Joe then said, "I would have also worn walking shoes."

"But then you wouldn't wear a suit and I wouldn't get to see this orange tie again," she replied.

"I ran out of the house," he admitted bashfully. "This was the first one I grabbed."

"Don't worry. It suits you very well." He looked over to see if her pun was intended and caught her smirking. "And besides, this was the best I could find from my cousin's closet. All I had for

Shabbos were my flats that give me blisters."

After a few minutes they turned onto a street that was flanked by big mansions enveloped by the thick woods. Joe wondered if anybody else ever walked along this road; there were crosswalks painted on the street, but no sidewalks.

"I hope that you aren't trying to hint to me what type of house you expect to live in," he joked.

"Not at first," she joked back.

They crossed a street and along one side of it was a high wall. Eventually the wall broke, revealing a parking lot, the sign on the side reading "Wave Hill," with admission hours and parking fees.

"Too bad we didn't come on Tuesday," Joe said sorrowfully. "Parking would be free."

"We aren't parking, anyway," she pointed out. "I think that admission is also free on Tuesday."

"This is where we're going?" Joe asked. Rachel nodded. "What is this place?"

"My aunt told me that it was once the estate of some very rich man who either gave it away or lost it to the government—she wasn't sure. But it was converted into a park and opened to the public."

"Have you ever been here before?"

"When I was a little girl, or so says my aunt. I probably won't remember a thing."

"So we'll get a map."

There was no map, so they sauntered around, happening upon the flower gardens where Rachel surprised Joe with her knowledge of horticulture and botany. The greenhouses were divided by climates and Rachel was explaining the reason why certain plants could handle extreme temperatures. Had Joe not been as tired as he was, he would've appreciated the information much more; instead he simply enjoyed getting a glimpse of an interest of hers. After the greenhouses they walked around the frog ponds where little children were kneeling dangerously close to the water in hopes of spotting unique wildlife. When they reached a bench set off from the path, Joe requested to sit down.

"Is everything all right?" she asked worriedly.

"Yeah. Let's just…enjoy where we are. We aren't in any rush to see the whole estate, are we?"

"Of course not."

Joe dropped down onto the bench. "I imagine that the owner of this place also came here to unwind. What else could he use this many shallow pools for?"

She sat at the opposite end of the bench, motioning for the lunch bag. As Joe extended his arm towards her he made a strained sound, returning to his corner of the bench with a yawn. He could sense her concern and felt he should come clean.

"I'm really fine," he said. "I just didn't get much sleep last night. I got back late despite my best efforts."

"You went away for Shabbos?" she asked.

Joe nodded. "My rabbi invited me to his bungalow colony."

She gaped open her mouth. "You went all the way to the mountains and came back last night? When did you leave?"

"We left right after Shabbos ended, but we took an unexpected detour for pizza around 10:30."

"Who drove you down?" she asked as she took out a Tupperware container from the lunch bag.

"This engaged couple who needed to get back to Brooklyn for wedding stuff today. Nice people."

She was taking out a red plastic fork from the bag and halted it in mid-air. "I'm so sorry. Had I known I wouldn't have dragged you all the way here."

"No, I'm glad you did. This place is very nice. I just want to sit for a bit."

"Would you like some fruit?"

"Sure."

Joe watched her hands as they opened the lid of the Tupperware. She stabbed a large ring of melon with the fork and placed it onto a similarly red plastic plate. With a wave of her hand she passed the plate to him, followed by a small bottle of water. He thanked her and made a bracha before tasting one of the sweetest melons he'd ever eaten.

He even told her, "This is one of the sweetest melons I've ever eaten."

She blushed. "I wish I could say I grew it myself. I didn't even pick it; I just nicked it from my aunt's house before I left this morning."

"You're taking my job in providing the refreshments for our date."

"Well, after your last successful choice of restaurant, I felt that I would give you a break. But if my spread isn't enough, there is a café in the mansion. I figured that a posh place like this only serves gourmet tea and watercress sandwiches."

"No, this is fine. We can save our appetite for lunch. Are the restaurants far from here?"

"Yeah," she said regrettably. "But we'll call my aunt and someone will get us."

"They offered this service?" She nodded. "And you agreed?" Again she nodded. "I see you're comfortable enough to let your family meet me."

Joe suddenly felt heavy in his chest after his last statement. With a few short words he had verbalized the silent backdrop to all of their meetings, something which hadn't even been eluded to up until then. Except for a general statement of "I had a good time" or "I had a nice time" that had concluded their previous dates, they had never directly discussed their personal feelings with each other. It wasn't as if Joe had gone so far to insinuate marriage, but he nonetheless had inadvertently, though not entirely, broken some sort of fourth wall.

"Sure I do," she replied after a moment, looking straight into his eyes. Joe admired her response; it seemed to accept the invitation into the next level of their relationship—however without any heaviness. After a prolonged stare, she added, "Just hope that the whole family doesn't come."

The day continued pleasantly as they casually perused the mansion and its lawns. For a while they sat at the café under the protection of a table umbrella, talking about their childhoods while gazing at the river and the Jersey cliffs beyond it. Eventually they were shooed away to make room for paying customers and after a short trip to the smaller mansion their hunger caught up with them and they phoned Rachel's aunt.

"Do you like the suburbs?" she asked him as they waited at the entrance for their ride, sitting on the sidewalk with their backs against the stone wall. "Or do you feel more like a city person after living in New York?"

He thought about it. "I don't know," he replied eventually. "I enjoy being able to easily get to minyanim and kosher food, but I don't love the crowds."

"What about where you live now?"

He huffed. "Where I'm living now is a fluke. I'm in a well-designed basement on a street lined with mansions—not like these mansions, but still sizeable. Besides the Brooklyn College students looking for parking, it's pretty much quiet."

"Where would you like to live, if you had the option?"

He picked at some strands of grass growing between the sidewalk lines. "It's hard to say. I really don't know the needs of a couple."

She picked a blade of grass and threw it into his lap. "So what would *you* choose if you were making the decision?"

He was taken aback by her directness, but he still answered. "I guess that I like Brooklyn."

"The people or the place?"

"Both. I feel more at home there, though I need more time learning to really feel like I can call myself one of them. I also like the availability of things…and the flatness. It makes riding my bike easier."

She raised her eyebrows in surprise. "I didn't know that you rode."

"Not that much. Just here and there. I rode to work for the first time ever last week."

"What prompted that?"

He shrugged. "It was Monday morning, after our Sunday date."

"You were so wired you couldn't sleep?"

"The opposite. I collapsed at home and woke up too early the next morning."

"Well, that's still nice." She paused as she watched a car pass. "I thought it was them," she explained.

"What about you?" Joe then asked. "Where would you like to live?"

"I guess somewhere where I wouldn't have to take a car everywhere I went. I got used to buses and trains from living in Manhattan and Yerushalayim."

"Would you want to live in Israel?"

She thought about it. "It would certainly be amazing. But I don't know how I would handle being so far from my family."

"You told me once that you didn't need to live in St. Louis—"

"Yeah, but Israel is a whole world away."

"True."

Just then a very clean black Toyota Camry slowed down and pulled up next to them. As it came to a stop, a teenage girl jumped out of the passenger seat, glanced quickly at Joe before looking straight at the ground as she opened the door to the back seat.

"Meira!" cried Rachel in a scolding manner. "What happened to cleaning-for-your-party all day?"

"I can't take a break for twenty minutes?" the girl asked before plunging into the car and sitting behind the driver.

Rachel then stood up and motioned to Joe. "I guess that means you should take the front."

Joe stood up, brushed off the back of his pants and walked towards the car. As he bent into the front seat, he was immediately addressed by an extended hand from the driver, a youngish-looking middle-aged man with a salt-and-pepper beard and hair and a warm smile.

"Shalom," the driver said. "I'm Ya'akov Shwartz, Rachel's uncle. And you are?"

"Joseph Charnoff," Joe answered.

"Joseph," he repeated, nodding his head as if Joe's name was a very interesting piece of information. The back door closed and the car started moving. "Is that what your friends call you?"

The question sounded strange to Joe. "Why do you ask?"

"It's just rare to hear someone by the name of Joseph."

There was audible but hushed conversation in the back. Joe hoped that Rachel wasn't listening. "I've had the nickname 'Joe' ever since I was in grade school, and I can't seem to get away from it."

"That isn't too bad, unless there's a story connected."

The car turned out of the residential maze onto a road that ran an alongside a highway. "It isn't much of a story," Joe said after a few seconds of debating whether he should say anything. "When I was little I had a Snoopy hat and my camp counselors would call me 'Joe Cool.'"

Rachel's uncle found this very funny, so much so that Joe found himself laughing too. "Yeah, there's something about summer camp. One counselor of mine used to call me 'Black Jack,' if you can believe it."

"What?" a voice from the back exclaimed. "I never knew that, abba."

"You never asked," Black Jack said to his daughter.

"And Joseph asked?" Rachel chimed in.

"We're chatting. So what do you do, Joe?"

He cringed; for sure Rachel heard her uncle call him 'Joe.' "Uh, I intern with a Wall Street research firm while I finish my Master's."

"In what?"

"Applied Mathematics."

He started nodding again. "Sounds interesting."

They were crossing over the highway and passing what looked like some sort of monument tower in the middle of a traffic circle. "What do you do?" Joe asked to fill in the quiet.

"I have a private dentistry practice."

"Here in Riverdale?"

"No, in Mamaroneck." Not knowing where that was, Joe simply nodded. "Did you two have a nice time?"

Joe didn't know whether the question was addressed to him or not. Rachel answered for them. "Very nice. Thank you for the recommendation."

"Can you imagine living on an estate like that?" Black Jack asked. "What a way to live!"

"I think Joseph would enjoy the view of the Hudson more than the huge house."

"Isn't it amazing?" Black Jack asked. "I never get tired of seeing it."

"What are those mountains across the river?" Joe inquired.

"Those are the Palisades. One of the Rockefellers bought all that land so that he wouldn't have his view disturbed. I guess we're the beneficiaries. So where are we bringing you two?"

"We want to eat," Rachel said.

"Well, we don't have anything too fancy in this town."

"Do you think I need fancy, Uncle Ya'akov?"

"No, but I didn't know what Joe here had in mind." He turned to Joe. "There's the café, the bakery, the deli, and pizza."

"Maybe we'll walk around first," Joe suggested. "Rachel will show me the town."

"There's nothing to see," Meira scoffed. "All the stores are on two streets."

"We'll drop you off on the corner," Black Jack suggested. They had reached an intersection where the continuation of the street was lined with small storefronts on both sides. "Here we are."

"Thank you very much, Uncle Ya'akov."

"It was nice to meet you," Joe said, offering his hand.

"Likewise, Joe. Will you be coming back afterwards, Rachel?"

"Uh, I was thinking of taking the train with Joseph later."

"You're leaving?" Meira whined, disappointment in her voice.

"I'll be back for your party, don't worry," she assured her cousin. "Can you pack my things for me?"

"What things? You're so neat everything's already in your bag."

"Put whatever I left in your bathroom into my travel case, you know, the hard plastic one. I think that that's all I left out."

"Can I call you if I see anything else?"

"Sure." They hugged. "See you later."

Joe stepped out of the car and saw the overhang of an al fresco café. Rachel waved to the passing car as it drove out of sight and then turned to Joe. "Shall we eat here?" she asked Joe.

"This place is kosher?" he inquired.

"It used to be. I guess it closed."

"So I guess it's the deli. I figure we should go fancier than pizza, what do you say?"

Rachel's countenance was visibly lifted by his suggestion. "Lead the way."

"Me? I don't know even know if we're still in New York City."

They started walking down the street, passing a restaurant that wasn't kosher and a bank. The next store in had advertisements for kosher meat, but inside only looked like a small market.

"Is this the deli?" Joe asked.

"I don't think my uncle would suggest this place."

A woman with a kerchief covering her hair exited the store in question with shopping bags. "Excuse me," Rachel asked her, "Is there a deli somewhere around here? Like, a sit-down restaurant?"

The woman looked at Rachel and then at Joe, particularly at his tie. "Yes, there was," she said gingerly. "It was a few doors down, but it closed."

Rachel frowned. "How long have I been out of the loop? Is there anywhere kosher to eat in this town?"

"There is a café," she said. Rachel and Joe shared a glance and smirked to each other. The woman then pointed them in the right direction and they started walking.

"I guess it'll have to do," he conceded.

"What do you mean? A café is great. Simple foods, choices of coffee…"

"I think I heard that jingle before."

They reached the place—a thin storefront with brick siding on the walls and two rows of black tables with wooden seats. There was a counter in front with elaborate desserts on display and various espresso machines lined against a mirror on the wall. A short Mexican waiter offered them their choice of seats and Rachel opted for a booth just behind the counter. Joe removed his suit jacket and sat opposite her.

"I don't need a menu," she told Joe after the waiter walked away. "I kind of liked the way they did it in that last restaurant we went to. It takes away the pressure of having the cost decide what you get."

Joe took the menu and opened it up. "And what if you were paying?"

She shrugged and picked up the other menu. "I hear."

He reached out and grabbed her menu lightly. "I didn't mean to suggest—"

"I know," she reassured him.

"How often do you come here?" he then asked.

"To this restaurant? I've never been."

"No, to your cousins?"

"More often since I finished college, but even then I only came once a month. It's just one subway from the Heights."

"So why did I pay $5 to take Metro-North?" Joe demanded to know.

"Because you'd be on the train for two hours if you came all the way from Brooklyn," she explained calmly. "Besides, the subway ends just outside Riverdale; someone has to pick me up whenever I come."

"Well, I need a minute to decide what to order."

"Go ahead. I'll be right back. If the waiter comes, order for me…" she looked quizzically into the menu before abruptly slamming it shut. "An avocado salad."

She got up and walked towards what Joe assumed was the bathroom. Once she was out of sight, he covered his face with the menu and sighed, but something felt different. He didn't feel a relaxation with his exhalation, but instead felt a warm pulsation under his ribs and a deep inner struggle somewhere near his stomach. He wanted to start laughing into the menu, as if his presence in the restaurant was indicative of something very significant that was all becoming very clear right then. The fact that Rachel was going to return from the bathroom in however long didn't scare him; on the contrary, he was awaiting her return with eager anticipation. Soon they would eat and bentch and perhaps find a shul where he could daven mincha and then take the subway together and *it all made sense*. There was no apprehension, no need to calculate the direction of the conversation or how to behave. He didn't mind anymore if she knew that his name was Joe or Joseph or Yosef. It all felt right.

She did return and she did order an avocado salad with vinaigrette dressing and a cherry soda. He ordered a cup of soup and a sandwich. They ate slowly and afterwards, on Rachel's suggestion, walked back to where they were dropped off and had cookies from the bakery they saw and shared a huge sprinkle cookie the size of Joe's hand for dessert. Black Jack picked them up from the pharmacy where Rachel wanted to buy a few things and brought Joe to a shul where they davened mincha and afterwards brought them to the subway station on Broadway. When Rachel had to get off the train, Joe stood up with her.

"Thank you for a wonderful day," he said. "Riverdale was a good choice."

"I had a very nice time," she said. "Get home safely."

"You too." He wanted to tell her more but he held back. It was, after all, still a shidduch. She stepped off the train and turned, waving goodbye one more time. The doors closed and through the glass he waved back, reluctantly letting the slow acceleration of the train take him away from her. He sat down and tried to calculate how many stops until he was home. He gave up counting after thirty.

However tired he was he couldn't sleep. The day had been a complete success—if the purpose was to convince him that he really liked her. He couldn't think of a single moment in which he felt that something was odd. Granted, he noticed a few times that she behaved a bit more casually than she had on their previous dates, but he didn't think of them pejoratively, but as a facet of her character. Or perhaps it was just an indication of how natural they were able to behave with each other. He still couldn't get over the fact that she felt enough at ease with him to have her uncle meet him. His mind was so preoccupied that he didn't even feel the length of the trip until the train approached 96th. He had to switch to the 2 anyway, so he rushed to the other track, but found no sign of headlights down the tunnel. When the local left the station, he heard a voice calling him.

"Joe! What are you doing here?"

He turned to see Avi Glass and his roommate Steven Broder, both dressed in solid polos and dark khakis, walking towards him. "Hey!"

"Woah, how stylish!" Steven said, turning over Joe's tie to check the label. "Did Sharon tell you to buy this?"

"Maybe," Joe said quickly. "What's going on?"

Avi answered, "Not much. Shabbat was quiet without you."

"Yeah, what are you doing up here?" Steven asked. "We didn't see you over Shabbat."

"I'm coming from further uptown. I just switched from the 1 train."

Avi looked down the tunnel of the 2 train. "Train's coming."

"So you're coming to Jessica's goodbye party?"

"Who's?"

"Jessica Farkas. She's making aliyah and they wanted to make a party before the Three Weeks."

"Farkas…" Joe repeated. The name didn't collate.

"Nati and Jessica," Avi added as he watched the train approach. Joe saw Avi's eyes fluctuating back and forth as the train decelerated and came to a stop just in front of them.

"Oh, right." Then he remembered his last conversation with Nati. "You think Nati'll be there?"

Avi and Steven exchanged a glance. "For sure," Steven said as they got onto the train. There was a line of empty seats and the three of them sat down. "He's been friends with her forever."

"It must be hard for him," Joe said. "Losing a friend like that."

Avi snorted, which made Steven shoot him a look. "I guess so."

Joe eyed them suspiciously. He tested his assumption. "If I was in Nati's shoes, I don't know if I'd be able to handle a goodbye party for a best friend."

"Best friend?" Steven repeated. "I wouldn't call her his 'best friend'…"

"She certainly wouldn't," Avi commented. Steven nudged him.

So I'm not the only one who knows.

"So why don't you come," Steven offered Joe. "It's starting now at Abigail's."

Joe shook his head violently. "Oh no. I'm beat."

"Come on. Come have a drink and wish her a Mazal Tov."

He tried to show his lack of interest by stretching elaborately. "Nah, I was up very early this morning, and this is my last ride on my card—"

But Steven didn't get the hint. "It's not even 8:00." He smacked Joe's leg. "So come. I'm surprised that you didn't get the message. Sharon texted us."

"My phone is off," Joe said, reaching into his pocket and turning it on. "I forgot."

They all watched Joe's phone load up, waiting to see if he had gotten the text message. The train stopped at 72nd Street and with the movement of people getting on and off they suspended their vigil. Avi then said, "You're not going to get any reception down here."

"I've gotten text messages in the strangest places," Steven countered. "It's like a double surprise."

"Like where?" Avi demanded to know.

"Like at 96th, on the platform."

Avi dismissed his answer. "That's because the platform is just below the street, not like two or three levels underground like most stops."

"Yeah, have you ever been to the 4-5 stop at 57th Street? The escalator is, like, three flights high and even at the top you're still not at the street."

"I don't know how you get texts at 96th. It's still underground."

"So what? You get phone calls in buildings?"

Avi shook his head and looked away. "That isn't the same as underground."

"Yeah, but the subway isn't really underground. It's under a thin layer of paved street."

"It can't be just a thin layer of street. With all those cars and trucks driving over, it must be at least twenty feet down."

Joe listened to their banter with mild amusement. For some reason he didn't feel included in their absorption in nonsense. He was still reveling in the absolute calm that had settled over him as his day with Rachel neared to its close and that made him feel aloof and distant from them. He hoped that they would continue long enough for him to extricate himself from joining them at the last minute.

"What about in an elevator?" Avi was asking Steven. "Do you get texts in an elevator?"

"What does it matter? I simply said that I can get texts in weird places, one of which you don't seem to understand how. So you don't understand. I don't understand either. Can we drop it?"

"Fine," Avi acquiesced, disappointment in his voice.

The train was passing by a station that only the local stops at. Joe felt inner relief that he had switched. "Do you guys also feel a satisfying feeling when you pass the local you got off?"

"Sometimes," Steven said. "I usually take whatever comes first and enjoy the air conditioning."

"We're getting close," Avi interjected. "You coming, Joe?"

Joe made a face, but before he could say anything they pressured him again.

"Come. It'll mean a lot to Nati."

"Just one drink and you can be on your way."

"You'll be home by 10 PM."

"She needs the encouragement after making such a big step."

Only when they both grabbed Joe's arms and hoisted him to his feet did he willingly accompany them. "OK, but ten minutes and I'm out," he informed them as they got off the train at Times Square.

Chapter Twenty-Eight

Sharon

WHEN SHARON HAD gotten off the phone with Joe on Saturday night, she was still lying in her bed when her father phoned.

"*Shavua tov,* Sharon," he said to her. "How was Shabbat?"

"Fine. What's up?"

Her father cut to the point. "Eh, *savta* is not well. The nursing home called on Shabbat, but we were all at the Young Israel. Your Ima called after havdalah, and she's there now."

Sharon sat up straight. "She's gone to Lakewood at this hour? Is anyone with her?"

"Your uncle Mendel will be here on Monday, but right now she's there."

"You're home with Aharon and Tehilah?"

"Yes."

She kicked her legs off the bed and stood up. "So who's at the store?"

"The managers are taking care of things tonight, but I have to be there early in the morning. I'm sorry to ask you, but can you come and be here?"

She stuck out her tongue. "Where's Eyal?"

"He was away for Shabbat. Went with friends somewhere."

"Did you try calling him?"

"He didn't answer."

She looked at the clock. It was nearly 10:00. "You don't want me to be with Ima? I'll get her to come home tonight."

"I don't want you taking a bus down there this late at night. I'll try and go meet her there tomorrow, if she's still there."

She threw her hands up to the ceiling. "You can't get a babysitter?"

"I need to leave the house at 6 AM. I can't ask someone to come that early."

"The babysitter could sleep by you."

"*Ma?* Let some girl to sleep in the house with just me and your siblings? *Lo ts'nua.*"

"Right." Sharon sighed, falling backwards onto her bed.

"I'm sorry."

"There's no need, Abba."

"I'll be up when you get here."

She quickly changed and by 11 PM was at Penn Station. As promised, her father was awake when she walked in the door just after midnight. He was sitting at the kitchen table, the cordless phone, his cell phone and an empty glass with Turkish coffee grounds in front of him. He stood up and hugged her when she entered. "*Toda raba*, Sharon."

"*B'vakasha.* Any news?"

Although he always had a serious look on his face, it was more intense than usual. He ran his fingers through his short beard, holding his hand in front of his mouth. His eyes opened widely and then closed before he looked at Sharon. "The dialysis isn't taking."

They stood there silently until a cough from upstairs stirred them. "How long?" Sharon eventually asked.

"No idea. Ima will be there until tomorrow."

"Can I call her?"

"She said she was going to try and rest. They have beds for visitors."

Sharon just nodded. Her father sat down and turned to her. "How was Shabbat?" he asked her solemnly.

"Very nice," she answered with a sigh. "I made a whole bunch of *salatim* on Thursday night. Madbucha, Moroccan carrots, roasted eggplant..."

He smiled. "Did you bring any for me to taste?"

"We finished them."

"Another time." He looked tired.

Sharon was still standing. "Go to bed, Abba. You'll be up early."

"So will you," he smiled.

The next day, Sharon woke up around 8 AM when Tehilah noticed her sleeping in the other bed and excitedly jumped on her. She treated her siblings to bagels, hoping that the novelty of being out for breakfast would satisfy their need to be entertained for at least a little while. After that Aharon went to swim in a neighbor's pool, so Sharon occupied Tehilah with construction paper and scissors while she cleaned the kitchen from Shabbat. It was 5:00 in the afternoon, as she was relieving her boredom by cooking macaroni and cheese from scratch, when her mother came home.

"Thank you so much," her mother said as she entered the kitchen.

She dropped the pasta stirrer onto the counter and ran to help her mother, who looked worn out and tired. "Please, Ima, there's no need. Sit down."

"I'm fine. How were things here?"

"Quiet. Aharon's swimming by the Lenders and Tehilah's cutting things."

"What is she cutting?" her mother asked worriedly.

"Construction paper."

Relieved, she sat back in her chair. "Don't scare me like that."

"Tehilah's a good girl. She wouldn't do anything like that."

"I know."

After a getting her mother a cup of water, Sharon sat down next to her at the table. "How's savta?"

Her mother shook her head from side to side. "I only left because there's nothing happening. She still isn't responding."

They sat at the table for a while until Sharon remembered the cooking pasta. She jumped up and tasted one of the macaroni from the pot. "It needs another minute."

"I only came home to see what we can do."

She waited before asking, "How much longer?"

"A few days, maybe a week. They have her on something very temporary but if she doesn't stabilize…" She didn't finish her sentence before putting her head into her hands. Sharon ran over and put her arms around her mother. *The pasta can be overcooked.* But after ten seconds her mother composed herself and even mustered a smile. "Thank you, honey. You can go, if you want."

"No, I'll stay. You need the help."

"It's fine. Mendy is flying in tomorrow and he'll be down there with her."

"I guess it's good he's coming now."

Her mother laughed a little bit. "I guess so."

Sharon went and drained the macaroni just as Tehilah came downstairs. "When's dinner going to be ready?" she asked Sharon.

"Hi Tehilah!" their mother said. "Come show me what you made."

"Where were you, Ima?"

"I went to visit savta. She wasn't feeling well over Shabbat."

"I made for her a flower," she boasted, producing from behind her back an elaborate folding of construction paper in the shape of a flower.

"That's so nice, sweetie." Sharon looked over and saw her mother mouthing to her, *Does she know?*

Sharon mouthed back, *No.*

As Sharon was rinsing the macaroni, her cell phone chimed. It was a text message asking if she was going to Jessica Farkas's goodbye party at Abigail's.

"What's that?" Tehilah asked Sharon.

"A goodbye party for a friend making aliyah."

"That's wonderful," her mother said.

"It's tonight," she said absently.

"So go," her mother told her. She looked at her mother peculiarly. "Is it in the city?" Sharon nodded. "Then go and sleep in your apartment tonight."

She put down her phone. "Are you sure?"

"I'm not going anywhere," then she added gravely, "and if anything happens, it's better you have more of your things."

Her mother was right. Sharon then ate with her family and got dressed, choosing clothes from whatever she had there. At 7 PM she got on a train and started texting a few people to see who was going. She called Joe but the call went straight to voice-mail. That meant that either his phone was off or he was on the subway; both possibilities didn't make any sense. Last night he had said that he was on his way home from the Catskills and it wasn't like him to leave Brooklyn on Sundays. It also wasn't like him to turn off his phone; even when she'd tried to reach him all last week it rang first. Then again, everything about him was strange these days.

Even on the train she still wavered. She kept feeling wrong, a sandy feeling tickling her eyes whenever she thought about her grandmother dying alone in New Jersey and her going to a party. But her mother insisted; perhaps the mitzvah of sharing in someone's *simcha* would be a *z'chut* for her grandmother's recovery. Then there was the chance—however unlikely—that Andy would show up when she hadn't yet thought about what she would do with him; she was still hoping for Joe's perspective on the matter. But besides all that she was simply worn out; every time she closed her eyes on the couch Tehilah came downstairs and demanded assistance or accolades on the progress of her artwork. Since the restaurant wasn't that far from Penn Station, and she was dressed already, she figured that she might as well go.

She reached Abigail's just before the scheduled time and found a nice-sized crowd congregating just by the entrance. She spotted Jessica as she walked in, excitedly entertaining well-wishers. At first nobody noticed Sharon, which she didn't mind. She didn't see anybody that she knew; in fact, they all seemed much older and she felt a little out of place. It was Nati who first spotted her and raised his eyes.

"Sharon!" he shouted over the shoulder of his conversation partner. "Thanks for coming!"

"Wow Nati," she said immediately, walking towards him. Sharon had guessed long ago how he really felt about Jessica. "How are you holding up?"

"That's nice of you to ask," he said plainly. Without elaborating, he indicated Sharon's approach to the man standing across from him.

"Eric, this is Sharon from the West Side."

Eric looked just like Nati probably looked five years ago. "Nice to meet you," he said in the way Nati talked.

"Are you two brothers?" Sharon asked.

Eric turned to Nati. "What did I tell you?" Then to Sharon: "No, we're cousins."

"Are you also from Maryland?"

Eric nodded. "Born and raised. Where are you from?"

"The Five Towns."

He scoffed in disgust. "Only in New York do they have the audacity to call a place 'The Five Towns' and expect that everyone knows which five towns they're referring to."

"I didn't give it the name," she muttered, turning to Nati. "How's Jessica? Getting nervous?"

"Ask her yourself," he said, pointing to her. "Hey, Jess!"

Sharon inwardly pitied him. Either he'd resolved his feelings for her or was further suppressing them. Jessica turned and on seeing Sharon her mouth dropped and her eyes widened. Sharon was surprised at her enthusiasm; it wasn't as if they were great friends. She knew Nati better, but then Nati and Jessica were one in the same package. Sharon never pictured what exactly Nati liked in her, but then she was so nice…

Sharon felt that she should at least share in the gush of the moment. "Oh my gosh! Jessica!"

"Sharon! Wow!" Jessica squeezed Sharon as if they were high school friends reunited at retirement.

"Mazal tov! What a big step!"

"I know!" She somehow smiled and seemed to cry at the same time. "Thank you for coming!"

Just then, Sharon noticed Steven Broder walk in front of the glass windows in front of the restaurant with two other guys behind him. While she didn't expect to stay much longer, she wanted someone familiar to help her escape from the giddiness. As he entered the restaurant, she saw that besides Avi Glass, Steven was accompanied by none other than Joe. Nothing looked different about him, except that his short hair seemed a bit wind-blown and he was wearing a suit with his tie somewhat loosened from its grip around his neck. He did have slight bags under his eyes and his cheeks and forehead had traces of tan. Otherwise, though, he looked as if he was completely overjoyed at the occasion. She watched him greet Nati with such empathy that one could be mistaken to think that they were brothers. For the first time she was seeing Joe not as her protégé but as someone from whom she was seeking advice, and with that he now had a certain air of maturity she never noticed before.

In the moment Sharon was looking at Joe, Jessica had turned to speak with a very tall girl with long blond hair who looked like the Scandinavian who almost crushed Sharon at the fireworks display. Sharon took her cue to excuse herself and walk over to Joe.

"You're a good friend," she heard Joe tell Nati, who was wearing a strained smile. "Really."

"Thanks Joe," Nati was saying blankly. "Thanks for coming."

"Hey Joey," Sharon interjected, causing them both to turn. He was surprised, but not alarmed, at seeing her. "Nice to see you."

His radiating happiness dropped a notch. "Nice to see you too, Sharon."

"How'd you get here?"

Nati took the chance to continue around. "Thank you guys for coming."

"We'll make a l'haim together, no?" Joe asked, turning to him.

"With everybody, later," Nati assured him as he walked away.

When he was gone, Sharon asked him quietly, "What was that about?"

Joe looked into her eyes. She could see that he was very tired. "I just think that Nati needed some encouragement."

She leaned in and looked over at Nati high-fiving Avi and Steven. "What do you know?" she whispered.

They shared a glance. "He's broken," Joe whispered.

"I know. Poor guy," she said simply.

"How does she not know?"

Sharon shook her head. "Maybe she does."

They both sighed. "What's up, Sharon?"

She was surprised by the way he asked the question—almost tenderly. "I'm all right," she told him, "but let me ask *you*, Joey. What's up with you?"

"I'm great," he said quickly. He felt very distant, looking around but not as if seeking anybody.

"Your phone was off," she said, matter-of-factly.

"I noticed that just now."

"So how did you find out?"

She could tell that he was hesitant to answer. "Uh, I ran into the guys on the subway. They were coming here as I was about to go home."

"What were you doing in the city?"

He coughed. "Meeting up with someone."

What is he hiding? "In a suit and tie?"

He laughed shortly. "Yeah. I ran out this morning."

"I remember that tie," she remarked, looking closely at it. She had insisted that he buy it one day at Urban Outfitters. It was a dull orange with white stripes that came as a set, though she doubted whether he even had the matching orange shirt. "It still looks good on you."

"Thanks."

She wanted to sit down with him at a small table and interrogate him, but before she could she suddenly became aware of something. Just behind her someone was talking about the scarcity of rain in Israel, and at the exact moment Sharon was looking at Joe's tie. Immediately her train of thought went express and she remembered that rainy day with Andy in Times Square, and the same tie that Joe was wearing poking out from under a big umbrella, helping a simply dressed religious girl cross a puddle. Her eyes narrowed and she realized that she was looking at the same build of the wearer of that tie but seven blocks from when she last saw him wearing it.

"You!" she pointed at him accusingly. She wanted to push him.

He suddenly became very alarmed, probably from the look of venom in Sharon's eyes. "What?"

She had many things to say, but the muddle in her mind could only produce, "You were in Times Square!"

He spoke to her quietly. "Sharon, is everything all right?"

"I saw you in Times Square wearing that tie!" she blurted out. "You were on a date!" His face froze, as if he were caught stealing. She interpreted his silence as validation of her conclusion. Excitedly, she guessed at everything. "You've been dating, and you haven't told me. This whole time…"

Avi Glass, who was standing ten feet away, turned to see. Joe stepped towards her, but she automatically retreated. "Sharon, calm down."

"Joey!" She started to cry, the shock of the intensity of her emotion made tears come even faster. "I can't believe you!"

"Wait…"

"What? Am I wrong?"

"Listen…"

She didn't want to listen, and with one turn she was out the door, running up Broadway and heading for the subway. She knew that she was already in an emotional turmoil with her grandmother's condition and her uncertainty with Andy, and now with Joe's return from the abyss she just couldn't handle it all and she didn't want to make a scene in front of her friends. With everything going on in her life she definitely didn't need Joe to have hidden something like this from her. She ran to the crosswalk at 38th Street while tears were flowing down her temples and down to her chin. Joe came alongside her while she waited at the light for a taxi to pass.

"Wait, Sharon," he started, but she didn't let him continue.

"How many dates have you been on?" she demanded.

"Will you please—"

"How many?" she again demanded, more violently.

He must have seen the fury in her eyes because he looked down when he said, "Six, but—"

"Six! When were you going to tell me?"

"I didn't tell anybody. It all happened so fast."

"What is it, a shidduch? You didn't even tell me you were set up."

"I was told not to."

"Not to tell? Not even your friends?"

"I didn't even tell my parents."

She began to walk away but turned back. "What's gotten into you? Last week you had a great time with Erica and now you tell me you went out with a girl six times?"

"Erica?" he exclaimed. "I was chaperoning your guest, so that you and Andy could enjoy your time together."

"Huh. It didn't look like that."

He turned around in frustration. "Sharon…"

"What are you going to tell me next, that you're engaged?"

"Will you please let me speak?"

"Are you engaged already?"

For the first time he spoke with annoyance. "No, I'm not engaged."

"Huh! Not this week."

He looked away. "Stop this already."

From the corner of her eye she saw that no cars were coming so she crossed the street and continued towards the subway entrance at 40th Street. Whatever Joe had to say she didn't want to hear it. With everything that she had done for him, the last thing she ever thought he would do would be to go behind her back and drop her out of his life like this. She dashed down the stairs and at the bottom took her Metrocard out of her purse and quickly swiped through the heavy metal turnstile.

After she had passed through, she heard Joe call from the top of the stairs, "Sharon, wait!" His voice had such force that she'd never heard from him that she had to stop. In a second he appeared and he came towards the barrier, his face flush and his eyes staring directly at hers through the bars. "Wait."

"Why?"

"You won't even let me explain?"

"What explanation is there? You left me out of a pretty important part of your life."

"I'm sorry," he said with remorse. "Everything happened very fast and I didn't realize how involved I was."

"You didn't even tell me you'd been set up."

"I didn't tell anybody."

"So what?" she held her hands out to the side. "We're not friends enough?"

"Friends?" he asked incredulously. Then his eyes narrowed and he pointed at her through the bars. "What's this all about, anyway? Why is it that when you've been getting dates for years and finally I get a break that you call *me* on it?"

The last thing Sharon was going to tolerate was an accusation. Coldly, she said, "I was always looking out for you, Joey. This argument is over." She slowly stepped backwards while keeping her gaze towards him. "You want to go off and get married and leave me out of it, go ahead."

"Wait, I'm sorry…"

"I won't stop you."

"No, Sharon…" he pleaded.

With tears filling her eyes, she mouthed to him: "goodbye."

She turned and started running down the corridor towards the trains. "Wait!" he screamed but she didn't stop. "My card is empty! Don't run away!"

Once out of sight, she stood against a wall to catch her breath and wipe her face with tissues from her bag. Even if he was apologetic for his behavior, he had accused her of being insensitive when she had done so much for him. When she reached the 2 platform and soon after got on a train, she sat down and breathed deeply, hoping that with some much-needed sleep she would deal with her problems, now on her own.

Chapter Twenty-Nine

Joe

WHEN THE ALARM BLARED at 6:40, Joe smacked the snooze with such force that the small clock bounced off the nightstand and skipped three times on the floor before coming to a stop. His first thought was to call in sick or to switch his day at work and catch a later minyan, but then he remembered that his tefillin were under the bimah at the shul on the corner. If he didn't go daven now he'd have to walk in during the minyan and get them, so sparing himself the embarrassment was enough to get him to roll onto the floor and land his back on the alarm clock. Once awake he dressed for work. He brushed his teeth and when he glanced in the mirror he snarled. For a minute or so he tried to give his reflection some form of motivational speech, even a one-line maxim, but just couldn't. On the way out the door he grabbed his phone and wallet from the table and as he put them into his messenger bag he saw his tefillin in the corner of the table. "That makes no sense," he said aloud with a scowl. He got to the shul just in time for the minyan.

With no food in his apartment, he went to the bakery hoping to pay with his debit card, but soon learned he would need to spend more than he was prepared to in order to use it. He considered the fruit store on the corner, but would they let him charge a small purchase? Maybe he should just buy a bagel near his office after a stop at an ATM. All this thinking was hurting his head. He lacked a desire to work and chose to have a late morning. At the fruit stand, he bought a half-dozen challah rolls in a bag, a quart of milk, whipped cream cheese, a box of Raisin Bran cereal and, as an impulse, a container of cut cantaloupe because it reminded him of Rachel. As he was paying, his phone began vibrating. It was Mrs. Rosenzweig.

"Good morning, Joseph," she said cheerfully. "It's Penina Rosenzweig."

"Good morning," he answered sullenly.

"Did I wake you?"

"No," he replied in a more pleasant tone, coughing as a cover. "No I'm awake."

"Very good. I didn't hear from you last night."

He reached for the pen in his pocket with his free hand, but the clerk slid one to him from the counter and presented his receipt. "Yeah, I got home very late."

"Really? Rachel called me just after 8 PM."

"We took the subway from Riverdale together, and I stopped in the city…" he didn't finish his sentence. "Can you hold for a second as I sign something?"

"Sure."

He signed the receipt, handed it to the clerk, took his shopping bag and walked out to the sidewalk. "I'm here."

"Very good. So how was it?"

"Very good," he joked, tapping his feet as he waited at the crosswalk for the light to change. "She picked a very nice location."

"Excellent to hear. What are you feeling?"

"Everything's great. We got along the whole day wonderfully and there's a good rapport…"

"That's what I'm hearing from Rachel. So how do you want to proceed?"

He was still tapping his foot and twisting his wrist so that the shopping bag would spin around itself. "What do you mean?"

"How do you want to continue?"

The light turned green but he didn't move. "I still don't understand what you mean. We'll go out again, no?"

"Well," she said slowly, "last night Rachel told me that she was ready for an engagement."

For a moment Joe forgot where he was—on the street, in Brooklyn, planet Earth. It was the honking of a distant truck that jolted him back to reality and in the readjustment he failed to detect the weight of the shopping bags he had been holding seconds before. Looking down he saw them sprawled to the ground, and it took another moment to conclude that he must have dropped them in his momentary escape from consciousness. "Hold on one second," he mumbled as he bent down to pick up his purchases and to ensure that nothing had exploded open on impact; besides the lid of the melon container giving way, everything but his grasp of himself was still intact. "What did you say?" he asked into the phone.

"She's seen enough and feels ready to get engaged. How do you feel about that?"

He crossed the street when the red hand began blinking and quickly walked home. His first feeling was disbelief. "After six dates?" he asked incredulously.

"Don't think that I didn't speak to her about it. She's very pleased with the progression of your dates and feels very confident about you, especially after yesterday. Was there anything special you did?"

He adjusted his kippah to its spot. "Nothing that I can think of"

"It doesn't matter. Whatever you did seemed to please her, and that's really all that matters, no? Do you feel similarly?"

His second feeling was uncertainty. "Don't get me wrong, I'm also very impressed and have had a great time with her. But is it enough to get engaged over?"

"Listen, it sounds like you need to think about it. Maybe talk to your rabbi and get back to me. Should I call you this afternoon?"

"No, I can call. I'm in the city today, but I'll try and extricate myself."

"Great, whatever that means. You college boys."

Immediately after they hung up Joe tried calling Rabbi Tzvi. His wife answered the phone and explained that he was still at shul, would be there most of the morning and when could he call Joe back? When he reached his apartment, he quickly threw his groceries into the refrigerator and ate a hurried breakfast of Raisin Bran. In between bites he made himself a cream cheese sandwich for lunch and went to work. He stopped at an ATM and found his balance tottering at a mere $400, whether or not that accounted for his purchase at the grocery. The latest bout of dating certainly took its toll on his available funds. It would have to last him until he got paid next Monday on the 15th. He got on a train just after 9 AM and allowed his mind to play games with him for the entire duration of the ride:

> I don't have the money to get engaged — But she
> likes me! She likes me enough to get engaged! How
> about that? — No, I've been stringing her along with
> no real way of giving her what she deserves — I don't

even know what getting engaged entails — Sure I do, there's a ring and a l'haim and a whole wedding to plan — Wait, I can't pay for that. I only have a small paycheck from Stadler & Klein and no guarantee of a job — She knows all this, and I'm not the only one involved in the story. There's her and her parents and my parents — My parents, I haven't even told my parents! They'll think I'm nuts! — Perhaps they'll trust me to make an adult decision, as they've trusted me until now — But what about Sharon? She hates my guts; forget Sharon for the moment. This doesn't concern her. I'm making a decision for the rest of my life — But I've never seen her that angry...ever. I've trusted her opinion on everything and now I'm going behind her like this? — Remember her 'advice' about Daniela? And what about trying to set me up with Erica? I need more mistakes like that? — But she's my friend — Since when am I keeping female friends? — I know, but I can't do anything now. I'd be kicking a dead horse — If not now, when?...

Joe was able to focus for about an hour at his cubicle before his same train of thought began repeating ad nauseam. He worked until mincha and then ate his lunch alone in the lunch room, his inner struggle his only company. Only after he finished did he try to call Rabbi Tzvi.

"Yosef, where have you been all day?" the rabbi asked him. "My wife says that you called around 8:30 this morning."

"I didn't want to disturb," he answered, leaning back in the chair. "I'm at work anyway."

"What's up? How was yesterday?"

He took a deep breath. "Yesterday…it was great. She had stayed by her relatives in Riverdale and so we met up there and visited this huge mansion with a whole garden and pond—it's called Wave Hill…it was very nice. And then we ate in the town there before getting on the subway home."

"Thank you for the play-by-play, but what are your feelings?"

He laughed nervously. "I…to tell you the truth?"

"I hope that you only do."

"It just felt natural, like there was no agenda. I was a bit tired, but I still cared to listen. Then, when we sat down at some restaurant two hours later, I suddenly felt this…overwhelming calm, I guess you could say. I nearly laughed like a toddler when she stepped out, like there was something very funny about me being there."

"Funny, like awkward?"

"No," he said, stretching the word. He was tapping his foot as he talked. "More like relief. I'd always felt this inner tension from the whole set-up, but suddenly it wasn't there and it felt pretty good."

"That's good. What's her take?"

Joe's leg was shaking so rapidly that he had to stand up. "So that's the thing. Mrs. Rosenzweig told me Rachel's ready to get engaged." Joe stood frozen, his eyes roaming around the room as he waited for a response, but none came. He hesitantly added, "and I didn't know what I should do about that."

"Did you jump for joy?" the Rabbi asked.

"What?"

"Come on, man, that's incredible!" the Rabbi cried into the phone. "How many people out there date for months and years before they hear something like that? After two weeks you've found a girl willing to marry you! Ha, how should you react—how did you react?"

He leaned against the counter. "I think that I had an out-of-body experience. I dropped the shopping bags I was carrying."

"OK, good. You still have blood pumping through you."

"But it's too soon," Joe posited. "I mean, we met two weeks ago, and Mrs. Rosenzweig told me Rachel finished working. Maybe she wants to finish up and go visit her parents or something."

"Maybe, but that shouldn't affect *your* feelings on the matter. How do you feel about it?"

He was pacing around the lunch room now. Mr. Siegel's secretary walked in, and Joe gave her a half-smile as he ducked into the corner by the fridge to let her get to the percolator. "I mean, it's certainly a big step—"

"I asked you this on Shabbos, but now it's serious. Try to ignore all the details. Informing your friends and family, adjusting your lifestyle to include another person, arranging a wedding and buying all the trinkets for your home—push that aside and ask yourself if *you* are ready—note what I'm stressing—to accept her, as she is, and devote your life to building a marriage."

Joe bit the inside of his cheek as he watched steam wisp into the air as the secretary slowly poured the dark coffee into her cup. *Is that a diamond on that ring?* "I mean, I've only really met her. How do I know I'm not settling?"

"First of all, she's not the only girl you know, if you catch my drift. You might need some time to really process this, especially with what we talked about."

Joe felt his lunch churn in his stomach. "OK."

"Furthermore, you aren't being asked to decide whether this girl is 'the one' of all the billions of women out there. We let ourselves think there's this unlimited pool of women out there and that with enough searching, we'll stumble upon the perfect one. Don't believe it. For some reason we don't go to such lengths when doing anything else. You wouldn't frown at the pitiful selection of milk cartons in one store because you can go to other stores and find thousands more to choose from."

Joe interrupted him. "OK, but there are still fifty cartons of milk in that one store." When Joe said 'carton of milk,' the secretary poked her head over the open door of the fridge and showed him a box.

"Do you want this?" she asked him.

Joe waved his hand in the negative. In his moment of interruption, he thought he missed something the Rabbi had said. "I'm sorry, what did you say?"

"I said that you're right, but it's really just fifty independent decisions—do I buy this one or not? That one or not? So here too, just weigh your decision on the one woman you've been given, as she is."

Joe's didn't answer right away, his focus directed at trying to see whether the secretary's hand was adorned with a new ring as it stirred her cup of coffee with a plastic stirrer. He diverted his eyes to the wall when she caught him. "I'll think about it."

Joe somehow put his emotional turmoil on hold and finished his work day without interruption. Like clockwork, though, the voices of his inner struggle returned just as he was gathering his things to leave at 5:30. They were reviewing the minutes from their last debate as he was leaving the building and on a whim he decided to find a serene location to think things through. The downtown breeze was softer than normal and so he turned southward and walked towards the great expanse of New York Bay. After a few minutes he found himself by the terminal of the Staten Island Ferry and he walked in search of a quiet spot. There was a fenced-off playground and a large fenced-off lawn, but he found a wooden boardwalk just along the water's edge. The entire bay was spread out before him and he leaned on the railing and watched the various tugboats and speedboats and tourist ferries maneuvering around. The breeze had picked up since his first contact with it on Water Street and the tide was high enough to occasionally push a gust of water up from under the wooden planks below him and lightly splash unsuspecting passers-by. While it was more action than he had hoped for, as long as it was silencing the voices he was content.

His first act of resolution was to call his parents. Perhaps after that hurdle he felt he could make a decision about where he was holding on the matter of engagement. He called the house number.

"Hello." It was his sister.

"Ellen?" he asked, surprised.

"Joe?"

"What are you doing there?"

"Aviva caught a slight fever so we stayed the night."

He cooed. "How is she?"

"Much better—aren't we Aviva?" she said in baby voice. "We're just waiting for Michael to bring us home."

Joe coughed. "He went all the way to Baltimore this morning?"

"Yep."

"And he'll have to drive down to Potomac and then back to Baltimore?"

"This is life with a baby. Soon by you. What's going on? How's your girlfriend?"

He almost choked on his breath. "Girlfriend?"

"Yeah, that girl you were going out with…what was it, two

weeks ago?"

"What girl?"

She made an exasperated moan. "Mom told me you were going on a date in the city. Was she wrong?"

He lowered the phone from his ear and rubbed his eyes. With a laugh, he said, "I can't get anything by her."

"No, she's astute. So, what's her name?"

Begrudgingly, he mumbled, "Rachel."

"Does she have a last name? Where's she from? You know, give me the basics."

"Rachel Rosen and she's from St. Louis."

"What are you doing out in St. Louis? Where are you, anyway? It sounds like a hurricane out there."

Joe looked around and the bay and the grandness of the scene made him smile. "I'm down by the Staten Island Ferry."

"Like I know what that's supposed to mean?"

"It's by the southernmost tip of Manhattan, right on the bay. No, she lives here."

"How long have you known her?"

He was afraid of that question. "Uh, a few weeks. It was a shidduch."

"Yeah, I figured that you'd go that way. Are you engaged yet?"

He stalled, making nonsensical noises. "No, but it's on the table."

"How exciting! Do you want me to tell mom?"

"I should probably tell her."

"Yeah, you should. Here she is."

Without any send-offs, Joe heard his mother's voice. "Hello Joe."

"Hi mom," he responded, mimicking her tone.

"What do you want to tell me?"

Joe resented that his sister didn't give him at least a few minutes to coddle his mother before having to jump into the serious conversation. "Oh, you know, I, uh, just told Ellen that I was dating a girl."

"That's nice to hear. How long have you known her?"

Why do they all have to ask that? "Uh, a few weeks. I met her for the first time that Sunday I called."

"Why didn't you tell me then?"

The conversation was getting to be too much for Joe, so he turned away from the railing and sat down on a bench next to a resting park sweeper. "I don't know, mom. I didn't want to get your hopes up or anything."

"Oh, Joe." His mother was in a good mood, her last statement more dismissal than disappointment. "So what's her name?"

"Rachel. Rachel Rosen. She's from St. Louis but she lives and works here in New York."

"That's great."

There was a pause in which he asked himself what he was actually calling for. "Yeah, it's great. It's really great."

"What did you say?" she asked after a moment. *What is wrong with their phone? This happened the last time.* "Aviva just started crying and I didn't hear you. Did you say something?"

"No, nothing intelligent."

"So, listen Joe, I have to help Ellen get ready to go. Anything else you want to talk about?"

Someone else was calling his phone but he didn't want to check who it was. "No. Just that I'm doing fine and to brighten your day, I guess."

"OK, Joe. Should I tell your father?"

"I'll call him."

"Call him now, while he's on his way home."

"Sure."

Before calling his father, he sat on the bench and thought. What exactly made him jump to call his parents? Dating Rachel was something significant enough to want to share with them, and he did. His secret was out. Now what?

He called Mrs. Rosenzweig. "Can I meet her again?" he asked after the preliminaries.

"Of course," she told him. "You mean that you want another date?"

He rolled his eyes. "Obviously."

"No…oh, you're being funny. Ha ha. I mean to ask whether I'm saying anything about…"

Joe furrowed his brow. "Isn't it my job to pop the question?"

"Yes," she said slowly, "but she usually knows it's coming. You wouldn't want to be this far and get blindsided by a rejection, right?"

"Right."

"On that note, can I trust you with her phone number?"

He detected an implied question of *so are you also intending on getting engaged and won't break her heart?* "Yeah, you can trust me."

"So get in touch with her and set up a time. It doesn't have to be right now, but it should be sometime tonight."

He stored Rachel's number in his phone and hung up. He jumped up from the bench and waved goodbye to the bay, and then to the park cleaner who was visibly puzzled by Joe's behavior. He floated on light feet to the subway, oblivious to the world as he stood the entire trip to Brooklyn. No buses came, so he walked to his basement but felt no fatigue. The positive feeling he had telling his mother and the forward momentum of his shidduch made him feel light-hearted. Soon, after his dinner of Raisin Bran, he would be calling a girl that he could be sure liked him, a certainty that he never had before with any girl he ever knew since Rebecca. Then it occurred to him that he couldn't remember the last time he thought about Rebecca.

At 7:00, on the dot, when he was satiated, he stepped out of his basement and dialed Rachel's phone number while sitting on the steps.

"Hello?" he heard her say, as if it was a question.

"Is this Rachel?" he asked in a sing-song voice.

"Yes. Who is this?"

"This is Joseph." Slight pause. *Which Joseph?* "Joseph Charnoff." *Faux pas #1.*

"Oh," she said in a way that made his heart race. "Hello Joseph."

He felt short of breath. "How are you doing?"

"Great. How are you?"

"Fine, just fine."

"Did you get back last night all right?"

Sharon! his inner voice screamed and he fell hard back to Earth. All his depression of the morning crept back into his chest. He wanted to just hang up and try again later, but he didn't. "Yeah. I ran into some friends in the subway—"

"Wow. What are the odds of that?"

"Not too high, I guess. They dragged me to a goodbye party for a gir…for someone from the West Side moving to Israel."

"That's nice. Do you go there often?"

"Where? Israel?"

"No, to the Upper West."

He bit his lip. "No. It isn't my scene."

"Exactly. Too much of a scene for me."

Joe laughed nervously. "Yeah. Uh, Mrs. Rosenzweig said that we should get together."

"You need her to tell you that?"

Faux pas #2. "No, I meant that I'd like to get together."

"Oh, that's better. Does tomorrow work?"

"Um, it could…" he coughed. "I'm coming into the city on Wednesday."

"Well, Joseph, the thing is that my cousin Meira—you remember her, right?"

"I only kind of met one."

"Yeah, that one. She was in the car when my uncle brought us to the restaurant."

"Right, sure."

"Well, my aunt is making her a sixteenth birthday party this week."

"Wow. Sixteen."

"Yeah, can you remember being sixteen?"

Math club, science club, APs and SATs? "Vaguely. Crazy times."

She laughed. "Well, I told my aunt I'd help set up the house and such, so if we meet on Wednesday it'll have to be before the party…which is called for 7:00."

Joe calculated with his fingers. "So let's meet in the Grand Central area. I can take a train there after work and hope to be there around 5:30. You can get a train right after."

"How long will we meet?"

He worried he was asking too much, but he still asked, "Can you go a bit late?"

"Sure. We'll meet in Grand Central itself. There's a Mendy's deli in the lower level."

"Great. So 5:30?"

"It's a date." They both laughed. "So, I'm in the middle of dinner here."

"Oh, sorry. What are you eating?"

"Just a salad. Nothing special."

"If you made it, it's probably special." *Was that too complimentary? Faux pas #3.*

She laughed nervously. "I just threw something together. It's edible, we'll say that much."

"Well, don't let me stop you." He heard Mr. Gruberman's husky cough from the window above his head. "Go ahead and enjoy."

"Thanks for calling, Joseph. Is this your number?"

"Yes it is."

"I'll see you on Wednesday."

"All right." *Let her hang up.*

She hung up. Joe sighed deeply and clunked his head against his knees.

For a long time he sat studying the lines in the concrete of the stairs. *What am I going to do about Sharon?* To leave things as they ended at the subway turnstile wasn't right, but what would confrontation help? He didn't even need Rabbi Tzvi's suspicions; he knew Sharon better than he knew anyone else and she knew everything about him. He had no problem cutting contact with every other girl he knew, but did nothing about the one he most had to let go. He couldn't continue dating Rachel with this looming over him, but with no real plan—or the guts—to deal with it, he hoped that their parting last Sunday would be the end. When he remembered that he had to get to the yeshiva, he jerked himself up and nearly slipped on the last step. He tried to learn but couldn't focus, unable to even see the words of his Gemara clearly. *How long can this funk go on?* he asked himself when he finished davening with no recollection of how he got to the end so quickly.

On Wednesday Joe left work on the dot and somehow got to Grand Central ten minutes before they were to meet. It was rush hour, much busier than he saw it on Sunday morning. The large lobby was filled with people who all seemed to be passing through very quickly, as if they all thought they were very late. Joe felt completely out of place as he stood in the main room and stared up at the constellation fresco on the ceiling while throngs of people passed by on all sides of him. When the big clock above the Information desk showed that it was 5:35, he walked downstairs to the food court.

There were small restaurant stands to his left and right, but Joe couldn't spot a sign for Mendy's. He scanned the various tables and when he spotted her, his heart jumped to a faster rhythm. She smiled when he approached but didn't get up.

"No tie?" she asked him jokingly.

"No sneakers?" he asked back.

"Touché. Go order."

"Did you?"

"Yes. I already paid and started eating."

He grimaced. "Once the shadchan's out of the picture all rules fly out the window?"

"Once the tie comes off, everything comes loose."

"Touché."

Joe was aghast at the prices. Even a half-sandwich cost close to eight dollars, but he splurged on a whole one. He washed his hands for bread and when he returned to the table he found her staring out at the crowd of commuters rushing to their trains. Only when he made his bracha did she turn her gaze back to him and smile. He could sense that she was distracted as they chatted and ate. At one point he dropped a napkin and when he bent down, he noticed a suitcase nestled under her seat. He asked her, "You take that much luggage every time you go?"

"No," she answered absently, looking around. "I'm going home."

All Joe could think to say was, "Really?"

She sighed. "Instead of helping my aunt I was packing. I'm going up to Riverdale for the Sweet Sixteen and then flying...hopefully before Shabbos."

He sipped his drink. "Which train do you want to get?"

"Whenever we finish," she said nonchalantly. "It's rush hour so there are trains all the time."

"Oh. But St. Louis?"

"Yeah," she conceded with sorrow. "Look, Joseph...does everyone call you Joseph? It sounded like my uncle called you something else."

"At work they call me Joseph—so does Mrs. Rosenzweig. In the yeshiva they call me Yosef, but since I'm a kid everyone calls me Joe. I didn't think it was proper to go on shidduchim as Joe, but that's what I'm known as."

She looked directly at him. "What would you like me to call you?"

He smiled. "Whatever you feel comfortable with."

"OK, Joe. Short and sweet." She smiled for a moment before returning to serious mode. "Look, you already know." She looked up at the low ceiling and sighed again. "I've had a really great time. I feel very comfortable around you—like I can be myself, and I think that you're the guy for me. I didn't lie when I said that I was ready to get engaged…" She paused after the last word, struggling to say what Joe knew was going to be a very emotional 'but'. His mind went through every possible 'but' she could throw at him, but she had just confirmed wanting to get engaged, so he surmised that her current issue wasn't a major emotional block but a particular detail that she was merely hesitant to address.

"It's OK," he reassured her. "Even if we haven't committed, per se, I'm still here."

She looked at him and Joe could see her lower lip quivering. She must've read sincerity in his face, because she continued. "No, it's nothing like that. It's just that I spoke to my parents yesterday and…" she sighed again, "and they want to meet you. I've been living out of the house for almost a decade, and I guess they feel left out of my life."

That's not so bad. "But I don't have anything with me. I need my tefillin, clothing…"

She lightened up, even chuckled a bit. "So do you agree?"

He put up his hands. "I don't know the protocol. I've been going along with whatever my rabbi says, and I'd like to consult him."

"Can you call him now?"

"Why? If you have a ticket —"

"I told my parents not to book the flight until we talked."

"Oh." There was a pause after she mentioned a joint decision. "When would you like to go?"

She spoke more calmly. "There's still space on a flight tomorrow night. I'd be in the airport when the fast ends."

Joe nodded seriously. "Right, there's a fast tomorrow. Good thing I ordered a whole sandwich."

"So you'd come for Shabbos?"

He shrugged. "Like I said, I need to ask my rabbi."

"Call him now, please."

He took out his phone and excused himself to call from the bench ringing the center pillar in the food court. The number of people on their way to the platforms seemed to have picked up from when he first came down. Rabbi Tzvi answered right away.

"Good evening, Yosef. I've been waiting for your call."

"Good evening," Joe replied pleasantly. "How's everything?"

"Great. Are you eating tonight? It's a long fast tomorrow."

"Uh, yes. In fact, I'm eating with Rachel right now."

"So what are you doing calling me? Talk with her!"

Joe looked in her direction and saw her bentching with a small *siddur.* "Actually, she insisted that I call. She just told me she wants to leave for St. Louis tomorrow."

"Why?"

"Her parents want to meet me and she wants to fly before the weekend."

The Rabbi hummed. "So when will you go?"

"Should I go? I told her I wanted to ask you."

"Let me speak with her," the Rabbi told him.

Joe didn't expect that. "All right," he said slowly. He went back to the table where Rachel was kissing her siddur. "He wants to talk to you."

She made a face he never saw on her before but could be expected for the situation. She put the siddur on the table and took the phone from him hesitantly.

"Hello?... Hello Rabbi... Thank you. Thank you for your help... OK...No, I decided... No, they know how I feel." She looked over at Joe and it made him have to sit down. "Yes, I'm sure... OK, I'll tell him... I'm looking forward as well... Bye." She held out the phone to him. "I guess I passed."

Joe took the phone. "Yes, rabbi."

"She sounds very confident."

"She is," Joe said, looking in her direction.

"So it looks like you're going to St. Louis," he concluded. "I'm glad that we had you for your last Shabbos as a free man, so to speak. Try not to go for Shabbos, but go within a few days. Be on your best behavior and get out of there as soon as you can. Give me a ring before you go."

"Thank you very much, rabbi."

"My pleasure. Goodbye."

As he closed his phone, he could see eager anticipation in Rachel's eyes. "Well?"

Joe deliberately and painstakingly put his phone slowly into his pocket. "So," he asked with a smile. "Which airport am I flying into?"

Chapter Thirty

Sharon

AT FIRST SHARON DIDN'T want to speak to anyone. Already on the subway she turned her phone off, something she hadn't done in… well, she couldn't remember. She practically ran to her building, not because she was afraid but because she needed to be alone. When she got to the apartment she was glad to find Tamar's door closed and no hint that she was awake. Sharon threw off her clothing and without brushing her teeth she was in bed within minutes. Then she thought that her mother might need her, so she turned on her phone, just in case. She was asleep in seconds.

She slept badly. Several times she awoke with the feeling that she had just experienced a very important dream but couldn't remember the details. Around 3:00 AM she realized that she had been turning for a long time and rolled onto her back and stared at the ceiling. She still couldn't believe that Joe would deliberately not tell her he was dating. Did their friendship mean nothing to him that he could go and leave her out of such a significant part of his life? It was indicative of how he was going too far with his religiosity and next thing she knew he was no longer going to speak to her. He deserved everything he got, she concluded, acting like her friend but all the while wanting to throw her over when he no longer needed her.

But it didn't feel right. What had he been insinuating with his comment that she'd had relationships when he hadn't? What had she been trying to do for him all along? Help him find a girl to marry. He was never interested in silly flings or immature relationships; even from among the girls at NYU he had been looking for a wife, and now he'd found her. Sharon wasn't sure that he was going to propose, but six dates was pretty serious — far more than with any other girl. He was probably boiling over with excitement. She saw his face when he was talking to Nati. He was beaming! Sharon should have been ecstatic for Joe, but why wasn't she? What triggered such a vehement response on her part — to start crying in the middle of a friend's party and run away like that? Sure she had her own personal conflicts that all combined made for one emotional explosion, but why couldn't she see past her own pain and celebrate with him? Yes, he had betrayed their friendship, and yes, he had met a girl in a way she disliked, but is that how a friend reacts to another friend's joy?

Maybe it was jealousy. As long as Joe had been jaded and forlorn and unable to find a girl, Sharon had someone with whom to commiserate and to share in her lack of relationship success. Her friends and friends' younger sisters were getting married and doing things with their lives, but as long as Joe was around she didn't have to feel too despondent. Once he showed that he didn't need her advice or her company and that he went off and found himself a kallah so quickly, she was ostensibly left alone and she blew up at him with pure, simple jealously.

As she went to the kitchen to for a cup of herbal tea, she decided it wasn't jealousy. She couldn't convince herself that she had selfishly maintained a friendship just to have a permanent shoulder to cry on. For years she had tried to help Joe find the girl he so desperately sought, mentoring him to not only drop his whole dorky image but to build his ego, to give him the confidence he needed to make the right moves. She couldn't understand, then, why nothing had worked out for him. After three years in school and many such crushes, he was never able to concretize his efforts into a single lasting relationship. She started to wonder whether she was somehow responsible for his consistent failures. Going through the list of Joe's pursuits, she realized that perhaps they had been out of his league — popular girls who were more whom Sharon thought he should be dating as opposed to girls that Joe might have really been happy with, like Erica. Sure she was a nerd then, but so was Joe. Was Sharon trying to make Joe into something other than what he was because that's what Sharon wanted him to be?

But why would Sharon want Joe to be more than he was? The very Joe she spent thousands of hours hanging out with was the Joe she knew and loved — in a platonic sense. Then she remembered what Esther had been insinuating on Friday night. While it didn't seem as if Joe was pining for her, seeing as how he went off and found himself a shidduch, could she be so sure that she was innocent? Could it be that she was trying to mold Joe into the guy that she could eventually see herself falling for, hoping that with enough experience he would be more the guy she was seeking? It felt so wrong, but she couldn't absolutely convince herself that it wasn't possible. In order to be sure, she would have to examine how she felt, now that she knew what she was examining.

The next day, on Monday, she had two serious conversations before she settled into her role as the Responsible Older Sister at home. She met Andy for dinner at Mr. Broadway on her way to

Penn Station and explained to him her conclusion, but she put it nicely.

"I've decided that I need some time to refocus. I think you're a very sweet guy and I enjoyed the time we spent together, but I realize the need to take my life seriously. Where that will take me I don't exactly know, but it can't be where I've been until now."

Whether he believed her slapdash 'it's not you, it's me' speech or not, he accepted it gracefully. "Can I still call you?" he asked.

"Give me a week or so," she requested, "I don't know what will be, if you'll even want to call me again after that."

They left the restaurant and parted ways. She watched him walk up Broadway and saw the square where she had yelled at Joe in the street. Right then she tried to call him—she knew that he was finished with work and perhaps she could catch him before he left the city. All she got was a busy signal. She decided not to wait; she had to get back to her parents' house and she didn't even know if Joe was in the city or if he could even meet. She didn't leave a message, but she called again as she walked into Penn Station, the call directed to voice mail. She got on the first train to her parents' house with the intention to talk to him and resolve her doubts when she got settled at home. The opportunity never came.

Chapter Thirty-One

Joe

SOMEHOW, DESPITE HIS heavy emotional state, Joe managed to learn in yeshiva on Thursday morning. He'd considered surprising Sharon at her apartment and letting his havrusa know he had a flight to catch as an excuse. Perhaps the gesture of pursuing peace would warm her up to hear what he had to say. He had tried calling a few times in the last few days but she didn't answer. Even if he reached her, what could he say? He was flying to the Midwest to meet his potential parents-in-law and could no longer speak to her? Still, his procrastination left things between them unresolved and him feeling unsettled.

Since they didn't have enough men for a minyan, Joe walked his bicycle with him as he and the handful of other guys who showed up on the fast day went to catch mincha at Landau's. The shul was surprisingly full for 1:30 in the afternoon but Joe found a corner where he could have his own space to pray. When he reached the additional tefilah inserted on the fast day, "*we are in a great distress*," he paused. He knew that however exciting his personal life might be and however much anticipation he might have for his trip to St. Louis, if every Jew wasn't experiencing similar joy then it was considered as if everyone was in great distress. He immediately thought of Sharon and finished his Amidah with a guilty conscience.

He carried the guilt all the way back to his apartment. As he came into his basement and realized he had nothing to do for the rest of the day, he wavered: should he sleep or take the time to find her? He even got into bed and set his alarm, but he knew he'd never sleep. How could he rest knowing that he was walking away from Sharon without having the guts to do it cleanly? However much he had to disentangle himself from her, it would be an affront to his gratitude for all she'd done for him if he didn't close things personally. Even waiting until he returned would be too long; he wanted to enter the next phase of his life without any emotional baggage. He had to confront her—fast.

It was after 3:00 PM when he left his apartment. The day was still hot and he was slightly weak but he had a deadline. On the way to the subway uptown he failed to reach her again. Sure, the possibility existed that she wouldn't be there, but where else could she be? She didn't like going home and he couldn't think of a logical reason that she wouldn't at least be somewhere in the Upper West. He spent the hour on the train figuring out what he was going to say. At 96th he ran to her building, somewhat doggedly with his messenger bag bopping against the back of his thighs. By 4:30 PM he was in her elevator. He rang her bell and waited a full minute, rocking back and forth with antsy energy. He rang the bell again and was relieved to hear a voice.

"Who is it?" he heard Tamar ask.

"It's Joe." He didn't need to say anymore. The door opened and Tamar appeared in the doorway, dressed as if she had thrown on appropriate clothing just a moment ago.

"Hi Joe," she said, looking at him funnily. "What are you doing here?"

He clapped his hands together. "I've come to talk to Sharon. Is she here?"

"No, she isn't," she said slowly. "Have you spoken with her lately?"

He shook his head in the negative. "We...kind of had a fight a few days ago."

"How long ago?"

"Sunday night." He was still rocking, wondering where Sharon was. "Listen, I'm in a hurry. Is she at the gym? What am I thinking? It's a fast. Do you mind if I chill here until she comes back?"

While Joe was nearly jumping off the walls, Tamar was practically lethargic. "I guess nobody told you," she said, leaning on the doorframe.

He stiffened up, imagining the worst. "Told me what?"

"Her grandmother died."

His heart sank, feeling as if it was deflating. He and Tamar both stood by the doorway for a long time. A door slammed shut down the hall and an elderly man slowly walked towards them with a shopping cart, addressing them with a slight nod. When he passed, Joe asked her, "When?"

"Tuesday. The funeral was yesterday. She's at her parents' house while her mother and uncles are sitting *shivah*."

A loud chime reverberated through the hallway when the elevator arrived. Joe considered his options. To travel to Long Island would take him very far from home, but he owed it to her to see this through. "So I'll go," he concluded. "Do you know her parents' address?"

"You're going to go to her house?" Tamar asked in disbelief.

"I know the family," he said shortly.

"I don't know the exact address—"

"Do you mind if I look for it?"

"No, go ahead."

She opened the door and motioned for him to enter. Joe went straight to Sharon's room, which looked as if she'd left in a hurry. Drawers were still open, her computer table was overrun with papers, and the pile of laundry was strewn about the floor. He shook the mouse of her computer and the photo screensaver displayed a shot of Joe standing in front of the two kosher restaurants on First Avenue with an indecisive expression. For a few months, they went to "the spot" every Tuesday night when the Caf would serve turkey, which Sharon hated. Every time, they'd stand out front and try to read each other's mind as to which restaurant the other wanted to choose. He sighed and looked through the papers on her desk for an envelope or something to indicate her home address. In a drawer under the vanity he found her old learner's permit. He wrote down the street name and number on a post-it note and went into the hall. Standing by Tamar's door, he knocked quickly and thanked her. "Sorry for intruding like this."

She opened her door enough for Joe to see half-full suitcases open on the bed. "No problem," she said.

"Where are you going?" he asked, figuring it rude to barge in and not be at least cordial.

She sighed. "I don't know, but I can't stay here."

"Why not?"

She leaned against her desk chair. "Sharon called me after the funeral. The apartment is tied to the will. Supposedly it's meant to be split by the children, and Sharon mentioned something about not getting in the middle of it."

"Sharon's moving out too?" he asked in surprise.

She made a face. "Something about her uncles not liking me here…I don't know."

"What are you going to do?"

She shrugged. "Well, I don't believe that they'll kick me out while they're sitting shivah, but I'm packing anyway."

Just then Joe had a thought. "Look, I know someone who left the Heights for the summer. Perhaps you can take her space while you figure something out."

"Maybe. It's a bit far for me, but if it's cheap…"

"At least take the number. It's an option."

"Thanks Joe. Who's this girl?"

He breathed deeply. "A girl I'm…dating."

"Hey, that's great to hear, Joe. How'd you meet her?"

"We were set up."

"Wow. Very nice. Should I tell her that I know you?"

"Know me?" he repeated. "How much do we know of each other?"

She nodded in agreement. "Thanks, Joe. You're a good guy. Sharon's lucky to have a friend like you."

He didn't say anything but looked at the floor. "I better get going."

Tamar walked him to the door. He glanced back for one last look at the apartment. It wasn't as significant a last glance as he'd given to Ben Gurion Airport after his eight months in Israel or his last minyan at the Bronfman Center before moving out of NYU. Tamar allowed him his sentimental moment before closing the door slowly behind him.

Again in the elevator he checked his watch and saw that it was

5:00. He would have to make his way through Penn Station during the peak of rush hour, and his hunger was beginning to catch up to him. But he still had time; he didn't know exactly how long the train to Cedarhurst was, but he figured that he would get there an hour before the fast ended.

Penn Station was buzzing as he waited with the rest of the herd of weary commuters for the large board to announce his track. When finally the information popped up on the big screen, he stood in awe as people who had been standing next to him moments before were suddenly running towards their train as if it were the last out of Manhattan. Slowly he made his way to the track and found the car particularly full. *So that's why they run.* He looked around the car and saw a few kippahs among the passengers, even one or two looking at seforim as they sat. A minute later, there bells rang and doors closed. After twenty minutes of cattle-car crowding he switched at Jamaica and settled into a seat. The time was just after 6:00 and for about fifteen minutes Joe closed his eyes.

Though there was an automatic voice announcing each stop, for some reason Joe was only startled awake when it called out the stop for "Hewlett." He dazedly pulled out of his pocket the schedule he got at Penn Station and saw that he had two more stops. Rather than invigorating him, his short rest had made him sluggish. His messenger bag felt heavier than before when he stood up to disembark. When he stepped onto the platform at Cedarhurst he didn't recognize the look of the neighborhood. He asked a Jewish man who was also getting off the train for directions. The weather was cooler here and Joe drew the strength to walk all the way to Sharon's house from the light breeze.

He remembered the house once he saw it. The small square of lawn was bare save for recently mowed grass that led to the thin path from the driveway. Small hedges lined the path on the front side of the house. There was the covered patio on the right side of the house, extending from the dining room in the back along the length of the house, with the familiar small bench and a barbecue grill visible under the awning. The front door of the house was open, but there was no sound from inside. Joe put his bag by the bench, walked over to the front door and composed himself. *I've come this far; I can do it.*

As he walked into the front hallway he found the house eerily silent and the living room empty. Across from the couches in the living room were low chairs for the mourners. Joe fell into one of the couches and waited. Soon an older man with noticeable stubble came up from the basement. He noticed Joe and walked towards him.

"Mincha's at 7 PM," he told Joe. "We also have a *sefer Torah* coming."

"I already davened," Joe said. The man nodded.

"Nobody's here now. The hours are on the door."

Joe quickly glanced towards the front. "I guess I didn't notice. The door was wide open."

Again he nodded silently. Then he asked Joe, "Who are you?"

"I'm a friend of Sharon's, Joe Charnoff. Who are you?"

"I'm her uncle Mendel."

"Oh," Joe said understandingly. "Did you come in...after she..."

"No, I came in on Monday." He looked down. "We knew it was coming."

"From where?"

"From Chicago."

"I was born in Chicago," Joe said.

"Really?" Mendel brightened. "Where?"

"I don't know," Joe admitted sadly. "We moved when I was a kid."

"How do you know Sharon?"

"We went to NYU together."

"Very nice."

Just then he heard the drop of a metal utensil and the clomping of heavy shoes on the parquet floors and a few seconds later Sharon walked into the room, drying her hands on a dish towel, an astonished expression on her face.

Chapter Thirty-Two

Sharon

SHARON KNEW THAT someone had entered the house while she was in the kitchen cutting vegetables, but she dismissed it. She wanted to get started on dinner before the minyan came and other visitors would fill the house. She even imagined that she heard Joe's voice talking with her uncle but the idea quickly passed; the only person who knew about her grandmother's passing was Tamar and Joe didn't have her number. Only when the stranger mentioned NYU did she suspect enough to drop the knife she was holding on the counter. In the living room she was amazed to find Joe on the couch. He gave her one contrite glance before turning his eyes to the floor.

"Sharon," her uncle Mendy said as he turned to her. "Your friend Joe just arrived."

"I see," she said. "Hello Joey."

"Hello Sharon," he replied uncomfortably, still not looking at her.

"How did you find out?" She was speaking tersely, though she didn't know why.

He shifted in his seat. "Tamar told me."

"You went to the apartment?" she asked, astounded.

Joe nodded. Looking up at her uncle, he told him, "Sharon kept your mother's place in very good condition."

"So I hear," Mendy replied. "Did it help you out?" he asked her.

Her gaze still fixed on Joe, she answered her uncle, "Very much. What brings you here?"

"Your mother's sitting shivah," he said matter-of-factly.

Despite the myriad of feelings she had towards Joe at that moment, she found herself growing impatient with him. "It's the longest fast of the year and you choose today to venture all the way out here?"

Meekly, he said, "I was already in the city and—"

"What were you doing in on a Thursday?" she demanded.

Her uncle must have detected something in her tone, because he slowly rose from his low chair and mumbled, "I think that I'm going to lie down before mincha."

"No, you stay Uncle Mendy," Sharon offered, softening her tone. "We'll go outside."

Joe stood up obligingly, muttering to her uncle the verse that comforters say to mourners as they leave their presence before following her to the dining room. Sliding open the screen door she motioned for him to join her on the patio. As she sat down, she saw that he was walking very heavily. When he settled into the bench he let out a quiet moan, as if he were in some sort of physical pain. She immediately regretted the harshness of how she greeted him.

"It's really sweet of you to come all this way," she changed her tone. "My mother will appreciate it."

He was silent for a moment. "I'm sorry about your grandmother."

"Thanks," she said quietly. She turned and saw him examining her face, his eyes roaming back and forth.

"Were you close to her?"

Sharon shrugged. "We used to visit more when I was younger… not so much once I started high school. There wasn't a falling out or anything."

"Oh." He didn't speak for some time, staring out at the trees that were the border between her house and the neighbor's. Eventually he added, "Really I came to speak to you." He was breathing deeply and talking slowly as if he were carefully choosing his words. "I've been calling you all week…since Tuesday, at least."

"You can understand why I haven't answered."

He snickered, if not cynically. "I've never seen you that angry." Then he added, "well, not with me."

"I know," she said quickly. "You were the target of a lot of pent-up frustration."

"I deserved it," he sighed.

"Not to that degree," she comforted him.

"Maybe not," he coughed, continuing in a raspy voice, "but you were right about everything."

He had made this last admission with such self-pity that the guilt he felt was punishment enough. It hurt Sharon to see Joe so heavy; blaming himself for everything she called him on last Sunday. She wished that they could forget the incident but she knew he wouldn't. Whether it would work or not, she had to do it anyway.

"I'm sorry Joey…for blowing up and running away. I…I was under a lot of stress and a lot of things together brought everything up at once."

He didn't say much for a while. Sharon saw a car park alongside their lawn and the driver emerged to join the minyan. Eventually Joe whispered, "I'm sorry too. I was confused from that whole Daniela thing and I didn't feel that you cared. I probably should've been honest from the beginning."

He then resumed his study of the trees, absorbed in some deep thought that even if she asked he wouldn't share. She sensed that he was hiding something, and it saddened her to think that their friendship had gotten to a place where there could be such distance between them. They weren't the same Joe and Sharon of even two weeks ago. Both of them had taken big steps and were no longer caught up in some relic of the past. As Sharon gazed over at Joe she saw in him that same look she had seen him wearing at Jessica's sendoff party and she wondered what it was about this new Joe that she had felt so compelled to run away from that night.

When the silence became oppressive, she changed the subject. "Tell me about her," she requested.

He examined her face, and she tried to convey that she was honestly curious. Whether he read her or not, he again looked away. "Her name is Rachel."

"Sounds Jewish. Is she from around here?"

Joe shook his head. "Nope. St. Louis."

Sharon let out her hair from its elastic band. "How'd you get set up with a girl from St. Louis of all places?"

"She boarded in Jersey for high school and after Israel went to Stern. Now she lives in the Heights."

She ran her fingers through her hair. "Is she...frum?"

Joe pointed to himself. "What do you think?"

Sharon turned and faced him, one of her knees resting on the bench. "But is she for you? She isn't cut-and-dry, is she?"

He glanced over and inhaled deeply. "No, she's cool. She's urban, like us."

A car pulled up to the house and Sharon spotted the rabbi of the *shteibel* walking towards the door. She dropped her head to bunch up her hair. "She knows where you come from?"

"Yeah. She knows."

She put the elastic between her lips as she held her hair with one hand. "How long have you been dating?"

"Two weeks. You saw us in Times Square on our first date."

The image of Joe crossing Broadway with the umbrella flashed in her mind. "She's pretty."

He smiled slightly. "Very much."

"When are you going to ask her?" she asked. Just then there was a sound of a loud splash beyond the trees. Joe didn't react at all. "Neighbors have a pool," she explained.

He nodded slowly. "I don't know," he eventually mumbled. "I'm going to meet her parents."

Sharon wrinkled her nose. "When?"

"Right after Shabbos. I have to be in LaGuardia at 11 PM."

"You're flying out to meet her parents?" she asked in amazement. "That's…"

"A big step," he admitted. "I know."

The sun was starting to hurt Sharon's eyes. This was the first time all day she was stepping outside the house. "I'm glad for you, Joey."

He glanced at her to see whether she was sincere. Apparently her look convinced him. "Thank you," he told her.

Another car pulled up to the house. "They're going to daven mincha," she said.

"I davened already," he replied. "I'll stay for ma'ariv, if I can."

"Will you? I made ziti and a big salad. It's the staple after-fast meal."

"You're always offering me food."

She smiled. "I'm a Jewish mother-in-training."

He huffed. "So no more address on West End?"

Sharon shook her head. "I don't think so. Not unless I buy it."

"Where are you going to go?"

She was silent and Joe understood she didn't know. The men inside began praying.

He looked away. "It must be hard to lose so much all at once."

"Yeah," was all she could say. She buried her head in her hands and rubbed her eyes.

"I guess it had to be," he offered. "It was a poor substitute for the spot."

"Though my food was certainly better."

"No question."

They laughed. Sharon was glad to see Joe happy, hoping he really had forgiven her. She felt the heaviness had lifted enough for her to ask, "When will I meet her?"

His countenance immediately dropped. He made a few dramatic gestures and facial expressions, as if her question was the breach of a subject he would have preferred not to discuss. After a series of deep sighs, he answered quietly, "I don't know."

She immediately understood. He had been morose from the moment she saw him. He didn't come all this way to apologize, but to tell her that he didn't know when, or if, she would meet Rachel. He was saying goodbye. Her eyes began filling with warm tears.

"We can't go on," he said in a low voice, looking out at the trees. "Not as friends, not as…not as anything. I already stopped talking to girls a long time ago, but…" he stopped. "I just couldn't tell you, not with everything you did for me. But I see that it only made things worse."

He became quiet again, hunched over with his hand covering his face. For a long time they sat there, her broken crying and sniffling the only sounds besides the crickets in the darkening evening.

An oven timer beeped loudly and Sharon jumped up from the

bench. She yanked open the screen door and dashed into the kitchen to switch it off, eliciting turned heads from the men trying to hear the Torah reading. She then put on the oven mitts lying on the counter and opened the oven. Sliding out the ziti tray, she bent over to lift the cover and a single tear splashed on the aluminum foil. She leaned her back on the counter and buried her face in the oven mitts.

> I can't believe he's doing this – He didn't want to hurt me, though – So what? He's hurting me now – That doesn't change his decision – He's only doing this because he's getting married – I also dumped Andy because I want a real relationship – What does that have to do with Joe? He's just a friend – Do I care about any of my other friends as much? – No, but that doesn't mean anything – He might as well be a boyfriend – Does not touching take away from being attached to him? – But to say that's it? Goodbye after four years? – He did come all the way out here…

After a minute of heavy sobbing into the oven mitts, she steadied her breathing and walked towards the porch. Through the glass doors she saw him staring up at the sky in silent contemplation. She stepped out onto the porch and he immediately turned to her with red eyes.

"Everything all right?" he asked.

"No," she blurted out. "I don't understand. I don't understand why you're just saying goodbye and that's it. I don't understand why everything in my life is changing all of a sudden, and I don't understand why it has to be like this." She stopped, and gazed above his head at the street. "One day I probably will, but right now it hurts."

After a moment, he said, "I was asking about the ziti."

She laughed, but it made her tear more. She sat down and they turned to each other.

"We know everything about each other," he said. "And we still stick with each other. We should only be so dedicated to our marriages."

"Is that admonishment or hope?" she asked.

Joe thought. "Both."

She sniffled and blinked rapidly. "I never imagined it would get to this."

He shrugged his shoulders. "Nobody does. That's the problem."

She thought about Esther's story, and about Nati and Jessica. "You're right." A car passed on the street and she turned to see Joe again gazing up at the sky. "What's so interesting up there?" she asked.

"There's green in the sky," he said flatly.

She rubbed her eyes with her sleeves. "What are you talking about?"

He licked his lips. "My rabbi told me this elaborate *mashal* about the sky and how it symbolizes upheavals in the stability of life—how the blue of the daytime thickens as the sun starts to fade and how the whole process is accompanied by high intensity colors—and I answered there must be green, you know, how all color transitions pass the full spectrum."

"ROY G. BIV," she muttered.

"Yeah," he said, snapping his fingers. "I heard the breeze shaking the leaves when you went in and I looked up and there it is—the green." Joe pointed up and at first all Sharon could see was a very blue sky with the last hints of light making the neighbor's trees look like dark shadows. But she humored him, running her eyes from directly above, then down towards the horizon. At the last vestiges of blue there was a very hazy transition of color that was mostly yellow with some pink, but much to her surprise she could make out a thin line of a different color, which she had to admit looked somewhat green.

"What do you think it means?" she asked.

He was about to open his mouth when they heard the sound of pressure on the wooden patio.

"There you are, Sharon," she heard her mother say. "I've been looking for you. Why is the ziti sitting on the stovetop?"

"Sorry," Sharon apologized automatically. "I wanted to check it and I forgot to put it back in."

Her mother then noticed who was on the bench with her. "Joey?" she asked surprised. He stood up and turned to her. "I didn't know you came."

He composed himself. "Yes, Mrs. Gilboa. I came right before mincha when no one was sitting."

"Yeah, we have hours. It's too much—an entire day."

"I'm sorry about your loss," he told her.

"That's so nice of you to come," her mother replied.

"Ima," Sharon interjected. "I'll put it back in the oven uncovered when they start ma'ariv. It'll give it a crispy coating."

"When are you going to make the salad?" her mother asked.

Sharon looked over at Joe. "In a minute."

"OK," her mother said before going into the house.

It was a long minute. The night had settled and they remained motionless on the bench. She could only see Joe between the shadows coming from the light through the sliding doors behind her. When they heard her uncle saying Kaddish, she stood up.

"Come," she requested. "I have to make dinner."

"Can I help?" Joe offered.

She smiled. "Of course."

He stretched and stood up. "Thank you for everything," he said, looking into her eyes.

She knew that "everything" meant exactly that. "Just wait," she said. "You haven't left yet."

Joe stayed for ma'ariv and then for dinner. He ate with Sharon and her siblings at the kitchen table while her mother and uncle sat with comforters who had come from the city. She had to mediate between her overtired siblings bickering over nothing at all, losing her last few minutes with Joe. Close to 9:00 he made an after-bracha, got up from his stool and stood up with a slouch.

"It's time I go," he announced. "The trains only run once an hour."

"I'll drive you," she offered. She peeked into the living room and frowned when she saw her mother still occupied.

"It's not a far walk," Joe assured her. "Stay here and put them to bed."

"Really, it's two minutes…"

He put up his hand. "Thank you, Sharon, but there's no need."

She didn't fight, her symbolic act of letting go. He went into the living room and flung his messenger bag over his shoulder. Sharon's mother was talking with an older woman when she interrupted and looked up at him.

"You're going, Joey?" Sharon's mother asked.

"Yes," he told her, smiling at the older woman. Quietly, he said, "I gotta go."

"This is Sharon's friend," Sharon's mother said to the woman on the couch. To Joe, "Thank you so much for coming."

Sharon appeared in the living room, and Joe almost collided into her when he turned around. He jerked his head towards the door and she nodded. Turning back to the living room, he murmured the verse said to mourners, and walked backwards towards the doorway.

Sharon was waiting there. For a moment they exchanged a last glance, inhaling deeply as they used to do before leaving one of their restaurants. They shared a smile before he pivoted and looked out onto her lawn. Then he lowered his head and stepped out. She followed him out the door and behind in the tracks he made in the green grass.

When he reached the edge of her lawn, her mother appeared in the doorway. "Don't let him walk," she called to Sharon. "One of us could drive him."

Sharon stopped where she was. "It's OK," she assured her mother as she watched him walk down the street in the glow of the orange streetlights. She breathed deeply and smiled. "He's going."

Joe was already across the street when he realized Sharon was no longer behind him. Mid-stride, he turned around and tilted his head with a puzzled expression on his face. Then he nodded in understanding and waved to her, a wide smile on his face. "Goodbye, Sharon."

She wiped away a tear and waved back. "Goodbye, Joey!"

THE END

Nathan Wolff would like to thank:

•Hashem, in short, for everything.

•His parents, for raising him and allowing him the room to choose his own path; for supporting throughout every stage of the book's production and always encouraging his work.

•His grandmother, for her unknowing generous support of the book and for constantly reminding him of how the world should be.

•His brother, sister, cousins and friends, for being great companions along the journey.

•His rabbis, for giving over the ideas contained in this book, for commenting on the manuscript several times, and for looking the other way when production seeped into his *sedarim*.

•His advisors, for taking their precious time to give vital advice on the proper direction of the book.

•His editors, for transforming *Outdated* into a real book.

•His production staff, for offering their services to a fledgling start-up without guarantee of pay.

•His children, for constantly keeping him on his toes, for sleeping soundly all those nights *Outdated* was being written, and for being the reason to smile when things got tough.

•His wife, for giving him countless hours to write, for sharing in his excitement over seemingly esoteric events in the process of the writing, for being a constant source of support, for encouraging every step of the way, and for everything else.

About the Author

Nathan Wolff has been writing creatively since elementary school, with scores of poems, short stories, plays, and novelettes waiting to be anthologized. After completing his BA in Political Theory from the State University of New York, he sojourned to Israel to learn Torah and twelve years later hasn't returned. He currently lives in Ramat Beit Shemesh with his wife and three children. *Outdated* is his first published novel. Contact him at nathannwolff@gmail.com